D1482320

WITHDRAWN

Music and Society

The masks of Orpheus

Wilfrid Mellers

The masks of Orpheus

Seven stages in the
story of European music

Manchester University Press

Published by Manchester University Press
Oxford Road, Manchester, M13 9PL, UK
27 South Main Street, Wolfeboro, NH 03824–2069, USA

British Library Cataloguing in publication data
Mellers, Wilfrid
  The masks of Orpheus: seven stages in
  the story of European music. – (Music
  and society)
  1. Music – Europe – History and criticism
  I. Title II. Series
  780′.94   ML240

Library of Congress cataloging in publication data applied for

ISBN 0 7190 2456 0 *hardback*

Photoset in Linotron Plantin with Gill Sans
by Northern Phototypesetting Co., Bolton

Printed in Great Britain
by Billing & Sons Ltd., Worcester

Contents

Foreword

We live, we are often told, in a museum culture, clinging on to artefacts of the past because we cannot invent appropriate ones ourselves. Yet even if this is true, it is also true that more people than ever before are interested in and enjoy some form of music: people who attend concerts of some or other kind and people who play music themselves, as well as the countless millions who buy records and tapes (themselves the products of a major industry) or simply experience the pervasive effects of music on radio and television and in films. Though heterogeneous, this public is enormous, including both those who are professionally involved in the production of masterworks and those who just 'know what they like' when they chance to hear it. For despite another of the claims often made about contemporary societies – that their rationalistic and utilitarian values have all but erased the spiritual, the emotional, in a word the distinctively human qualities of life – it is evident that the clamour for music not only survives, but indeed is intensified, in such societies.

In short, music matters. For some it is the paramount expression of human creativity, for others the symbolic affirmation of the Western cultural tradition. Others again hear in their music an explicit denial of the values of such a tradition: for them music may mean the sound of protest, rebellion or even revolution. What is common to each of these, and other, orientations is an undeniable, if usually unstated, belief in both the power and the importance of music in society. In this context, the usefulness of the books in this series – to students, teachers, and the general public – should spring from the fact that they aim to enhance enjoyment by way of understanding. Specialist knowledge will not be assumed, the volumes being written in a lively style, primarily for non-specialist, albeit thoughtful, enthusiastic, and diligent readers.

We take it as axiomatic that, since music is made by human beings, it cannot but be a manifestation of human experience – of the problems and despair, the triumphs and joys which are an integral part of living together in particular social contexts. Some of the books have a musical, others a sociological, bias, but in all the musical and sociological aspects are inseparable. We are concerned simultaneously with the external manifestations of music as revealed, historically and anthropologically, in ritual and in religious, civic, military, and festive activities, in work and in play; and also with the social, psychological and philosophical undercurrents inherent in music's being made by human creatures. Although matters have been complicated, over the last century, by the fact that industrial capitalism in the West has to a degree fragmented the cultural homogeneity of earlier societies, this interdependence of music and society has not been radically changed. It is true that in our 'pluralistic' society we may detect at least three overlapping musical discourses: a folk or ethnic tradition, a classical or art tradition, and a commercial or commodity tradition. Even so, Music & Society starts from a recognition of the fact that these 'discourses', however distinct, cannot be independent, since they are coexistent manifestations of the world we live in.

The classical myth of Orpheus plumbs deep into our subconscious minds, for he was a patriarchal male – possibly a shamanistic priest of ancient Thrace – who aspired to Godhead through the exercise of Reason and Art. He failed; and was punished for his presumption by the avenging matriarchal maenads, through his severed *head* sang on through the ages. European man, haunted by his story, has interpreted it in many ways, in accord with changing needs and desires. Whereas for medieval man Orpheus was a post-lapsarian seeker after reunion with the oneness of God, for High Renaissance man he was a humanist Hero asserting man's potential rivalry with the divine. Monteverdi, in his version, balanced the claims of Flesh and Word; composers of the classical baroque, such as Purcell and Handel, had little doubt that Man as absolutist monarch might take God's place – though the greatest of the classical baroque masters, Bach, was in this respect as in others out of step.

By the time of the Enlightenment Gluck gives an optimistic twist to the tale, for his Orpheus's failure is transmuted, through the hero's and heroine's human courage, into rational triumph. Mozart and Beethoven bring back the metaphysical implications of the myth. For

Tchaikovsky it becomes a romantic dream of the Eternal Return, while Offenbach debunks it in hedonistic cynicism. In our own battered century Stravinsky reinstates the primal version of the legend, not shrinking, in the wake of two world wars, from the tragic denouement. Harrison Birtwistle, in the opera that bears the same title as this book, explores the theme's relevance to our electronic and nuclear crises.

So, in effect, the rather grand theme of the book (as of Birtwistle's opera) is the evolution of ideas of artistic creation down the centuries. Art, especially music, emulates God in that it is *our* creative act, which to some degree implies in-spiration. Sometimes man has been, as the Abbess Hildegard put it, 'a feather on the breath of God'; at other times he has come near to claiming that it is he who puffs. For the most part, however, he has prevaricated, veering between confidence and doubt. Such is the heart of the human condition: which must be why it is often called a 'predicament'.

Most unequivocally of all the arts, music is a social activity. It has evoked and does evoke strong collective sentiments; it has generated and will support complex social institutions. Even the solitary composer, who may think that his personal motivation is to transcend the society he finds himself in, owes his 'loneness' to the world that made him. Beethoven himself – who in his middle years believed that his music should and could change the world, and in late years knew that his transcendent music had changed the self, ours as well as his own – could not but be dependent on his music's being *heard*; and this inevitably involved other people – as performers and listeners, but also as patrons, sponsors, agents, managers, instrument makers and the whole host of unseen but vital others without whom musical performances would be no more than unfulfilled dreams. Unlike the solitary experience of novel readers or contemplators of paintings, communities of musicians and listeners, whether in tribal gatherings, peasant communities, 'classical' concerts, jazz clubs or discos, depend on contact with one another, and on a shared cultural perspective.

Music does not create or realise itself, but is always the result of people doing things together in particular places and times. To understand music is to understand the men and women who make it, and vice versa. The approach promulgated in Music & Society is, we believe, basic. It needs no further explanation or apology, except in so far as its self-evident truths have sometimes, and rather oddly, been forgotten.

Wilfrid Mellers
Pete Martin

Prefatory note

This book is a product of a course I was invited to give, in 1986, at the Humanities Department of the University of Syracuse, NY. Thanks are due to the students, undergraduate and graduate, who participated.

Some paragraphs of the book have appeared, in slightly different forms, in the *Times Literary Supplement*; a few other sections are adapted from books of mine long out of print; the discussion of Beethoven's *Missa Solemnis* incorporates material from my (still in print) book *Beethoven and the Voice of God*.

The book is dedicated, in homage,

To Harrison Birtwistle.

Chapter I

Dionysos, Apollo and Orpheus: the mercurian monarch from Classical Antiquity to the Renaissance

Alfonso X as King David-Orpheus; Il Favola di Orfeo (1480)

Looking back on the European centuries we may observe how great and less than great composers have helped reconcile us to the appalling cruelty of life, the agonising ecstasy of love, and the scary inevitability of death; and have done so by seeking, sometimes attaining, an identity between flesh and word, the physical and the metaphysical. Throughout European history one myth has haunted man's consciousness, attaining fanatical intensity during the Renaissance when the modern world was in labour. That myth is the legend of Orpheus, a direct projection of this unconscious theme which, basic in the sense that any artist may be and usually is an intermediary between worlds natural and supernatural, has repeatedly, since the Renaissance, been formulated in ritualistically theatrical terms. This book will examine these formulations, scattered over five centuries in several disparate worlds.

There was probably a real Orpheus, a shamanistic priest in ancient Thrace who combined the professions of poet, composer, lyre-player, magician, religious teacher and oracle-giver. Although a human being, he must have possessed gifts uncommon enough for legends about super-human qualities to accrue around him until his 'meaning' was inseparable from his protean amorphousness. A synonym for impulses deep within the psyche, at once individual and archetypal, he equivocated between two gods who are polar opposites; and his equivocation is his truth.

Dionysos, often confused with Bacchus because wine is apt to induce dionysiac abandon, was a god of instinct, of energy free and untrammelled. If this makes him a Father who plays the phallic flute, it also relates him to the Dark Goddesses and Terrible Mothers of a matriarchal society – Dionysos was often depicted as 'a youth of effeminate

appearance, with luxuriant hair'. Apollo, contrasted with Dionysos's
exuberance, is the Son of the Father, the power of intellect that would
discipline Dionysiac frenzy. His order is beautiful and heroic, for it is
humanity's victory over chaos; and, in so far as he is associated with
the rationally canny head against the irrationally wayward heart, the
Son becomes a sun high in the sky, patriarchally 'managing' terrestrial
affairs. Yet at the same time the Apollonian order is a *fall* in that it
dams and stifles, possibly destroys, Dionysos's generative potency.

According to the legend Apollo had acquired his art – his lyre –
from Hermes or Mercury, the traditional trickster and messenger
between the human and the divine. Hermetic Hermes secretly stole
cattle tended by Apollo; pursued by Zeus's secret police he hid in a
cave and fashioned a musical instrument out of tortoiseshell and
cowgut. When captured, Hermes appeased Zeus's wrath by playing
his lyre ravishingly and by presenting it to the delighted Apollo in
exchange for the cattle. Committed neither to God nor man, Hermes
is as volatile as his alternative name of Mercury suggests. He is a liar
and a trickster whose strength lies in his mercurial two-way traffic.
The Lie is incarnate in his seven-stringed lyre★ which represents – in
English, punningly – the sevenfold structure of the physical world.
Hermes' theft parallels Prometheus's theft from the gods of power in
the form of fire; but whereas Promethean fire generates energy in the
external world, Hermes' spiritual power is 'sealed' in the materiality
of tortoiseshell and cowgut. Through the sound of music, however,
materiality may be returned to spirit; the equilibrium between the
dionysiac flute (phallic shaped, plucked from the wood of the forest,
activated by human breath) and the Apollonian lyre (strung with
animal gut, struck by the human hand and controlled by the mind) is
perennial and eternal.

So musically, as in the philosophical formulation of the myth,
intellectual knowledge is at once a boon and, as man loses contact with
irrational levels of being, the root of a Fall. Yet this fall is redeemable,
since as man relinquished the spiritual levels of his being, so was he
given the potential to regain them through the utterance of sound.
Music, of its very nature, prefigures as Eternal Return; as becomes

★ But according to some accounts the lyre originally had five strings, and
was probably pentatonic as well as monodic. It was Apollo who added the two
extra strings, thereby making 'Western' (harmonic) music feasible. As we will
see, this makes some sense in relation to the story of European music.

explicit in the myth when at some ill-defined point in time the Dionysos-Apollo-Hermes-Mercury figure merged into his quasi-human counterpart Orpheus, who was possibly Apollo's son and certainly an apostle of his art and reason, while being at the same time possessed of, and by, dionysiac energy. In any case, he is man himself, who sings with his human voice and plays his humanly constructed instrument, unmasking a way back to the source of creation. Having fallen, he teeters irresolutely between the realms of free energy and of formal control. Although his music aspires to the recovered Whole, a marriage of the sundered poles, its form, once achiveved, leads back to generative impulses which predate such discipline. Thus music is potential magic, as is evident throughout recorded time: in the aborigines' incantations that would summon forces of air, sun and water; in the guile of the Indian snake-charmer; in the singing and harping of the Biblical King David; in the village priest's chanted appeal for his God's blessing on crops, royal personages, or us 'miserable offenders'; in the American negro's blues, wherein the guitar-lyre may alleviate distress in harmonically canalising primitive vocal lament.

As the Dionysos-Apollo figure was metamorphosed into quasi-human Orpheus, other mythic strands were gathered into the story. Like shamans everywhere, Orpheus could not only through his music arouse or pacify birds and beasts, the instinctual creatures of Nature; he could also defy natural laws, counteracting gravity and telescoping time; and could even confront the gods themselves, defying death. Since the heart of the Orpheus myth is a psychic rebirth, this personal theme merged into seasonal rites concerning the rebirth of the year. Orpheus's wife Eurydice relates to the Demeter-Persephone story: the human life that descends into the nether world of Hades at the winter solstice and has to be wooed back in the spring of the year. 'Stolen' Eurydice recalls Hermes' theft of the cattle; both thefts may be redeemed by music. The seasonal rite in Eurydice's story also functions on a psychological level, for her tale is another fall. A literal fall, indeed, since, pursued by an ardent illicit lover, she falls to the ground, where she is bitten by a serpent of mortality, prophetic of Eden's snake. In early versions of the story she dies and Orpheus, armed with his lyre, descends into Hades to appeal to the gods to reprieve her. His singing and playing are so magically enchanting that Pluto, god of death, relents, but with a condition – one of the traditional wagers between god and man. She may follow Orpheus out of the underworld so long as he does not look back to check if she is following. He must have total faith in the divine will, the more so because he cannot hope to comprehend it. He fails the test because he is not in fact a god, but fallibly human. He is impatient because egotistical, insisting on personal, if partial, knowledge instead of accepting the cosmic order. For human Orpheus the self and the world, like life and death, must be incompatible, since he cannot evisage the Whole of which Eurydice is now a part. Given the facts of the human condition, rebirths must be temporary – as is patently true in psychological terms, since we must all die in the body.

In some versions of the story Orpheus, having lost Eurydice a second time through his own fault, kills himself or is, for his disobedience or cowardice or both, destroyed by Zeus's thunderbolt. But the version of the tale that prevailed tells us that Orpheus, ashamed of and appalled by his failure, spent the rest of his days in melancholy misogyny, eschewing all women. Though his point is that no living woman could compete with twice-dead Eurydice, it is disingenuous to dismiss women in general because his patriarchal pride had failed one of them. Not surprisingly, 'women' decide they have had enough of him; avenging maenads or bacchantes – elemental earth goddesses harking back to pre-patriarchal, dionysiac societies – sacrificially dismember him, scattering his remains on the unconscious waters of the river Hebrus. These Terrible Mothers are pre-Oedipal, a legacy of our infantile history, unboundedly good to the young child yet also terrible in that their displeasure seems the end of all loving and of life itself. Even so, Orpheus's detrunked head, bobbling on the waters, sings on, prophesying to the winds. On earth he had found his Eurydice, the 'wise one' of social solidarity and of sacral marriage; on earth he had lost her to the serpent of mortality. Beneath the earth, in the dark labyrinth, he had heroically found her again, being reunited to her as Eternal Beloved, *anima* to his *animus*. Then, through his dualistic impatience and retrospection, he had lost her to death for ever. So the story is about human hope, and fortitude, and failure: the very heart of our human predicament. Man seeks a balance between passional Dionysos and rational Apollo. If he could achieve it, he would be whole and holy, not far from a god himself. Being human, he cannot achieve it; and the reason why he cannot, usually involving a wager between god and man, is some imperfection that would be trivial were it not a defect of pride, regarded in the Middle Ages as first of the seven deadly sins. This is still manifest in the 'flaw' in Shakespeare's tragic heroes: the essence of Lear's fault is that it is foolishly egotistical.

Stories of a severed head that sings on recur in numerous cultures over vast periods of time and areas of space. It seems possible that the Greek cult of an idealised and idolised homosexuality had something to do with this fear and evasion of commitment of soul to body: since male love could not involve total genital union it could be the more readily intellectualised. Nor is it surprising that such a dichotomy between head and heart, spirit and body, should have been among the legacies of Greek civilisation to Christendom. Small wonder that medieval theologians, shifting from a humanistic to a theocratic stance, should have latched on to this lapsed Dionysiac priest who composed Apollonian songs describing the creation of heaven and earth; who used Apollonian music therapeutically to calm the beasts and our own bestialities; and who, descending to hell, confronted with music the furies of sin and death. As early as the second century the Church detected analogies between Orpheus and Christ; by the ninth century – despite dubiety about Orpheus's parleying with the creatures, which might be construed as submission to sensuality and the wiles of Satan – Orpheus is firmly established in the Christian hierarchy. Far from being seen as a threat to God's almightiness, he becomes, in his wooing of the beasts, an analogy for Christ the Shepherd-Saviour, while his descent into the nether regions is equated with Christ's 'Harrowing of Hell'. Much is made of the analogy between the seven strings of the lyre and the seven phases of the Music of the Spheres, which Christianity had appropriated from Platonism. As Macrobius put it: 'every soul in the world is allured by its (the lyre's) sounds, for the soul carries with it the memory of the music which it knew in the sky, and is so captivated by its charm that there is no breast so cruel or savage as not to be gripped by its spell'. The New Song of Christ and the Neo-Platonic Harmony of the Spheres are near-identified.

Later authorities, such as Bersuire in his *Metamorphosis Ovidana,* turn myth into rigorous allegory:

Orpheus, the child of the Sun, is Christ the Sun of God the Father, who from the beginning led Eurydice, that is the human soul. And from the beginning Christ joined her to himself through his special prerogative. While she collected flowers, that is, seized the forbidden fruit, the devil, a serpent, drew near to the new bride and bit her by temptation and killed her by sin, and finally she went to the world below. Seeing this, Christ-Orpheus wished to descend himself to the lower world and thus he retook his wife, that is, human nature, ripping her from the hands of the ruler of hell himself.

Christian apologists thus give the story a happy ending, which it does not have in the myth except *in potentia*. In psychological terms, however, potential is what counts. Orpheus, healer and prophet, attempts to exist here and now in a series of resurrections, alternating free energy with formal constraint. Subconsciously, Christian theologians of the Middle Ages seem to have been aware of this too, since they depict Christ as playing not only Apollo's lyre but also, on occasion, Dionysos's flute. In the Gnostic Hymn of Jesus he leads his people in a *ludus puerorum* – a round dance and 'loving game' – to heaven, the relation of Christ to the soul being that of bridegroom to bride. But although the sexual and the sacred ought to be one, body and spirit are, since the Fall, 'divorced, sheer opposites, antipodes', to be reunited only in the wish-fulfilment of an afterlife. Christian Orpheus's head can sing only *because* it is severed. Pauline Christianity made a very partial use of the Orpheus story.

In so far as Orpheus is Mercury or Hermes he is, as we have observed, a messenger between the human and the divine; and he may travel in either direction. For the humanistically-orientated Greeks, with their anthropomorphic view of Nature and their multiple gods and goddesses made in their own image, Orpheus is a creature who attempts to take the creator's place as controller of Nature and confronter of death. For people of the Middle Ages, however, Orpheus-Christ is a god who, assuming human flesh, serves as a gateway to transcendence, helping us to recover spirit in 'putting off' mortality. This is evident at the heart of the doctrinal music of the Christian Church: plainsong, intermediary between the human and the divine, worked by sublimation rather than by incarnation; and monodic vocal line, floating a-temporally from the Holy Word and eschewing intervals inducive of tension, served to levitate singers and participants from awareness of self into communion with God. Even so, the experience was not *purely* sublimatory. We are apt to forget, because Gothic cathedrals survive today only as austere, if tatty, edifices of mouldering grey stone, that they were focal points of the community. Blazing in light and colour, reverberating with bells and with ululating voices, they served as art gallery, museum and concert-hall as well as temples of worship; they were also market places, centres of industry, society's economic hub. It is not therefore surprising that many varieties of experience were embraced within the Church's purlieus: as is demonstrated by an eleventh-century picture (in the Cotton Manuscript Tiberius CVII in the British Library) of a kingly troubadour playing the harp under the inspiration of the Holy dove, who lands beak down on his crown, while an attendant juggles and others play rebec and horns. Willy-nilly, men lived in their 'everyday' experience; what gave it meaning, however was the Dove's descent, and man's Orphic task was to render actual his potential.

In medieval secular monody, as practised by the troubadours, the Orphic implications of monody are even more patent than in plain-chant. A revealing example is provided by culturally-segregated medieval Spain, in the four-hundred-odd *cantigas* of Santa Maria garnered together, and perhaps in part composed, by Alfonso X (1230–1280), King of Castile and León. Justifiably nicknamed *El Sabio*, he was a man of high cultivation in poetry, music and the visual arts; he was also interested and probably trained in mathematics and science, and was, under Arab influence, well versed in astronomy. That art may override anthropological and geographical boundaries was proven at his brilliant court, at which Christians, Muslims and Jews worked amicably together under Christian rule. Musically, this equation between East and West encouraged traffic between spirit and flesh.

The texts of the *cantigas*, many written by Alfonso himself, are mostly hymns in praise of the Virgin Mary, extolling her deeds and the miracles performed in her name. Although they are not popular art, being constructed on elaborate principles derived from Provençal troubadour poetry and music, they efface boundaries between sacred and secular. Most troubadour monody pays homage to a real woman; but although the passion with which the poet-musician hymns her is more erotic than agapeic, she is still, within the convention of medieval chivalry, unattainable, and liable to instant metamorphosis into an Eternal Beloved and/or the Virgin Mary. In her turn Mary herself, in the *cantigas* of Alfonso X, becomes a creature of grace and light, a harbinger of the Renaissance who is celebrated in the Rose windows of Chartres Cathedral – as contrasted with the patriarchal authority of a God the Father, let alone the abstraction of a Holy Ghost. Since Mary is Christ's mother, and he is a man as well as a god, the troubadour, singing to his absent beloved, and Alfonso, singing to the Virgin Mary, are alike paying homage to female humanity and to God at the same time. This ambivalence was inherent in the status of women in the Middle Ages. Since a married woman was her husband's vassal, romantic love was impossible within a marriage contract. Outside it a woman could be worshipped but, since she was

usually married to someone else, could be adored only guiltily. This
gave her a dual identity: first as the seraphic Virgin who, though
sensuously lovely, is intangible; secondly as the Dark Goddess of
Gnosticism, at once a lure and a threat.

Alfonso X, collating his *cantigas*, poised between God and the
World, man and woman, spirit and flesh, specifically compared
himself to Orpheus and to the harping King David, healing the pain
of duality through music. *His* Orpheus is not a human spirit aspirant
to godhead but a creature who seeks the eternal return to the creator;
clearly a Beloved who is at once a celestial Queen and a Dark Goddess, and is unattainable in either role, gives to the Dionysiac-Apollonian relationship of the Greeks a changed emphasis. Terrestrial
passion, Christianised and sublimated, induces a thread of melancholy within monodic aspiration. Whereas the essence of plainsong is
that it seems, in its winging continuity, eternal, the most characteristic *cantiga* melodies counteract their airborne flow with cadentially-
falling fourths and fifths. The *cantiga* singer does not invite us to participate in a rite, as does the cantor in Jewish synogogue or Roman
cathedral, or as does the Indian *vina* player, who induces ecstasy
unless, being untalented, he merely promotes boredom. King
Alfonso sang of his desire, and of his sorrow because desire is unap-
peased and unappeasable. The latent wildness of his song was
enhanced by the nasal twang of Arabian-styled instruments that
heterophonically (not harmonically) embellished the monodic line –
though precisely what the singers did with their instruments is still a
matter for speculation. At the same time the pentatonic innocence of
the tunes themselves sounds wistful: perhaps more so to us than to
Alfonso, though melancholy is intrinsic to music that tells us that
though the Mother of God was a woman, he the singer cannot but be
battered and bruised by his *awareness* of the flesh, and his consequent
awareness of the inescapable fact of death. The Renaissance is thus
already implicit in troubadour song; the celebration of the Knight's
lady in association with the Virgin Queen is a move towards human
grace; the Christian life of St Louis complements the chivalric symbolism of Dante's Beatrice.

It is significant that at a time when women were still regarded as
chattels there should have been female troubadours, some of them
talented. Most distinguished among them is the extraordinary
Abbess Hildegard of Bingen, born at Rheinhessen as early as 1098
and by the mid-twelfth century internationally celebrated as

visionary, naturalist, playwright, poet and composer. Her poetry and music are contained in a monumental collection called *Symphonia armonie celestium revelationum*, and the Orphic implications of the title are fulfilled. She is Orphic in the multifariousness of her gifts, which embrace most that was known of the visible and invisible world, and in the manner in which the Latin verses, drawing on traditional sacred texts, are imbued with a personalised fervour, flowing into convoluting melodic lines. Passion is subliminated in an airborne melody wherein power and pathos coexist. Like Alfonso, she is Orphean in revealing the interdependence of natural and supernatural worlds, not in elevating the human *to* the divine. There is something deeply moving, and psychologically revealing, in the fact that the visionary art of a woman – a creature regarded, even when celebate, by monkish medieval man as ancillary to the devil – should thus consummate the melodic essence of the Middle Ages. We may recall the story she told of a King on his throne: around whom 'stood great and beautiful columns ornamented with ivory, bearing the banners of the King with great honour. Then it pleased the King to raise a small feather from the ground, and he commanded it to fly. The feather flew, not because of anything in itself, but because the wind blew it along. Thus am I: *a feather on the breath of God.*' Woman was flesh, sin and death; yet in being a creature of instinct, she was also an Orphic agent of the numinous and a gateway to the unknown. Medieval man's uneasiness about woman plumbs to the heart of human paradox, and effects transition to the 'new birth' inherent in the word 'Renaissance'. At this point the latent Orphic theme becomes patent.

Among many other things, the Renaissance was a rebirth of classical antiquity precisely because the Greek world had been humanly, rather than mystically, orientated. This is why with the Renaissance the Orpheus story regains its significance as a parable about man's attempt to arrogate to himself godly powers. Not unexpectedly, the tale is now dramatically projected, imitated on some form of stage. To this development, however, two basic modifications in music's nature and function were necessary: one was the evolution of the 'Western' notion of harmony as progression in time; the other was the partial subservience of music to words not, as in the Middle Ages, as invocation, but as communication from one human being to another. The harmonic evolution was associated with the growing significance of dance as an organising principle; the verbal development was inseparable from the birth of what we now call opera. In this chapter we are concerned with the first of these modifications, though the one is implicit in the other.

During the Middle Ages the 'Western' world had used music to basically religious ends. The Christian Word – reputed to be God's, rather than man's – is incarnate in the plain song, releasing us from personal identity. Borne on its apparently endless line, we hopefully lay aside the burden of mortality, sin and guilt, floating aloft to join the angels in the stratosphere – or at least in the vaulted roof of church or cathedral. The modern world emerged over several centuries as Renaissance man learned to think of himself as the focal centre of the universe, rather than as a cog in the cosmography of God. This changing view of man's destiny involved the most fundamental watershed in musical history: which was manifest when monophonic gave way to polyphonic principle. Other cultures, of course, fortuitously created music in more than one voice or part; only Renaissance Europe, however, became obsessed by the phenomena that occur when two or more voices are sounded simultaneously. It is true that in the twelfth century *ars antiqua* of Léonin and Pérotin at Notre Dame there is little interest in the harmonic consequences of the simultaneously-sounding tones, for both organum and heterophony are techniques for embellishing a single line rather than alternations of 'chords' existing in time. Even so, the acceptance of 'poly-phony' – a music of many voices rather than one – must sooner or later imply mensuration if the parts are to keep together; and mensuration imposes the pulse of time and the recognition of 'events' occuring within it. The more man thinks of himself as a creature existing within time, rather than as a being who seeks to transcend it, the more meaningful must harmonic sequence and consequence become. This is evident if we compare with the thirteenth century *Ars Antiqua* of Léonin and Pérotin the fourteenth century *ars nova* of Guillaume de Machaut, or still more with the Italian *ars nova* contemporary with it.

Partly perhaps for climatic reasons, Italy rather than France was in the vanguard of the new humanistic music, so it is hardly surprising that Francesco Landini (*c.* 1325–97), who had several monastic appointments and offered advice on organ construction in eccesiastical buildings, should have owed his renown almost exclusively to his secular music; of his one hundred and fifty-four extant compositions only two are religious motets. His secular love songs are sometimes affiliated to 'mystically' chivalric traditions, but may also encompass a vibrant responsiveness to everyday life: as is true of his specifically

Orphic piece, 'Sy dolce non sono'. The verses, which may possibly be Landini's own, compare the sweetness with which Orpheus's voice charmed birds and beasts with the crowing of his pet rooster in the woods. Nature, and the sensuous pleasures it evokes, deflate the spiritual pretentions of Orpheus, not to mention Philomel and Phoebus. True, the humanism of Italian *ars nova* does not entirely deny the linear-mathematical principles of *ars antiqua* since the lowest of the three parts – traditionally called the 'tenor' since it is *held* – is built on the old, god-like predeterminacy: a metrical pattern of seven bars is repeated consistently, though the pitches change. At the same time the music is moving from the metaphysical towards the physical. The piece is not in the metrically-patterned *aaab* of the fourteenth-century madrigal, but is through-composed, in anticipation of the madrigal of the sixteenth century. Moreover, Orpheus's human powers in relation to Nature are stressed at the expense of his religious heritage, as is manifest in every aspect of the music's technique. Above the authoritarian tenor, the two upper parts are free, complicated in cross-rhythms and, to our ears, 'jazzy' in their syncopations and melismatic embellishments within the triple pulse.

Renaissance man, at the dawn of the Western world, capers proudly but a shade fearfully on the visible and tactile earth – as, at the Western world's twilight, the deracinated Negro will do in his New Found Land. The medieval technique of the *hocket* or 'hiccup' (a truncation of rhythm originally made on mathematical principles) becomes physical excitation. Similarly, the harmony, though still derived 'horizontally' from the movement of parts individually composed without reference to vertical progression, relishes what we would consider ungrammatical passing dissonances, while manifesting increasing partiality for the euphonious third, at the expense of the Middle Ages' more austere fourths and fifths. Moreover, although the fragmented rhythms are medieval in permitting no expressive interpretation of the text – indeed the text may even be omitted if one or more parts be played instrumentally – it is possible that the music embraces 'naturalistic' illustration. Not only do the so-called 'Landini cadences' – which the composer did not invent but was fond of – ornamentally resolve cadential dissonance, stressing the sharp leading note in a way which implies direction rather than the timeless circularity of plainchant; we may even hear in some of these cadences the crowing of that Orphic cock! Presumably the verses, deflating Orpheus to one of Nature's braggarts, are a witticism; point is added to the joke if we recall the sexual symbolism of cocks – at least in English.

The harmonic revolution, only latent in the secularity of this medievally-conceived madrigal, ripens throughout the fifteenth century, notably in the music of Dunstable, which counteracts the sensuousness of newly-discovered triadic harmony with the a-temporal suavity of melodic lines still affiliated to plainchant. Only later in the fifteenth century are the implications of the harmonic revolution fully revealed; and one can almost date a moment when it happens. In 1463 the canon-composer Guillaume Dufay composed, towards the end of a long life, a four-part *Ave Regina* which he asked to have sung at his deathbed. The motet, calling on the Virgin Queen as Orphic intermediary between man and God, incorporates into its liturgical text an appeal that the Lord should have mercy on his dying Dufay. This unmedieval intrusion of the personal into the liturgical also provokes a 'modern' harmonic technique. Up to this point the music has absorbed its triadic sensuousness into the continuous flow of plainsong-like melody. With the words 'miserere tui labentis Dufay', however, the liquid major thirds are abruptly contradicted by a *minor* third; and the dramatic effort of this *false relation* is inseparable from the fact that it involves opposition, and therefore dualism, rather than monism. Moreover, the effect is inconceivable except in relation to Time. Because it is a shock, we are conscious of *when it happens*: momentarily, the music no longer carries us outside time but makes us aware that the sands of Time – our time, for we are dying – are running out. The metamorphosis of the communal 'miserere nobis' into the personal 'miserere tui labentis Dufay' tells us that henceforth our separateness from God is the wondrous heart of our 'miserable' condition.

Only a century later was Western man brave enough to confront this discovery head on. For the nonce he drew back, appalled, sidestepping the threat of mutability and mortality. In his evasive action he called on temporally-based dance rhythms and clearly-defined, simple triadic harmonies to express his hopeful satisfaction with himself as a social being, sporting with his fellows in harmony and grace, in potentially civilised societies. Of course the greatest composers of the late fifteenth and early sixteenth centuries, notably Josquin de Près, revealed the shape of things to come, as supreme geniuses must. As a Renaissance man he excelled in every kind of music current in his day, from tragically penitential psalm to ribald chanson. And it is characteristic that for him sacred and secular genres

overlap: from which point of view the *Déploration* he composed on
the death of his beloved teacher Ockeghem is revealing.

Josquin opens with an unambigous reference to the medieval and
Roman Church, for he quotes plainsong from the traditional liturgy of
the Requiem service, with text in hieratic Latin. This leads, however,
into a setting in the vernacular of a modern French poem paying
homage to the master who was also a friend. Basically, its idiom is that
of traditionally 'spiritual' polyphony, non-metrical, long flowing. But
the civic aspects of Renaissance style are no less evident, for the song
of mourning is sung by Renaissance courtiers masquerading as shepherds and shepherdesses. The recurrent falling minor thirds, tolling
like funereal bells, impart harmonic density to ecclesiastical idiom;
dance rhythms pervade their song, even though the individual lines
efface metrical time. These elegiac nymphs and shepherds relate to
the Arcadian landscapes of classical antiquity *because* they are Renaissance humanists – human and humane, even in the act of mourning –
before they are mystically-inclined Christians. This is why the flowing
lines and corporal rhythms between them generate a third dimension,
which is personal sorrow, incarnate in progressively modern, 'functional' harmony. Though there is nothing as stark as that isolated false
relation in Dufay's *Ave Regina,* there are alternations of tension and
relaxation, existing in time. Unlike Dunstable's music, this piece has
beginning, middle and end; an elegiac lament leads to consummation,
or at least to resignation to the fact of mortality. The chanson is
Orphic in a significantly ambivalent sense. The 'nymphes des bois,
déesses des fontaines, Chantres expers de toutes nations' summon
sound to assuage human grief, in music of incipiently operatic
intensity, while at the same time the plainsong cantus firmus grants to
the dead master rest and light everlasting. The last stanza calls on
composing friends and colleagues – specified by name, for they are
real people, in the real world – both to share in human sorrow, and to
appeal for superhuman beatitude. Monody is basically a religious act;
polyphony is also a social act as, facing mortality, we comfort one
another.

Here is the essential technique of the High Renaissance: the horizontal flow of the lines is inseparable from the vertical harmonic sense
they make when sung together; Josquin is the first composer *known* to
have thought of composition as a process simultaneously horizontal
and vertical. But the fulfilment of this could not have attained classical
formulation in the age of Palestrina had not the civic aspects of music

first become aware of their unalienable rights, as they had never been in the Middle Ages. A minor near-contemporary of Josquin, Clement Jannequin, illustrates this neatly. Despite his clerical office, Janne-quin wrote not for the Church nor even for the old aristocracy, but rather for the affluent bourgeois upper class who congregated in, and established music publishing houses in, the mercantile centres of Paris, Lyons and elsewhere. Giving his public what it wanted, Janne-quin composed a mere brace of masses to some three hundred chan-sons: which are fascinating not so much for musical distinction as for the fact that they banish the last trace of scholasticism. In his music there is no plainsong, no canonic puzzle, no magical mystery, but an outdoor sunlit music for dancing folk, in an urban, not bucolic, context. Often the pieces are descriptive and illustrative, in homopho-nic textures that celebrate the social concord of people living together in emotional as well as aural euphony. Cadences with metrically-defi-ned leading notes prevail, and if the tunes are sometimes modal, they resemble rural folksongs rather than plainsong; rhythms are cosily symmetrical.

The love-songs paralled the poetry of Ronsard, whom Jannequin set, evoking a 'green paradise of childish loves' with no more than a wistful recognition that love's dream is not likely to be true, at least for long. One of the most beautiful of his love songs, 'Ce joli moi de Mai', became immensely popular, no doubt because its pristine simplicity precariously encapsulates the 'premier matin du monde' that Renais-sance man, in his more hopeful moments, celebrated. The descriptive pieces parallel Rabelais, paying homage to the blithe mindlessness of birds who are not 'conscious' as we are, or to the perhaps hardly less unconscious aggression of War. The chirruping birds make us laugh, as Jannequin surely meant them to. Indeed the birds are surrogates for us as, momentarily released from consciousness and conscience, we merrily relish the Renaissance's New Day. In the battle pieces, bellicosity encourages the square-rhythmed tread of marching feet and the togetherness of homophony rather than free individuation of line. The war pieces too make us laugh, and we cannot be certain that Jannequin intended no ironic undertow.* Men in their competitive combativeness may be as daft as birds; male prowess may be risible

---

* The deepest and most complex of all the problems involved in 'authenticity' is that although we may know what happens in a work of art, and how it affects us, we cannot be sure how it affected *them*. Looking closely

even as we pay it the homage of imitation. Birds and war in Jannequin are complementary inanities and wish-fulfilments, occasions for mirth in both the medieval and the modern senses.

The 'never-never land' Jannequin presents in his vocal chansons is echoed in the dance music for instruments that proliferated in manic euphoria throughout Europe. While dance music had, of course, always existed, it was regarded during the Middle Ages as for the most part too trivial to justify notation. Now in the sixteenth century it is not only notated but also published, as a distributable commodity, functional in towns and cities as well as at courts. The instruments were not usually specified; one could employ any that came to hand, and town waits had different instruments from those at aristocratic courts. All this vivaciously dancing music celebrates confidence in the hedonistic present, as do Jannequin's chansons. On the tide of this this confidence rode the earliest explicit dramatisations of Orpheus's story: which hopefully affirmed humanity's potential while skirting the the pain and terror inherent in the notion of man sufficient unto himself.

This nervousness is manifest in Robert Henryson's beautiful poem on the Orpheus and Eurydice story, the late fifteenth-century date of which is contemporary with the first musical-theatrical treatment of the tale we are to examine. The Scots poet tells the story with a human empathy that plumbs the depths of feeling in the famous lament, 'Quhar art thow gane, my luf Eurydice?'. Yet the bulk of the poem is in the 'ornate' manner of medieval rhetoric, while Henryson transports Orpheus, on his way back from supernatural realms, through a medieval stellar landscape wherein he hears the Plantonic Music of the Spheres, described in obsolete technical detail:

In his passage among the planeitis all
he hard a hevinly melody and sound,
passing all instrumentis musicall . . .

Thair leirit he tonis proportionat,
as duplare, troplare, and emetrious,
aeolius, and eik the quadruplait . . .
          [etc.]

Moreover, after the telling of the tale Henryson – or it may have been Bannantyne who collated the manuscripts – appended a Moralitas

at Renaissance portraiture, however, I suspect they were more like us than we might superficially expect. In a sense, the likeness is what survives through so many hundred years.

which, in medieval terms, negates the myth's humanistic burden, bluntly reproving Orpheus for pride and presumption:

Thairfoir downwart we cast our myndis E,
blindit with lust, and may nocht upwartis fle;
sould our desyre be socht up in the spheiris
when it is tedderit in this worldis reairis,
quhyle on the flesche, quhyle on this worldis wrak!
and to the hevin full smale intent we tak . . .

Apollo than for this abusion,
Quhilk is the god of divinatioun,
for he usurpet of his facultie,
put him to hell, and there remanis he.

Renaissance man, it seems, could believe in human self-sufficiency only so long as he did not think too hard. Absence of thought was easiest if material conditions were relatively comfortable: as they were at the courts of the petty princelings who, at their festive junketings, products of affluence, attempted to bolster their slightly jittery self-esteem. Basically the Renaissance masque was a party of like-minded men and women, usually masters and mistresses of lesser breeds without and within the law. Frequently these masques graced the weddings of important persons, or of persons who believed themselves to be important. A marriage is a contract, sexual, sacred and, above all, economic.

In 1480 two grand marriages were celebrated at the court of Cardinal Francesco Gonzago of Mantua: that of Chiara Gonzaga to Gilbert de Montpensier and that of Isabella d'Este to Francesco Gonzaga the younger. For the occasion the Cardinal commissioned Angelo Poliziano to produce an entertainment. He wrote *La Favola di Orfeo*: a fashionable theme which could be construed, with a little sleight of hand, as apposite to weddings. Its performance was so successful that it was repeated several times in Mantua and elsewhere, and was published in 1494. For one of the later performances no less a person than Leonardo de Vinci designed sets which, for their elegance and ingenuity, caused a sensation. Poliziano, if less prestigious than Leonardo, was also a quintessential Renaissance man, nurtured in Florence on ancient languages and philosophy, versed in Greek and Latin rhetoric, familiar with Platonic doctrines of Proportion. His *Orfeo*, described as a 'rappresentazione profana', was his most substantial work: it recounts the story straight, not omitting the Bacchic denouément. As a true Renaissance man, however, Poliziano

eschews Henryson's quasi-medieval *moralitas*; adhering to the model
of Ovid and Virgil, he celebrates Neoplatonic love as a power purpor-
ting to be stronger than fate.

Since *La Favola di Orfeo* was conceived as classical drama it was
provided with song and dance as well as words, emulating what the
Renaissance believed to be the theatrical principles of antiquity.
Oddly enough, in view of its popularity, no music for it has survived.
Yet there may be point in this anonymity since the production is not a
'work' of art but a party, a communal entertainment to which many
contribute. The music, springing from the exigencies of the moment,
lived in a hedonistic present, as does much pop music today. There
was a capacious well of such music in the *frottola* tradition, an Italian
complement to the French *chanson* as practised by Jannequin: brief,
four-part pieces, consistently homophonic, concordant, metrical, the
words sung tunefully, one syllable to a note. Instrumental dance
music, similar in idiom, likewise abounded: childishly tuneful, boun-
cily rhythmed, hopefully without a care in a careladen world. Instrumental *intromesse* were used to cover scene changes, and in the course
of time developed into independent mood-pieces, often with allegori-
cal associations. At this date there was no recitative for the protagonists musically to converse in. For the most part they spoke, breaking
into song and dance as occasion offered, in a manner closer to what we
would call musical comedy than to opera.

While there is no score for this production, we know that the chief
court composer was Bartolomeo Tromboncino, who was born at
Verona around 1470 and died, probably in Venice, in 1530. Other
composers associated with the court were Serafino dell'Aquila
(1466–1500), Michele Pesenti (*c*. 1470–after 1524), and Marco Cara
(*c*. 1470–*c*. 1525). A considerable amount of music by these
composers is extant; some of it has been adapted for a recorded
performance of this *Orfeo* by the Huegas Ensemble, directed by Paul
van Nevel. We cannot of course be certain that the lost original music
would be the same in effect as that used in the recorded version. We
can, however, be fairly confident that it would have been similar in
range and character, and certain that it would have made no attempt
to plumb the depths of the story it intuitively needed to dramatise. It
still fumbled, half blind and deaf, in the darkness of Renaissance
light, not yet able to comprehend what was happening; one reason
why no score survives is because much of the music was improvised,
or developed ad hoc from rudimentary notations.

We may therefore comment on the recorded performance 'as though' it were a live performance in the present moment: when the festivities open with jolly music for brass, to which the nobility processionally enter. Similar music accompanied the junketing of civic dignitaries, middle as well as upper-class, all over Europe, and the jollification is for active participation; listened to 'cold', it sounds forlorn. To some degree this applies to the whole of the Prologue, which is appropriately introduced by the messenger-god Mercury, and takes place both here and now at this very court, and also in an Arcadian Golden Age wherein nymphs and shepherds carol, as they do in contemporary madrigals and chansons, of love's joys and sorrows: especially the latter, given that human sensuality is of its nature ephemeral.

The opening dialogue is between an old shepherd, Mopeus, apt to moralise from the presumed experience of age, and a young shepherd Airisteus – Eurydice's *other* lover who was chasing her when, stumbling, she was bitten by the serpent. But Aristeus is not simply the villain of the piece; indeed in the original myth he is more like Orpheus's *alter ego*, since they both shared the same father – Apollo. Although Aristeus's maternal ancestry – Cyrene, a water-nymph – hints at a connection with waterily unconscious depths, he is presented not as fallen man and vile ravisher but as himself a lovelorn swain for whom Eurydice displays, if not heart-felt affection, a teasing partiality. That she falls, literally, and is snake-bitten, is not his or her fault but an accident of fortune, well known to be blind. The play, in this version, seems to be saying that since we live in a fallen world, all we can hope to do is to keep our peckers up: which is why, though Aristeus himself suffers love-grief and prophesies that of Orpheus, these dark feelings leave no stain on the music's melodic blandness and harmonic euphony. All the frottola-like choruses and solo airs are brisk-rhythmed, innocently concordant, delicately ornamented, haloed by chattering plucked strings and bubbling recorders.

So awareness of mutability scarcely sullies that 'green paradise of childish loves' such as we heard in Jannequin's chansons. As in Jannequin, the transient wistfulness may derive from the tunes' ambivalence between 'modern' diatonicism and medieval modality. But the young Arcadians will not overtly admit that Eden is a Forgotten Garden; they prefer to make sorrow itself a pleasure, so that Aristeus seeks no cure for his 'dolce doglie'. Even his outpouring of grief to the impervious forests, wherein he admits that time destroys all, is not more than gently melancholic. 'Dite che la mia vita fugge via E consuma come brina al sole', he pipes, his vocal line cooing while guileless recorders spatter dew on the grass. In such contexts the *tierce de Picardi* – the major cadential resolution of a minorish mode – sounds more than normally touching. Its bliss is frail.

When the action switches to Orpheus, the music acquires more gravity; and Orfeo, being a hero and demigod, sings in Latin rather than in the pseudo-shepherds' vernacular. But he begins in real, not mythical, life, with fulsome compliments to His Eminence Cardinal Francesco Gonzaga, who is grand enough to warrant a Latin oration and whom he equates with Apollo, the divine poet. Apollo-Gonzaga can alone save Orfeo (and he represents Mankind) from the ravages of fate and time. All this praise-music sounds (at least to us) faintly sad in its modality, perhaps because it is asking whether, even in this court of courts, human pretentions can be valid. Of course they cannot: for immediately after this rhetorical solo and choric invocation to Maecenas's glory and bounty, a shepherd-messenger enters with the 'crudel novella' of Eurydice's death. The song is slightly slow, compared with most of the music, and was probably accompanied by regal, traditional instrument of death. Even so, though the manner is religiously incantatory, there is no musical evidence that this snake can bite; and in the sacral music for trombones and drums that follows the message, Time marches on in metrical solemnity but with little dramatic impact. Orpheus 'tries out' his lyre-lute in the diatonic concords of Renaissance optimism, and decides that he and it are strong enough to challenge death. The mutability theme of the Prologue thus acquires a measure of substance, and the succeeding solo with choric interludes – appealing to the 'spiriti infernali' to tame snakes, open portals and have pity on his suffering – is the most affecting music in the piece. It is an interestingly odd mixup, since the spirits of the underworld behave like Christian angels who may, if he is lucky, waft Orfeo to peace. Death is unanswerably peace of a kind. The melismatic music for the taming of the snakes induces hypnosis, if not *rigor mortis*.

Pluto, answering Orfeo, is naturally a bass and naturally accompanied by funereal shawms and sackbuts. He sings in rigidly metrical rhythm, imposing fate's Law. When Orfeo tells Pluto what has happened to Eurydice, slyly pointing the parallel with Pluto's own wife Proserpina (Latin for Persephone), the music is again fairly merry,

elaborately ornamented. There is little musical evidence of his suffering, let alone hers, though the liveliness of the music may testify to
human resilience as well as insensitivity. Man seems to win, for Pluto
relents, though he delivers his warning about backward glances with
still stricter metrical rigour and with schoolmasterish repeated notes.
An orchestral interlude of rejoicing over the reprieve is briefly
rumbustuous. Even Eurydice's second rape by death is gentle, not
dramatic, let alone desperate. Similarly, Orfeo's lament, after the
second death, when he bids farewell to women and the world, has no
tinge of desperation. Again it is no more than gravely wistful, and
even that may be more in our ears – after several more 'fallen' centuries
– than in his. When the chorus advises submission, *faute de mieux*, to
destiny ('Segue chi fugge: a chi la vuol s'asconde: E vanne e vien alla
riva l'onde'), the music resembles that of the Arcadian Prologue. We
live in a dream we have no choice but to accept – until we can learn to
grow up. It cannot be an accident that throughout the Middle Ages
and the Renaissance, almost up to the turn into the seventeenth
century, most of the greatest – and most humanly aware – music was
associated with the church and with man's relationship to God.
Courageously trying to do without him, Renaissance man at first
stumbled – as did Eurydice herself.

That Poliziano gives the story its original horrific end seems, in this
context, surprising, though it may be a consequence of his, and
Renaissance man's, very failure to confront the tangled human realities inherent in the tale. On the whole text and music evade suffering,
sin and guilt: so at the end he can offer no more than a shrug of the
shoulders. Momentarily, we have made a paradise on earth: now it is
over; there is nothing to be done about it. That shrug is incarnate in
the music of the Bacchantes who appear to tear Orfeo to pieces. Their
choral music is fierce, maybe, but remarkably cheerful; indeed it is
not radically different from the euphoric music of the Prologue's
Arcadian shepherds, except that its manner is low, bucolic rather than
sophisticated. In this it forms an antimasque to the masque; and we
shall see in the next chapter that although the antimasque in celeb-
rations of the Mercurian Monarch presents the negative, libidinously
inchaote elements in our fallen natures coexistent with our presumptive earthly paradise, it is always comic if grotesque, never frightening. Such is the case with this late fifteenth-century *Orfeo*: for after 'lo
scellerato' has been briskly dismembered the Bacchantes – idiot
travesties of those archetypal Terrible Mothers – invite everyone to

the 'real' wedding feast, recommending mass amnesia through inebriation. Such opportunist escapism, such dismissal of tragedy in farce, obliterates distinctions between high and low as well as between life and death, making an odd denouement to a piece ostensibly about man as a semi-divine hero. The play is dismissed as being, after all, 'only' play-acting, what might be or might have been. Renaissance man has not, as yet, made a very brave showing. It will be a long time before a composer appears who, facing man's solitariness, is strong enough to confront his tragic destiny.

Chapter II

Christ-Orpheus Platonised in the High Renaissance

Dowland as 'the English Orpheus'; Monteverdi's
Favola in musica, L'Orfeo (1607)

The 1480 *Orfeo* which graced – and at the end perhaps disgraced – a Cardinal's dual wedding ceremony tells a tale the human implications of which the entertainment, in song, dance and spectacle, did its best to evade. Yet it seems that men and women needed to dramatise those themes. Over the next hundred years they acquired the necessary techniques, technique being the external manifestation of experience and self-knowledge. In the process masque, a party and fiesta, grows up into opera, a drama and *tragoedia*.

In the 1480 *Orfeo* harmony and symmetrical dance rhythms are synonyms for social concord; they are musically what keeps us going, in 'togetherness'. But the communal aspect is an end in itself; there is little evidence here that communities are collocations of individual human beings. As personal identity begins to complement communal anonymity, harmony, especially when explored on instruments, learns to become expressive; and melodic line learns how to reflect the vargaries of human feeling contained in a poetic text. The transition is clearly revealed in the history of the lute during the sixteenth century, both as a solo instrument and as an accompaniment to solo voice.

Although we do not know what the precise instrumentation of the 1480 *Orfeo* was, its Orpheus indubitably played lute, lyra da bracchio and/or harp, emulating the man-god's lyre. Because of its Orphic properties, the lute was accepted as king of instruments throughout the sixteenth century. As early as the first two decades of the century the Italian virtuoso Pietrobono de Burzellis was explicitly compared to Orpheus, a man aspiring to Apollonian divinity. To hear Pietrobono play was to be transported from earth to heaven, for he made the Platonic music of the spheres audible to our mundane ears; it was even claimed that he had the power to raise the dead, or conversely to

metamorphose flesh and blood into stone. Again he was a two-way
Orpheus: either his virtuosity might seem to elevate him to godhead,
or he could lose selfhood in being united to the Whole. Like Orpheus
himself, Pietrobono is a somewhat legendary figure. Since his music
was largely improvised, we can have no adequate notion of its extraordinary effect; but it must have been melodically, harmonically and
rhythmically exciting in a manner lacking in the emotionally-neutral
social music of masques and fiestas. A little later, in 1517, we have
notated evidence of the music of another lute virtuoso, Vincenzo
Capirola, a collection of whose works was copied out by a pupil in
order that his improvisations might be preserved for posterity. Much
of the expressiveness of the music must again have been dependent on
the heat of the moment, but enough comes across in the notations to
indicate why Capirola was known as 'il divino'. Platonically he reveals
the divine music as it exists in the eternal mind of God; his instrument
is 'instrumental' to an Eternal Return. Aspiring to godhead himself,
he uses his ears as Mercurian messengers, as though they were
'chinks' in the muddy darkness that surrounds us. 'By the ears, the
soul receives the echoes of that incomparable music, by which it is led
back to the deep and silent memory of the harmony which it previously enjoyed. The whole soul then kindles with desire to fly back to
its original home, so that it may enjoy that true music again.'

Similar accounts were given of the playing of Francesco da Milano,
who transported listeners into states of *ekstasis* and whose music we
can today examine in publication and listen to in potentially divine or
frenzied performance. Given his Orphic propensities, it is not surprising that Francesco da Milano should, even more than his pre-
decessors, relish all the formal varieties of instrumental music curren-
tly practised, from quasi-ecclesiastical polyphony, to symphonically-
developed dance, to rhapsodic prelude, to symmetrically-disposed air,
effecting transmutations of and between the genres; indeed quasi-
improvised evolution from imitative 'points' may itself be conceived
as an Orphic process. Soon the lute tradition, centred on Italy where
the Renaissance had most vigorously flowered, spread over Europe:
especially to France, where the lute became the essential instrument
of aristocratic *ruelles* and *salons*, being capable of the utmost tonal and
rhythmic refinement. The lute's sounds were a language through
which Orphic man spoke; Antoine Francisque's collection of lute
pieces published in 1600 was in fact entitled *Trésor d'Orphée*, while
the anthology that le vieux Gaultier – the eldest of a distinguished

family of lutenists – called *L'Entretien des Dieux* implies in its title that divine voices might reach us, and that we might humanly attain to the divine. Significantly, the pieces are both polyphonic, in continuity with old ecclesiastical traditions, and also dance music, dance being an embodiment of social concord. The Mercurian nature of Gaultier's music is endorsed by the published edition's exquisite calligraphy and emblematic visual illustrations, documenting the therapeutic effects of musical modes and manners.

At the end of the sixteenth century lute tradition reaches its climax in England, in the work of John Dowland – an even more legendary figure than the lute virtuosi referred to above. Born in 1563, possibly in Dublin, he was London-nurtured in indigenous musical traditions, but soon acquired a European reputation. Converted to the Roman Catholic faith while in the service of the English ambassador at Paris from 1580 to 1584, he later travelled in Italy and Germany, partly because he found advancement at home difficult, whether because of his religion, or his somewhat prickly temperament, or a mixture of both. Between 1594 and 1606 he was lutenist to Christian IV of Denmark, at the very court of Elsinore where Shakespeare's Hamlet had the 'cursed spite' to be required to set right the consequence of the Fall. Although the unreliable Thomas Fuller surprisingly described Dowland as 'a cheerful person, passing his days in lawful merriment', this account accords neither with the (often Hamlet-like) temper of his music nor with the valedictory cadence of his prefatorial prose. After his return to England he belatedly obtained appointments at the Courts of James I and Charles I, the situation perhaps being alleviated because, disillusioned by Jesuitical casuistry, he had relinquished the Old Faith. But he was never a churchman in the conventional sense, and his approach to the world seems to have been as much stoic as Christian. He took the malcontent's line that, in the words of Gibbons's noble choral ayre 'The Silver Swan', 'more geese than swans now live, more fools than wise'; and had no doubt that he was the swan with the most silver voice and the sleekest plumage. Ultimately his contemporaries agreed with him, dubbing him, as was only to be expected, 'the English Orpheus'.

Of course Dowland's lute repertory embraced many domestically functional pieces – brief dances and 'puffs' dedicated to friends and colleagues, variations on folk and popular tunes communicable on several levels. His temperament seems to have had a fair share of Elizabethan exuberance – and perhaps of Irish charm – as well as of

Jacobean melancholy; had this not been so it is doubtful whether his greatest works could have attained their excellence. These supreme works – dances, notably pavanes and galliards, developed to 'symphonic' proportions, and large-scale polyphonic fancies transforming vocal techniques instrumentally – are those in which the Mercurian ambiguity is most potent. He explores, and seems almost to *discover*, the maximum human intensity through harmony and texture; at the same time he 'reveals' the divine order on Platonic principles assimilated into Christian tradition.

Renaissance man believed that the proportions inherent in music's harmonic series (discovered, relevantly enough, by the Ancient Greek Pythagoras) offered a blueprint for the order manifest in Nature and endemic in men and women, if they could behave as their god-given reason dictated. Since the primacy of the octave's relationship of 2:1 and of the fifth's relationship of 3:2 is scientifically demonstrable, similar proportions must govern the ordering of visible space in architecture and painting, and of the movements of human bodies in dance. They ought even to apply to social institutions; good taste in life and in art had been proved to be not merely subjective but founded on rational principles. Sir Henry Wootton adapted Vitruvius's terms *Eurhythmia, Symmetria, Decor* and *Distributo* to contemporary architecture in a way that amounted to a humane social philosophy. But of all the arts music remained most susceptible to philosophical formulation, to which the Orphic lute was basic. As Mersenne put it in 1636, 'the lute hath gained such influence over the other stringed instruments either because people have given it this advantage, or it has achieved this great success by virtue of its excellence and perfection. A lutenist will succeed in everything when playing his instrument. So, for example, he will be able to represent the two geometric means, the duplication of the cube, the quadrature of the circle, the proportion of the movements of the stars and the speed of falling bodies.'

The most profound, and also the most systematic, manifestation of Dowland's Mercurianism is in the twin polyphonic fancies, 'Forlorne Hope' and 'Farewell'. Both are harmonically plangent, since the 'theme' polyphonically imitated is a chromatic scale, of its nature inducive of harmonic shock. In the first fancy the scale descends through a fourth: an inversion of God's interval of the perfect fifth, which had acquired symbolic significance alike in medieval Christianity and in Renaissance neo-Platonism and hermeticism. The falling fourth 'represents' man's descent from kinship with God into Shakespeare's 'muddy vesture of decay'. The declension, being chromatic, creates harmonic disturbance, obliterating the lucidity of quasi-vocal modality as the tessitura sinks. The chromatic cry is repeated seven times in the opening ten bars, both numbers being magic; at the unlucky thirteenth entry the music slows to heavy crotchets, descending to murky depths. Traditionally, the strings of the lute were associated with the four elements, of which the lowest was earth. Having been buried in earth, however, battered man desperately rallies, for the final stretch of the fancy explodes in extravagant virtuosity, the theme momentarily rising instead of falling, the figuration glittering in rapid scales and roulades. The extreme difficulty of the music is part of the point, as its exhibitionism reflects the follies of the temporal world whilst it is at the same time a kind of pride, so that the chromaticism is not, after all, totally destructive. As Anthony Rooley has put it in notes to which I am already indebted, 'there are sixteen statements of the chromatic theme in all, which is four times four. The final statement falls a seventh, through all the chromatic tones, and actually splits into two fourths pivoting on a central note. John Dowland combines a thorough plan of number symbolism based on the number four with an emotive work of the first order.'

If 'Forlorne Hope' is 'about' man's submission to the mire and the melancholic desperation that induces, the complementary fancy, 'Farewell', concerns the possibility of redemption. Since its theme is still a chromatic scale, it too is harmonically emotive; but since the scale in this case *rises*, it may balance its companion fancy with a hope that is not forlorn, but purgatorial. There are again seven magic statements of the theme in the first section, each being (in Rooley's phrase) an 'expansion of awareness'; the piece attains a point of 'profound awakening' when the theme returns in bar 49, rising a whole octave in four bars. In the middle reaches the fugal entries pile up in chromatic ascent, in a double spiral of seven plus seven. After the climax the music descends to calm by way of chains of dissonant secundal appoggiaturas. Despite the passionate, even dramatic, intensity of these suspensions, they are 'numerologically' ordered by the number eight, hermetically symbolic of union with the divine. The piece is called 'Farewell' not in valedictory lament but in a literal sense. Saying goodbye to the world, Dowland musically demonstrates that man – the more so when powerfully aware of the joyous or horrendous contagion of the world – must lose himself to find himself. This, indeed, is *how* we may 'Fare Well'; the two sides of Dowland's Mercurian temperament have become one.

This evidence suggests that Dowland was a profoundly if precariously religious man whose faith was personal rather than the property of an Established Church. Almost all his music is for solo lute or for voice, usually solo voice, with lute accompaniment. Late in life, however, he published alternative versions of some of his solo ayres harmonised in four parts; some of these set religious verse which, being introspective, is far from simple affirmation. The choral version of 'Thou Mighty God' – which includes in its three biblical narratives the Orphic story of Saul and David – is noble but *intensely* dramatic; relatively short, declamatory phrases, rhetorical rhythmic gestures and 'pathetic' chromatically-altered harmony extract the maximum human pith from religious experience, or rather from a painful approach to it.

Whereas the divine intricacies of late medieval and early Renaissance polyphony, seeking transcendence, had little interest in specific verbal meaning, single syllables being spread melismatically over many notes, the reforms of the Council of Trent and then of the English Reformed Church aimed to encourage in church 'the best sort of melody and music' – as the Preface to the Queen's Prayer Book of 1559 put it – 'that may be conveniently devised, *having respect that the sentence of the hymn be understanded and perceived*' (my italics). Dowland's late 'spiritual madrigals' such as 'Thou mighty God' – which comes from the significantly titled *A Pilgrimes Solace* published in 1612 – mark a further stage in this humanising of polyphony. Obviously, however, a more basic means of emphasising verbal meaning is to eschew vocal polyphony, and even homophony, altogether and to concentrate on a single vocal line discreetly supported by instrumental harmonies on the lute, the most portable, as well as the most subtle, of accompanying instruments. It is not therefore surprising that Dowland's most substantial and – notwithstanding the range and potency of his music for solo lute – most significant contribution lies in his solo ayres, of which he published four volumes between 1597 and 1612. It is oversimple, but perhaps justifiable, to say that the first volume concentrates on love and life, the second volume introspectively on tears and melancholy, the third on love as Platonic assuagement and the fourth (a Pilgrimes Solace) on love as spiritual purgation.

A religious or at least spiritual dimension is latent in many of
Dowland's ayres, though they are ostensibly secular love songs unri-
valled in the history of English song both in lyrical potency and in
responsiveness to words. It is no accident that his famous 'Lacrimae',
'Flow my teares', should, judging from the number of literary
references to it extant, have haunted the popular imagination no less
than it appealed to upper-class connoisseurs. Its subject is fundamental to the Elizabethan-Jacobean consciousness and, indeed, to that of
humanity itself. Although superficially the anonymous poem might
be mistaken for a conventional outpouring of the Wailing Lover, we
recall that that theme was rooted in medieval chivalry and troubadour
convention. With the weakening of religious impulse, or at least faith,
the loss or unattainability of the beloved receives a more humanistic
interpretation: she may be difficult of access because man, seeking
self-dependence, is crying for the moon. 'I freeze when present;
absent, my desire is hot', says the archetypal Renaissance poet
Petrarch, summing up the essence of romantic love, and anticipating
the contemporary tag 'You can't win'. Since the realisation of earthly
desires is improbable and even their apparent satisfaction disap-
points, we can understand why the greatest madrigals and ayres do
not so much deal with particular love-relationships as make
statements about the mutability inherent in being human. Any
expression of *human* love, after the Fall, longs for an eternal return.

The stylised verses which Renaissance poets wrote for music are a
means of distancing personal passion without denying it, for this is
what is asked of a courtier aspiring to *cortesia*. The rhetorical tropes
characteristic of the Astrophel and Stella sequence of that 'parfit
English gentleman' Sir Philip Sidney had musical counterparts in no
less rhetorical devices of phrase balance and ornamentation; this is
one reason why Dowland, most powerfully emotive of the composers
of ayres, is also 'difficult', his complexity being related to his Mercurian ambiguity. The tears of his best-selling Lacrimae are emblemati-
cal, the song being based on the same motive of the falling fourth as is
'Forlorne Hope', though it is not chromaticised. Since the melody
balances the declining fourth against the uplifting interval of a minor
sixth it musically mirrors the tear, which rises, swells, then bursts
with the burden of human grief. The effect is at once passionate and
majestic; and the heart-easing loveliness of the tune is inseparable
from its response to the words – not in a declamatory manner but by
using keywords as impetus to lyrical elan: consider, for instance, the

sustained initial note on the word 'happy'. Complementarily, the plangency of the lute harmony is assuaged in the ceremonial rhythm of a dance, relating personal grief to a social situation. The song is a pavane – grandest and most aristocractic of Renaissance court dances – in three strains, each having an ornamented repeat. No wonder the song became a universal synonym for the quasi-religious transcendence of private sorrow to which man, facing the dark alone, had committed himself. Another 'tears' song, 'I saw my lady weep', is also a pavane with even deeper personal intensity. If it did not achieve the celebrity of the archetypal Lacrimae, the reason may be that its tune is less hauntingly memorable. As an interlacing of verbal, melodic, rhythmic and harmonic subtleties, however, it stands supreme among English songs; and if we accept Rooley's view that the Lady loved and bewept is also a personification of Music, through whom God speaks, it must count as a crucially Mercurian testament.

Yet if one had to choose a single song to sum up Dowland's achievement it would probably be 'In darknesse let me dwelle', from the collection of songs by several composers, assembled in 1610 under the title of *A Musicall Banquet* by Dowland's son Robert. Though this late song is neither strophic nor in dance form, it resembles the Lacrimae in its climacteric use of falling fourths. Gradually, the vocal line rises from a long sustained tone, low in register, *de profundis*, its contours being pointed with expressive dissonances in the polyphonically-conceived lute part – which is independent, no longer mere chordal support to the voice. Augmented fifths and false relations intimate, perhaps imitate, 'hell's jarring sounds' until at the climax the slow ascent, having reached its highest note E, precipitately descends in fourths both perfect and imperfect (i.e. diminished, C to G sharp). Yet although human fortitude seems here to triumph over a religious heritage in music that complements the melancholy of Hamlet and the introspective love poetry of Donne, the song is also Orphically purgatorial. The tomb becomes a womb; acceptance of death proves a paradoxical gateway to life. Unlike the promise of the fancy that invites us to Fare Well, that of 'In darknesse let me dwelle' remains tentative. After the lute postlude has returned to the depths from which we started, the voice appends a whispered repetition of the opening phrase, its penultimate note sustained still more lingeringly and lovingly over the dissonant major seventh until it echoes into silence, awaiting – on a half close, not a final cadence – the release of death. This is a dramatic, even operatic, effect. When will the cadence be completed, the axe fall?

Such intensity of life, complemented by so acute a consciousness of death, recalls the no less stylised, self-dramatising histrionics of Dowland's contemporary, John Donne. His notorious portrait of himself in his shroud became his domestic companion, giving explicit formulation to a motif familiar from the sculptured effigies on Jacobean tombs. Here the fairly great ones of the earth are depicted in their lavish worldly accoutrements, gaudily bedecked, blazoned with coats of arms, with their tribes of children living and dead lined up as testimony to man's linear durability. In close attendance lurk cadavers, shrouds, skulls and skeletons, not so much to remind us of the vanity of material possessions in the context of a hopefully blissful eternity, as to point the contrast between life and death. 'To this favour shall you come' – even you who value the world and the flesh so much and have been, as mortals go, so materially 'successful'. Donne's obsession with shrouds – not to mention that of Webster and Tourneur – complements Dowland's identification of womb and tomb; both involve an element of self-dramatisation, the ultimate end of which is operatic.

The climax of descending fourths in 'In darknesse let me dwelle' does in fact suggest the declamatory techniques of the Italian monodists who were Dowland's contemporaries. Although he must, through his continental travels, have been familiar with their work, he, as a solo performer whose music was passionately introspective rather than theatrically outward-going, had no incentive to turn to opera; nor, indeed, is there any English equivalent to the Italian experimentalists, perhaps because our dramatic fervour was so richly absorbed in Shakesperean poetic drama. None the less, Dowland's songs embraced the techniques necessary for opera; lyrical vocal line at once intrinsically sustained and sensitive to words, and corporeal movement springing from dance as a social institution. Dowland's contemporaries and successors at the Jacobean and Caroline courts did combine poetry, song and dance with theatrical spectacle, projecting the myth of the mercurian monarch, hopefully linking earth to heaven. Projection was physical since the heart of the masque, in the seventeenth as it had been in the fifteenth and sixteenth centuries, was dance, viewed as a man-made order triumphing over chaos. If God made man in his image, man returns the compliment, seeking spiritual self-aggrandisement, rather than (like Dowland) transcendence, by way of the Orphic theme.

In the Elizabethan age Sir John Davies, in his poem *Orchestra* (1596), had called dancing 'this new art': which of course it was not, though it seemed so to modern folk in that they made of it a new social philosophy – almost a substitute for traditional religious belief. Although the discussion in Davies's poem takes place in classical antiquity, the point lies in the concluding prophecy: the ultimate realisation of love's order (dance) will occur two thousand years hence, in 'our glorious English Court's Divine Image, as it should be in this our Golden Age'. So the masque was essentially contemporary, re-enacting the Mercurian theme, for when the masquers are unmasked they prove to be not legendary creatures from classical mythology, but the King and nobility, who are the temporal State; the gods are ourselves. The finest writer of masques for the Jacobean and Caroline court was Ben Jonson, especially in his collaborations with Alfonso Ferrabosco the younger as composer and Inigo Jones as designer. Jonson's tough intellect and sinewy verse allied terpsichorean to poetic grace, refusing to countenance the mindless vacuity whereby corporeally mortal masquers pretended that in their earthly paradise Time might be immobilised. They could imagine it might, only if too high on self-esteem and fermented liquors to notice it. They were not so far beyond the bacchic revellers in the 1480 *Orfeo*, and bathos was not uncommon, the grandiose ceremony being in more than one sense dissipated in a fit of the giggles from the fine ladies, or even in the collapse of the monarch himself.

Theoretically, the masque allowed for human fallibility in the antimasque, a grotesque rout of satyrs representing the libidinous undercurrents in our fallen selves. But such 'things that go bump in the night' are still admitted, as they were in the 1480 *Orfeo*, only to be laughed away. In our pretend-paradise they carry no real threat, as they do in those adaptations of masque convention, Shakespeare's *The Tempest* and Milton's *Comus*. The Shakespeare and Milton poems are art; but such pieces as the Jonson-Ferrabosco *Oberon*, or still more the later *Triumph of Peace* concocted by Shirley and William Lawes, are entertainment that is also humanist ritual: in which again, as in the fiesta which is the 1480 *Orfeo*, so much bland homophony grows tedious unless one is oneself participating in the social and spiritual harmony it venerates. We are left reflecting that the seventeenth century was waiting for a composer of a sufficiently audacious genius to confront the antimasque, not to dismiss it as a gaggle of fey fairies (as does Jonson in *Oberon*), nor to demean it to contemporary Low Life (as does Shirley in the labourers who gauchely want to play a part in the aristocratic revels, thereby hinting, in ways that Shirley cannot have been conscious of, that 'our revels now are ended'). Such a composer appeared in Monteverdi who in 1607, contemporaneous with the greatest plays of Shakespeare, adapted the Mercurian theme to modern life in his *Orfeo* and who, much later in 1642, lifted the lid off the libido to reveal the cauldron of human horrors simmering beneath society's polished pretence. That is an experience as enthralling, and as terrifying, now as it was then: perhaps even more so, since it sheds obliquely penetrating light on our own bewilderments. Our electronic revolution is their scientific revolution, writ large.

Claudio Monteverdi was born, like Dowland, in the mid-sixteenth century, but his creative life covered a longer span, since he was vigorously active almost until his death in 1643. The place of his birth is significant, for Cremona was the town of the master violin makers, Amati, Guarnieri and Stradivari, and the contemporary efflorescence of this instrument – lyrically vocal in tone, brilliant in sonority, sharply defined in attack – was not fortuitous. The violin became the supreme instrument of the new, humanistic world because it lent itself equally well to voice and dance and was audible, as the relatively intimate voils were not, in the large spaces needed to accommodate men and monarchs in increasing pomp and circumstance.

Monteverdi was trained, however, in the old school, the *stile antico* of Palestrina and Flemish polyphony, and in youth composed old-fashioned church music as part of his ecclesiastical duties. When professional advancement permitted he turned to his interests as a passionate modernist and composed secular music, at first in the form of canzonetti ('little songs' celebrating the sunny present, deriving from the *frottola* tradition already flourishing in the 1480 *Orfeo,* and from its French complement as represented by the *chansons* of Jannequin). More significantly, Monteverdi transformed the four, five and six-part madrigal as practised by Marenzio into miniature dramas or operatic scenes. Dissonant harmony and illustrative arabesques become more important than traditionally imitative 'points'; structure is based not so much on fugato and linear evolution as on a kaleidoscopic interplay of harmonies and sonorities, following the rhythms of speech. We can trace the metamorphosis of polyphonic madrigal into incipient opera in the sequence of Monteverdi's Fourth and Fifth Books of madrigals, published in 1603 and 1605 respectively.

The madrigals in the fourth book are all *a cappella,* in the conventional manner, and their highly stylised techniques, both verbal and musical, are means of distancing passion without denying it; this is what is asked of a courtier aspiring to *cortesia.* The rhetorical tropes in the pastoral sequence *Astrophel and Stella* by Sir Philip Sidney are exactly complemented by the stylisations of phrase, gesture and illustrative ornamentation in English madrigalian verse. Sidney had picked up these modish manners from Italy; shortly after his death they were to attain an apex in the work of Monteverdi's favourite poet Guarini, whose *Il Pastor Fido,* published in 1589, was as modish as a man could get.

Yet from the first tones of the first madrigal in Monteverdi's Fourth Book we can hear that convention is being dramatically reborn. This opening madrigal has a theatrical context, since it is a musical insertion into a masque-like pastoral play – *Il Pastor Fido* itself. The first soprano initiates 'Ah dolente partita' with an isolated high 'Ah' that pierces silence with an intensity not far from a yell; only to merge into an excruciating semitonic dissonance. That is drama, an event occurring in time; and the rest of the piece, following the rhythms as well as the meanings of the words, stems from it, aurally depicting 'la pena della morte' and the 'vivace morire' inherent in it. The civilised control – which needs impeccable tuning and metrical precision, and must have received them from reputedly highly skilled performers – renders pain not merely supportable, but relishable. Similarly, in the grander setting of 'Pign'e sospira' from Tasso's immensely popular *Gerusalemme liberata* of 1589, the weird rising chromatics of the opening are Manneristly mannered even in their pathos. And the same stylised elegance distinguishes the whirling scales in parallel thirds and the prancing rhythms of pieces celebrating the delights of being alive, well, and *young* in a Renaissant morning, such as 'Io mi son giovinetta' or 'Quel augellin che canta', with its chirruping birds both feathered and humanly downy-skinned.

Sex, as distinct from love, occasionally proves stronger than decorum: as in 'Si ch'io vorrei morire', which deliciously embroiders the pun on the literal and sexual meanings of dying and becomes, in its rapidly panting, overlapping 'points', an imitation of licking and nipping ('Datemi tant'humore Che di dolcezza' in questo sen m'estingua') that might be indelicate were it not in part a game. But Monteverdi, knowing that even for *homo ludens* the game must also be for real, had to develop the genre towards theatrical projection, in

which other people, outside his charmed circle, could imaginately
participate. In the Fourth Book passion precipitates from precarious
awareness of, and respect for, the rules of the High Renaissance game.
From the Fifth Book, published when Monteverdi was thirty-eight,
the game has become a ritual of humanism; and in its second half
instruments are added to voices, enhancing theatrical projection. In
Monteverdi's later madrigalian works lutes, theorbos and gamba
function as continuo instruments; sometimes bowed strings insert
interludial dance music, which may have been literally danced to.

In the fifth book's unaccompanied first part the verses are again
from Guarini's *Il Pastor Fido*. The texts of the accompanied madrigals
are from the same poet's *Rime*, and these carry the conventional
theme of the Wailing Lover several stages further, asserting the
interdependence of pleasure and pain in a world wherein religious
sanctions are dubiously operative. Here and now on the earth, they
accept sex and death as the only absolutes. The imagery is overtly
sexual, riddled with wounds, darts, penetrations and blood. The
sado-masochistic puns on the literal and sexual meanings of dying
never reach the clinically certifiable extremes which will be
encountered later in the work of Monteverdi's contemporary Gesualdo, being restrained perhaps by his Christian heritage, certainly by
his respect for Renaissance Platonism. None the less, the violence that
lurks beneath the polished surface of both words and music conditions their strength.

Even the (courtier) nymphs and shepherds who babble like
Nature's prattling brooks and twittering birds in Arcadian pastorals
such as '*Questi vaghi concenti*' differ from their conventional proto-
types in that they are aware of the complex vagaries, light *and* dark, of
human feeling. This makes their joyousness not less but more reward-
ing. The implications of this are more deeply revealed in the sixth
book, notably in the second of Monteverdi's two settings of 'Zefiro
torna'. The first, in madrigalian polyphony, was all delight and
ordered ecstasy; the second – one of Monteverdi's most justly celebrated pieces, both technically and emotionally – is a chaconne for two
tenors, with an instrumental bass enunciating an ostinato. To begin
with, the tenors jubilate melismatically, but then lament in dissonant
suspensions and wailful chromatics. Both states, seemingly interdependent, approach operatic extravagance, and the rapture seems to
spring from the awareness of impermanence. Love's mutability calls
for both pride and fortitude if it is to be withstood; the pride explodes

in vocal arabesques, the fortitude is stably affirmed in the ground bass. We can understand why the technique of chaconne or passacaglia – an instrumentally harmonic modification of the old *cantus firmus* technique – should pervade seventeenth-century music; it offers a secular complement to the ancient plainchant Law, since its *harmonic* bass is man-made yet becomes a means whereby man, even through the heights and depths of his most passionate excesses, may *hold on*.

One of the most heart-rending instances is the famous *Lamento della Ninfa*, from the Eighth Book published much later, in 1638 (by which time Monteverdi had turned seventy). The 'nymph' grieves not merely for love but also for the sorrow inherent in the human condition, in so far as it is subject to Time. The poet, Rinuccini, produces strophic verses similar to those he had devised, early in the century, for operas by Peri, and allows for theatrical antiphony between the lamenting soloist and three male choric voices whose harmonies, though often dissonant, prove consolatory in relating the girl's plight to Everyman's and Everywoman's. Meanwhile the most rudimentary form of ostinato bass – a descent down four tones of a diatonic scale – continues unbroken, at once measuring time and effacing it. Since the pulse is unruffled, we become habituated to it; it even seems a release that makes possible the exquisite grace of the girl's lament – a manifestation of melodic genius, startling in its simplicity, if ever there was one.

Monteverdi's sorrow, like that of his nymph, exists within the glamour of the dancing world. He lives fully in living dangerously, and it is worth recalling that the word experience derives from the Latin *ex periculo* – from and out of peril. He is more than a Renaissance Man; he may not extravagantly be called Shakespearean, and it is no accident that Shakespeare's greatest plays coincide in date with the maturing of Monteverdi's talent. This we may associate with two major masterpieces: the *Vespers and Magnificat* in which he consummates the Orphic equation of Flesh and Word; and his explicit dramatisation and musicking of the Orpheus story, wherein masque at last grows up into opera.

Although liturgical, Monteverdi's *Vespers* of 1610 belong equally to Church and State, and, by inference, to the theatre also. It is to the point that scholarly disputation continues as to the senses in which the Vespers are and are not liturgical music. Composed for and performed in theatrically resplendent buildings, they fuse what Monteverdi called the old and new practices, thereby effecting a synthesis of spirit

and flesh, heaven and earth. We have seen that some such marriage
has been fundamental to the Orphic experience throughout European
history; but at no other time had the human and divine been more
intimately related than they are in Monteverdi's work. The opening
states a dichotomy which startles, as it was surely meant to. We hear
the age-old plainchant unaccompanied, as it was in the beginning,
now and ever shall be; into its timeless serenity bursts a fanfare,
manifesting worldly glory, on dancing rhythmed trumpets and violins.
It is as though confidence in man's splendour here and now sweeps
aside the old spiritual aspiration: proud monarchs (at least momentarily) need no more than the glamour which hopefully identifies them
with gods. There is nothing to this fanfare but colour and rhythm – no
melody and little harmony. The rest of the work is to reveal how
hollow this glamour is. The complexity of human impulses is inherent
in the technical infiltrations of the 'old' and 'new' techniques.

Thus Monteverdi calls on the old doctrinal device of *cantus firmus*:
but does so in order to induce sensual excitation! Whereas in the
Middle Ages plainsong *cantus firmus* was 'held' as tenor in long,
impersonally instrumental notes which the human voices garlanded,
in Monteverdi's *Sonata sopra Sancta Maria* the plainsong is *sung* by
human voices in unison, while the surrounding counterpoints are
instrumental, scored for the most brilliant orchestra at Monteverdi's
disposal. The polyphony is now not so much a synonym for divine
many-in-oneness as a simulation of men and women dancing together
in metrically ebullient, vividly coloured 'divisions'. There is a comparable transition from the divine to the human in the hymn 'Ave Maris
Stella'. Here the plainsong is first treated in solemn antiphonal
counterpoint halfway between traditional liturgical style and a ceremonial masque dance. Then it is transformed into a song-dance in
lilting triple time, with corporeally stimulating cross accents of 6/4
and 3/2. The tune becomes majestic, yet also tenderly humane,
haunting as a folk or popular song. The divine has found Mercurian
incarnation in human feeling.

If such pieces show old-style techniques reinterpreted in the light of
post-Renaissance humanism, the antiphons are unambiguously in the
new secular manner which, stemming from the inflectionalism of
Monteverdi's madrigals, became operatic recitative. In 'Pulchra es'
and 'Nigra sum' luxuriant ornamentation, parallel thirds and bouncy
dance rhythms make for sensuous splendour, while dissonant suspensions and fragmented melody evoke human suffering, as though

actor-singers were momently undergoing it. Yet even here operatic recitative may recall liturgical incantation, especially in exotic manifestations. In 'Duo Seraphim' the glottal trills suggest Hebraic synogogue music and the incantation of the Islamic Church; Venice was a melting-pot where cultures clashed and, in the process, generated energy.

Monteverdi's ultimate fusion of the liturgical and the humanistic occurs in the Psalm settings and Magnificat: wherein personal passion disrupts the serene continuity of vocal polyphony, while the human solidarity of dance seeks a new criterion of order. Thus the 'Et miserecordia' of the Magnificat starts with plainchant and a Palestrinian suavity; but 'Fecit potentiam', taking its cue from the motif of power, garlands a plainsong *cantus firmus* with frisky instrumental divisions. In the 'Deposuit' voices again have the *cantus firmus*, while cornetts and violins dialogue in echo. The obsession of the seventeenth century with echoes is fascinating, for it is as though the physical world were mirrored in the metaphysical. Heaven is like us, only purer. In the 'Esurientes' the voices, cooing in parallel thirds, sound simultaneously sensual and angelic. The echo is blissful, but a long way off.

A still stranger piece, 'Gloria Patri', takes us to the heart of the Counter-Reformation spirit, for baroque opulence itself becomes mystical ecstasy. As Renaissance humanist, Monteverdi delighted in world, flesh and devil; but his delight tingled the nerves more acutely because he still knew God. The Word become Flesh was the first miracle whereby man, fearfully frail yet potentially divine, recognised himself as, in Sir John Davies's words, 'a proud and yet a wretched thing'. This Gloria hints at a more wondrous miracle: perhaps the Flesh might become Word. The visual as well as aural conditions of performance of Monteverdi's church music, in Mantua or Venice, would have made this the more apprehensible.

Such too is the explicit burden of Monteverdi's dramatisation of the Orpheus story. He was not the first Italian composer of the late Renaissance to music the tale; and he inherits the philosophical and to a degree technical muddledom that we have seen to be inherent in man's attempt to play God. Renaissance man had discovered or rediscovered his human powers, his potential responsibility for his destiny, and had invented artistic techniques to render incarnate his hard-won representation of Nature. Painters had explored perspective naturalistically to imitate 'reality'; musicians were evolving a 'science' of harmony, based on the presumed laws of the Pythagorean series, to give 'body' to human feelings, which could be acted out on a stage. None the less people nurtured in a Christian hierarchy still believed that the process of self-discovery ought also to be a revelation of divine origins: *musica humana* ought to put us in touch with *musica mundana* – the Music of the Spheres – and might do so if man-Orpheus, through the joy and suffering his music manifests, could move the gods to pity and succour him. For late Renaissance man music, projected on to a stage, is an act both of incarnation and, it is hoped, of revelation.

This is implicit in a version of Orpheus's story which anticipates Monteverdi's by a few years. It was made by the poet-dramatist Ottavio Rinuccini and the composer Jacopo Peri, for the wedding of Maria Medici on 6 October 1600 – a New Art appropriately ushering in a new century. We noted that Poliziano's version of a hundred-odd years earlier had been a spoken play in which musical interludes – songs, dances, occasionally scene-setting mood pieces – were inserted. Rinuccini and Peri preserve the ceremonial intradas, the dances, and the occasional choruses as auralisations of the public world; but transform the spoken play into recitative based on the inflexions of speech, yet consistently sung, the implication being that mere speech is inadequate to human beings aspiring to godhead. Like the other members of the sophisticated court Camerata, Rinuccini and Peri thought they were accommodating the dramatic principles of classical antiquity to Christian philosophy – Greek tragedy was chanted and possibly sung precisely because it was concerned with life in contexts wider and deeper than the human. Peri's piece is still a cross between a party and a work of art. The public music of the dances and choruses is rudimentary notated, for it lives dispensably in the present moment, gracious in its triple-rhythmed lilt, enlivening in its intermittent cross-metres. The vocal recitative, which *is* the play, is meticulously notated in vocal line, but is supported only by string bass; at this date no 'figures' assist its realisation, nor is there indication of the instruments to be employed, though they must have embraced many or all of the plucked stringed lutes and harps available, plus harpsichord and chamber organ. All the source materials which Monteverdi is to develop are present in Peri's *Euridice*: preludial toccata, interludial dance and chorus, homophonic *frottola*, polyphonic madrigal, symbolic instrumentation and – most of all – recitative and arioso, the dimension lacking in the 1480 *Orfeo*. Peri's recitative is developed to high malleability and expressivity; it is often, especially at Eurydice's death, deeply pathetic. But it is not tragic; and tragic awareness is the ultimate dimension that Monteverdi brings to the story, as he fuses and metamorphoses its multiple strands and Peri's multifarious techniques. This is the force of his originality, itself an Orphic activity.

Monteverdi's *Orfeo* was composed to a libretto of Alessandro Striggio, for private performance before members of the *Accademia degli Invaghiti*, an aristocratic institution closely involved with the Gonzaga's court of Mantua – the same court for which the 1480 *Orfeo* had been devised. Monteverdi had worked for the Gonzagas for eighteen years and was to continue his association for a further five. Striggio borrowed heavily from Poliziano's original version, still extant in the Gonzaga records, though on second thoughts, before the first performance in 1607, he or Monteverdi radically changed Poliziano's ending, for reasons that will be considered in due course. Technically, both librettist and composer learned more from Rinuccini and Peri's *Euridice*, for the obvious reason that it explored the possibilities of recitative as the Poliziano original had felt no need to.

In Monteverdi's opera there are four levels of experience. First, there is the temporal, public world: an Italian court for the delectation of which this entertainment, like the 1480 version, was produced. This piece too starts as a masque presenting the illusion that civilised man may create paradise on earth. This is why the opening toccata is a music of *carne*-val, celebrating the flesh in a would-be eternal present. Festivity exists in this very moment, which is all we can be certain of. As in the almost identical toccata that was, three years later, to launch the Vespers, only one chord, brilliantly scored and rescored, is either necessary or feasible. The concordant major triad (notated in C but sounding as resplendent D major) is presented 'circularly', without progression let alone development, and is repeated three times. If the symbolism is Trinitarian, that gives the lordly ones of the earth a further boost; in their charmed and charming court they purr as they pretend that Now needs no before or after, since eternal perfection has been achieved. Even when the play (of passion) succeeds carnival it is at first in ideality, still a pretence: though the danced Ritornello in modally inflected D minor, as distinct from the unsullied D major of the fanfare, offers communal music in which paradise on earth is more *tentatively* envisaged.

This Ritornello introduces not L'Amor, as in Peri, but La Musica, who identifies herself with Orpheus in singing of her power both to enflame and to pacify passion. The heaven she delineates is an apotheosis of the dancing movements of the human body, harmonised in concord and grace. Hence the importance of dance rhythms in Monteverdi, even more than in Peri. They are vibrant in sensuality, yet elegantly disciplined, for a true earthly paradise must reconcile Dionysos and Apollo. Her vocal line is Mercurian from the opposite direction, for it springs from the rhythms and contours of human speech, to which it gives harmonic corporeality. Even in the Prologue, La Musica intimates that there are two related harmonies: that of the golden cittern she plays, and that of the heavenly lyre. Bodily concord, attainable here on earth, will be consummated only in a spiritual heaven, though this spiritual dimension is no longer mystical as it had been in the Middle Ages. It is rather a produce of man's (admittedly God-given) Reason which, by way of Renaissance Platonism, had disciplined Palladian architecture on mathematical proportions. But there is a paradox latent here in that the Pythagorean 'laws' Leonardo had discovered a century back were those of 'Nature', and the more man learned about Nature the more ambiguous she seemed. If natural laws are not identical with divine laws they may be not absolute but arbitrary. As will be seen, the contrast between a physical heaven (sonorous in singing strings and resonating wind instruments) and a Christianised Platonism (seeking a polyphonic many-in-oneness in abstract metrical proportions of which the foundations, if they are only natural, must be dubious) is the paradoxical theme of Monteverdi's opera.

The first act makes a transition from the Prologue's ideality to a real world wherein the marriage-masque of Orpheus and Euridice, at first barely distinguished from royal persons in the audience, is being celebrated by those legendary nymphs and shepherds who have been seen to be denizens of the court. They hymn their Golden Age in songs and dances both polyphonic and homophonic, with colourful interlacings of voices with string and wind choirs. This music is similar in character to, though more developed than, the Arcadian music of Peri. The hope that human order might prevail is inherent in the act's structure, which is sectional and mathematical like that of the Prologue – to which, indeed, it gives earthly embodiment. In the centre praise songs are sung by Orpheus and Euridice to one another, framed by two choruses of homage repeated mirror-wise in inverse order. The congratulatory choruses of 'shepherds and shepherdesses' are linked by a three-fold repetition of the string ritornello, and are

consummated in a final chorus, 'Ecco Orfeo', vigorous but somewhat
nervously animated by hemiola cross-rhythms. All this ceremonial
music might well refer to a wedding of real people, as did the 1480
Orfeo and the 1600 *Euridice*. The difference between the earlier and
Monteverdi's Arcadian music is the same as that between a fifteenth-
century *frottola* and a Monteverdi madrigal: Monteverdi is not
emotionally and technically infantile. Vocal lines flow lyrically, rhythms swing exultantly; 'for the time being' we can *believe* that man is
in his heaven and all is well with his world. Verse and music celebrate
the harmonious union of Man, Society and Nature.

The second act opens in the same pastoral serenity still more
exquisitely civilised since the dance music is Frenchified, perhaps as a
result of Monteverdi's continental travels. As Orpheus grows in confidence, so it seems to be he himself, the man-god-leader, who has
promoted through his music this celestial-seeming harmony between
men and women, birds and beasts, woods and streams. But a masque
is no more than a dream of what might be; as soon as an individual
man is made responsible for the human condition – his own, and that
of the community – masque must grow to operatic maturity. Musically this is manifest in the second level of experience, that of the
human passions interactive in this presumptive earthly paradise:
which turns out to be no paradise after all since individual human
beings, left to their own resources or at most with the support of
man-made laws, are fallible. *Their* experience is contained not in
pastoral polyphonies and nympholectic dances but in the reality of
accompanied arioso which, extending the fragmentation of line
passion-promoted in madrigals, follows the minutest inflections of the
spoken-sung words. There is some contemporary evidence that Monteverdi's later madrigals were sung-acted with much mopping and
mowing, rolling of eyes and gesturing of hands; his recitative, physically expressive in sighs, sobs, gasps and wails, has far greater dramatic immediacy than Peri's. At the same time action is sublimated into
inherently musical conventions, underlined by the fluctuating harmonies of the continuo instruments – lutes, citterns, harps, harpsi-
chords, organs, in varying combinations. As La Musica says in the
Prologue, 'by my singing I charm and comfort the most despairing
spirit; with noble fire, or with consuming rage the heart inflaming'.
Music's Mercurian power is at once to inspire and to assuage.

The key point of the opera is the central arioso of the Messenger,
who inverts the function of the Mercurian Trickster in the original

myth. For he-she, far from being a harbinger of the divine, brings dark veracity into the dream-world the nymphs and shepherds hoped to live in. Her message upsets the paradisal applecart, and the apple metaphor is pertinent since she comes to tell Orfeo that his beloved wife, whose handmaiden she is and with whom he had been living in this ostensible Eden, has been snatched from him. While in a meadow gathering flowers, Persephone-like, she has trodden on a vicious serpent, who bit her fatally. The passage – one of the most famous in European music – is remarkable for its immediacy. Whereas the pastoral prologue and first act exist within conventions of vocal polyphony and instrumental dance which we are habituated to and respect, the Messenger's arioso creates itself before our astonished ears and eyes. It is nasty, brutish, and short, as a later seventeenth-century philosopher thought life was. The shifts between triads of E major – which as the sharpest key in common use will acquire heavenly associations in later baroque music – and of G minor – to become a key of tragic reality in the baroque and still more the classical age – splinter the dialogue, the human communication between the Messenger, Orfeo and attendant shepherds, while delivering a stab to the nerves, and even the solar plexus. The E major triad is sometimes embellished with a C sharp 'added sixth', enhancing its dreamy yearning – as will, centuries later, the same chord in cocktail-lounge jazz pianism! Though its fleeting vision breaks the heart, it is impotent in the context of the arioso's reality, within which desperately mortal beings must live.

Striggio omits from the story Euridice's pursuit by an intending rapist, either as a force of evil or as evidence, if she is wilfully but will-lessly dallying with him, of the insubstantiality of human morals. In Poliziano's version Aristeus, apparently fancied by Euridice, is vocally evident and himself suffers the pangs of amatory frustration. In Striggio stumbling Euridice is the cause of her own fall: perhaps because a Great Lady should not be subject to indignity, but more because it is admitted that since the Christian Fall she and we cannot escape the serpent in the grass. Even in Arcadia one can no longer pretend that human malice (and indignity) can be discounted, though the chorus, as the social world, do their best to counteract the Messenger's severity. Nymphs and shepherds try to palliate Orfeo's distress with choruses of consolation on a larger scale than those in the first act, with vestiges of ecclesiastical polyphony tempering their madrigalian harmonies. Tentatively ceremonial grandeur again suggests an equilibrium between fallible flesh and hopefully infallible spirit. The act concludes with a repetition of the Ritornello of the Prologue which, although unchanged, is different in effect since in this context earthly happiness seems not only lost but also illusory.

The third act opens with a complete change of instrumentation. Violins, organ and harpsichord as played on earth are ousted by cornetti and trombones: sacred instruments to which Orfeo moves into the kingdom of the dead. After a solemn Sinfonia symbolising the supernatural, Speranza appears. Not so much a character as aspect of Orfeo's psyche, she hazards in arioso that there may be a glimmer of hope; mortality may not be totally unanswerable if man, through music, may aspire to the divine. She and her arioso are related to La Musica in the Prologue since it is by way of music that hope may be manifest. Her line is less fragmented, more floatingly spiritual than the Messenger's, or Orfeo's in dialogue with her. But it still contains harmonic stabs and rhythmic hiatuses since, if allied to superhuman music, she is part of a suffering human and evidence of his courage. She offers to conduct Orfeo to the nether world, to appeal for Euridice's restoration. Sepulchral brass of the dead heralds the approach to Hades. Though the Sinfonia opens in mixolydian G, it soon shifts to the flat regions of G minor, C minor and B flat major – which latter key, perhaps because it had been the flattest transposition permitted in Renaissance polyphony, had become associated with 'lower' regions. That G minor is B flat major's relative may bear on its later association with tragedy; there may even be point in the fact that B flat major became for Beethoven a key of power triumphant, for no man confronted the forces of darkness as unflinchingly as he did.

Caronte, guardian of the Lethean gate, is naturally a bass who, being beyond human agony or joy, sings a relatively neutral recitative, while at the same time introducing us to the third level of experience: the supernatural that man may aspire to. Orfeo is a man who through his music challenges the gods; but it may be significant that his challenge is not direct to Pluto, god of death, but to Charon (Caronte), a middleman and not so far from a comic character, whose basic key of F major is a degree less flat than that of death himself. It is to Charon that Orfeo sings the arioso which, as Monteverdi pointed out in a famous letter of 1616, is the climax of the opera and a sublime paradox. For the arioso – so lyrical that is may count as an aria – wherein he woos and wins over the powers of darkness (during the subsequent sinfonia Charon, hypnotised by the quasi-celestial music, falls asleep), employs all the sensual artifice of which Renaissance man was capable, rioting in vocal arabesques of fantastic virtuosity, doubled and echoed by voluptuous violins and cackling cornetti, reinforced by a luxuriance of parts for continuo instruments, including of course lyre-emulating lutes and harps; and does so in order to achieve an extra-sensory purpose! Echo effects, as has been noted, are pervasive in seventeenth-century music, though nowhere so excitingly as here. They usually imply an equation between the physical and metaphysical such as is common to seventeenth-century echo poems, in which the echoing rhyme word is often a pun, and therefore illusory. Double meanings suggest how man is, in Sir Thomas Browne's phrase, 'an Amphibian', living in divided worlds of body and spirit. The symbolic use of instruments – singing strings for heroically human passions, flutes and oboes for the pre-conscious simplicities of the pastoral life, brass for supernatural beings and the dead – reinforces these ambiguities, as we pass from one level of experience to another.

The circular form of this sublime 'Possente spirto' aria functions similarly, being far more complex than the strophic pastoral songs of the first two acts. Striggio writes the verse in archaically Dantesque, stylised *terza rima*: on the first three stanzas of which Monteverdi lavishes a cornucopian fecundity of roulade. Each verse is followed by an instrumental ritornello on the same bass. With the fourth verse the vocal line grows broader, but more rather than less impassioned, while for the fifth and sixth verses the line returns to even more intense recitative, ending with a recapitulation of Orfeo's original plea. The effect is both powerful and profound. It is as though Orfeo gradually relinquishes his divine-seeming ostentation, admitting that although all that post-Renaissance opulence of ornament may be good enough to put a buffoon to sleep, he must in the last resort rely on his basic humanity. The first phrase of the fourth stanza of his song of seduction is an immensely inflated melisma on the words *Orpheus I am*. We remember that Monteverdi remarked that his Ariadne moved people so much 'simply' because she was a woman, his Orfeo because he was a man.

The third act ends, again in mirror fashion, with a literal repeat of the sacred sinfonia, now played by 'human' strings in conjunction with 'divine' wind. The thematically related chorus of 'infernali spiriti' which follows is the grandest and most traditionally Christian music we have so far encountered. A further repetition of the sinfonia

at once ends the third act and begins the fourth. Yet although Orfeo
has, in crossing the threshold of the dead, entered a different realm
(symbolised by the changed instrumentation), this involves a paradox
that will become overtly ironic. The chorus praises Orfeo for his
heroic courage: which is not to be substantiated by the events of the
fourth act. It proves untrue that 'Nought avails against man's will', for
Orfeo's courage is not equal to his desire – or more accurately, his love
is deficient, being self-regarding. At this point Striggio brings in the
Persephone story, as does the original myth: for Proserpina (Latin for
Persephone) intercedes on Orfeo's behalf, appealing to Pluto, god of
death, her husband and one-time ravisher, for Euridice's restoration.
Her arioso resembles Speranza's, for spring is seasonally *hope* for the
year's renewal. Her lines, giving an anthropological dimension to the
personal story, are long-flowing but emotive; whereas the music of
Pluto, who is of course a deep bass, is relatively neutral – like Caronte's but grander. Proserpina, if a goddess, is also a woman who, in
touch with Nature and instinctual feeling, may hope to soften even a
godly heart. This is implicit in Peri's version (which is significantly
named after the heroine, not hero), but in Monteverdi it becomes
'incarnate' in a thawing of the wintry earth, as well as of the heart, by
way of evolving tonalities. The underworld characters are centred
flatwards, in F and B flat. Pluto relents but imposes his condition: that
Orfeo, having total confidence in and submission to the divine will,
will not look back to see if Euridice is following him. At this point the
key changes to G major, counteracting the flat keys, though we should
not forget that G minor, relative of B flat major, is the key of the tragic
arioso in which the Messenger had recounted Euridice's death. This
makes its effect, though it is improbable that we consciously recall it
as the music prances in the jaunty dotted rhythm traditionally
associated with physical energy. (We have noted that it pervades
Monteverdi's superbly physical *Sonata sopra Sancata Maria*. By the
time of Purcell it has become a swagger, generating sexual confidence:
as, in more rawly-deprived circumstances more than two hundred
years later, it will in the boogie rhythms of the black ghettos of
Chicago.)

On the portals of the Kingdom of the Dead are engraved the words
of Dante: 'Abandon hope, all ye who enter here'. So Speranza, being a
human attribute, has to leave Orfeo to make the last stage of his
pilgrimage alone. Without her he finds no superhuman succour, while
his humanity quails, his weakness being his egotism and his inability

to see beyond his nose. Muttering that the God of Love would surely permit a tiny peep, and it would be a nonsense if love were not stronger than death, he looks back. His moment of failure is marked by an ungrammatical shift from a dominant-tonic cadence in 'positive' G major to an F major triad, and by what Striggio's stage direction calls a *strepito*, offstage: an inchaote *noise*, as contrasted with the musical sounds Orfeo has so artfully, and up to then successfully, uttered. The *strepito* is indeed a thing that goes bump in the night: one of those arbitrary accidents that may defeat man's noblest intentions. But that Orfeo's self-indulgence is more foolish than wicked does not discount its fatal effect. In a wonderfully immediate passage of arioso Euridice wails her disconsolate farewell. With structural point as well as emotional poignancy this recapitulates the Messenger's report of her first death: only it is now the other way round; tragic G minor is followed by heavenly E major since 'heaven' is no longer a dream of paradise on earth but, in whatever metaphysical realm it may be, her immediate destination. The tritone at her cadence lacerates the heart through its musical tension, apart from its symbolic significance as *diabolus in musica*. The serpent in the grass who occasioned her first death is thus equated with the man who has betrayed her a second and final time.

There is no parallel to this in Peri's *Euridice*, for she does not die a second time. Monteverdi's Euridice, inverting the medieval view of her as the soul-bride of male Christ, is rather humanity's heart. Though her humane arioso at her second death does not aspire to the lyrical *ecstasis* that Orfeo attains when wooing the powers of darkness, her truth is the heart's truth which, with potent rather than comfortable calm, accepts human limitation; her name means 'the Wise One'. Even so Monteverdi, as High Renaissance Man on the crest of the wave, cannot intellectually accept what his music tells us, since he presents her henceforth as subservient to her would-be heroic husband. We have to wait until Purcell's Dido for a tragic heroine who, pricking the bubble of patriarchal pride, becomes the mainspring of the action.

Given this context, it cannot be fortuitous that after Euridice's second death Orfeo's courage seems less heroic, if it can be said to survive at all. He laments his lot, forgetting that it was his own fault; the chorus proffers severer consolation, telling him in gravely harmonious polyphony that virtue is its own reward. These polyphonic-harmonic choruses are an interesting modification of traditional ecclesiastical style, for their contrapuntal many-in-oneness is humanly and harmonically ordered, the square rhythm, rigidly-marshalled chords and moderate tempo being the best mere human beings can manage. The hard, cold, netherworld sonorities are re-established; so it is not surprising that Orfeo finds the chorus's moralising hard and cold comfort. Their music grows grand, however, accompanied by supernatural brass as well as human strings, as the chorus reprovingly tells him that man must win victory over himself. The act ends with another repetition of the Prologue's Ritornello, the gracious dance tune now embellished with whirling scales on Orphic harps grown ironically distraught, even desperate. The desperation is understandable, since to achieve victory over himself is precisely what Orfeo cannot do.

Irony deepens when in the fifth and last act Orfeo finds himself, after all his (nearly) superhuman efforts, back where he started from, in a pastoral Arcadia that now sounds as insubstantial as the dream it always was. He is fobbed off with pie in the sky, instead of a wife in bed and palace: for Striggio and Monteverdi, as High Renaissance Heroes, cannot bring themselves to countenance the horrible conse-quences of Orfeo's failure as recounted in the myth, yet are unable, as does Poliziano, to shrug off the Terrible Mothers as a black joke. Striggio's original end, incorporating the dis-memberment, was changed, an act of transubstantiation being substituted. Though Monteverdi had gone much further than Peri in facing the tragedy – in the Greek sense – inherent in man's Orphic presumption, he draws back from accepting Eurydice as Demeter and Earth Mother. There is irony indeed in the fact that Apollo himself, whom Orfeo has hope-fully but disastrously emulated, should enter to the *same* supernatural music that in Act IV had accompanied the advent of Pluto, God of Death! His purpose, admittedly, is to transport Orfeo 'aloft' where he will be apotheosised – but only in spirit: which is Monteverdi's way of saying that his *head* sings on. Though he cannot have his Euridice up there she can be looked down on and back at, as pretty as a picture, itself an illusion. This eternal looking back is a very wry coda, considering the nature of Orfeo's fault and sin. But the last act seems to be saying that sex is better abandoned since it is the source of human divisiveness, forgetting that it is also the source of human life – a muddlement that harked back, of course, to the Fathers of the Christian Church. So the Apollonian metamorphosis points to the inadequacy of the sex-death, love-war dichotomy of the seventeenth

century, while being in itself no more than a wish-fulfilment and
probably also a cheat. In his heart Monteverdi surely knew it to be
such: which is why his treatment of Euridice, despite the wondrous
music his heart accorded her, is intellectually shifty.

Yet although he degrades woman in assuming that she is incapable
of Apollonian intellect, his point is not crudely anti-feminist. Psychologically Eurydice is the passional, not merely animal, element of
Orfeo, anima to his animus. She has to be sloughed off because
post-Renaissance man was not yet ready to rediscover the Whole; he is
still struggling to do so three hundred years later in Wagner's *Tristan*.
In 1607 Proud Man has to be left high and dry in the sky, wretchedly
womanless if blessed with a blond god. The music of transubstantiation which Apollo and Orfeo sing together is lyrically beautiful and
sensuous, for they chime in stepwise-moving parallel thirds in the
dotted rhythms of physical animation, to which Orfeo had bootlessly
escorted Eurydice from hell. Moreover, although they levitate
skywards with human Orfeo singing the underpart to divine Apollo, it
is Orfeo who ends on top. This is a hollow victory for humanism,
however, since the music is – compared with the consummating fire of
the monody that solitary Orfeo had sung and played to the darkness,
in the dark – blandly uncommitted and, like the 1480 Orfeo, pre- or
post-tragic. The severed head cannot sing to much effect, and the
flowing scales and concordant harmonies carry us all too easily back
from sky to court, where nymphs and shepherds are rejoicing over
Orfeo's apotheosis. The music they rejoice to is precisely the same
kind as had been heard in the Prologue and first act: the inadequacy of
which to the realities of human experience is the central theme of the
opera that had grown out of the masque! So in my end is my beginning. The process has to happen again and again; and is happening
still.

These euphoric choruses and dances are not in fact the very last
music we hear in *Orfeo*. For Monteverdi's exit dance is a *moresco* such
as was danced by the pretend blackamoors often featured in antimas-
ques to Renaissance masques. Monteverdi's *moresco*, though not
blackly evil, is far wilder than the rumbustiously comic bacchantes
music at the end of the 1480 *Orfeo*. This is what one might expect,
since although he shuffles out of tragedy in his epilogic *deus ex
machina*, the substance of his opera owes its durable power, and
indeed its modernity, to the fact that he was the first theatre
composer, and remains one of the greatest, to face up to the psyche's

depth, height, terror and joy. *Orfeo* testifies to the *tragedy* of humanism, despite its cheating end. For the rest of his long life he no longer cheated but unflinchingly confronted the barbarity and horror, even at the expense of the power and glory, of fallen, post-Renaissance man. His Orphic vision was tarnished, for better and for worse.

Chapter III

Orpheus crestfallen and restored

Gesualdo, 'musician and murderer'; Monteverdi's *L'Incoronazione di Poppea* (1642); Cavalli's *La Calisto* (1652); Man-Orpheus restored in the High Baroque of Purcell, 'Orpheus Britannicus'; *Ode to St Cecilia* (1692); Orpheus and St Cecilia in the music of Handel; Mercurian Christ-Orpheus in the music of Bach

The muddled ethics of the end of Monteverdi's *Orfeo* reflect those of Renaissance humanism, which could not believe in man *enough*. Orfeo had to be transubstantiated in wish-fulfilment, Euridice to be repressed. One might even say that not until Beethoven is the Renaissance hope that man might be responsible for his destiny fulfilled musically, though humanists like Handel and Mozart made a brave showing.

We have seen that the failure of Orpheus as man-god had been latent even within the musical techniques of the High Renaissance itself. Palestrina's near-identity between the divine and the civic may have attained classical status, and has remained a guideline for textbooks precisely because of its purity which belied the contrariness of Renaissance life. We have noted how Leonardo's enquiring mind had demonstrated the inadequacy of man-made pseudo-scientific theories of harmony and proportion to the realities of experience; the negative consequences of this became more apparent with the passage of time. Man's condition, independent of laws once considered absolute because divine, became as volatile as the continuous energy and whirling grace that Leonardo, towards the end of his life, delineated in his meticulous drawings of water. 'L'aqua è il vetturale della natura', he remarked; and human experience proves no less subservient to the universal flux. Sir Kenneth Clarke points out how Leonardo's late Deluge drawings appear at random in his Notebooks, along with geometrical drawings that are now 'the doodles of disillusion. His beloved mathematics are no longer employed in the search for truth, but cynically as a mere intellectual pastime.' Yet this awareness of mutability, as against the certitudes of mathematical law, is also the secret of Leonardo's magical power, which makes the

Mona Lisa 'the most mysterious picture ever painted'. Her famous smile, that of the cat who has eaten the canary, seems to express complete self-absorption along with total possession of the loved object. Yet Leonardo has discovered that this process has 'the same rhythm as that in which the rain pours from the clouds, wears away the earth, flows to the sea and is sucked into the clouds again'. If this is so, attributes of grace like the famous smile and the turning movement become 'extremely sinister' because indistinguishable from the flux which, being beyond human reason, must be inimical to human security. Leonardo is no longer a scientist seeking measurable truth, but a magician whose skills are in some ways necromantic. By the early years of the seventeenth century unheroic man can seem to John Webster to be lost 'in a mist. My soul, like to a ship in a black storm, is driven I know not whither.'

The supreme genius of Monteverdi in *L'Orfeo* – in this again we may bracket him with Shakespeare rather than Webster – is that he came near to triumphing undismayed over this tragic predicament. Even so, his triumph involved, as we saw, an element of deceit; and it was short-lived. A response to the situation which is more normal in its very abnormality is offered by Monteverdi's contemporary Carlo Gesualdo, who might almost be identified with Webster's melancholic malcontent. Gesualdo, Prince of Venosa, was an aristocrat of the Old World: but also a murderer who, like Mozart's Don Giovanni, destroyed the world he came from. Though his sexual procilivities seem to have been kinky, he married a beautiful, aristocratic woman in order to propagate his line. After some years he had her and her lover, and possibly his or the lover's child, murdered, not as a *crime passionel*, but as a planned act of vengeful misogyny. On the other hand he was passionately devoted to music, played the lute expertly and established at his castle an academy wherein composers and performing musicians consorted with fashionable poets such as Marini and Gongora.

The extravagance of Gesualdo's empiricism is evident even in, perhaps most in, his church music, composed mainly after the murder, as a self-dramatising penitential act, accompanied literally by self-flagellation. He chose consistently gloomy Biblical texts, as in the motet *O vos omnes* of 1603. The theme is the terror of the grave and, implicitly, the *loss* of faith. The unity of traditional contrapuntal technique dissolves in chromaticism; chords succeed one another, prompted by an unwonted chromatic alteration rather than by continuous line. The music sunders the positive values of the past, as did Gesualdo in his life. That it should be very difficult to sing is appropriate since, 'in a mist', we are driven we know not whither.

But the arbitrariness of Gesualdo's harmonic progressions is sometimes evidence of genius: as in 'Recussit pastor', with its wild octave leap at the beginning, its sepulchral chromatics for the devil and its celestial open octaves at the end. Gesualdo's most aberrant moments often have autobiographical implications; 'Aestimatus est', a religious motet about descent into the pit which enacts musically the terrors evoked by the pall of darkness, seems the more scary because it was written by a psychosopathic asthmatic. Similarly, in his secular music the Mannerist preoccupation with sex and death approaches lunatic obsession. His poets pun even more febrilely on the literal and sexual meanings of dying; the music, in 'Ardo per tu', flares in flickering melismata until it expires in chromatic deliquescence. 'Ardite zanzaretto' might seem a light-hearted madrigal about a mosquito, but the sado-masochistic joke is cruel as the insect nips, in sharp, fast dissonances, the woman's breast. Most extreme of these Mannerist madrigals is 'In pur respiro', an even more asthmatic piece than 'Aestimatus est', fusing expressionism, naturalism, symbolism and self-confession. Such music, though deeply introverted, is dramatic enough to call for externalisation and operatic projection if it is not to end in lunacy.

Though hardly a 'great' composer, Gesualdo represents a turning point in European consciousness. We can relate him not only to the Mannerist poets he set but also to the Mannerist painter Parmigianino, who distorted visual perspective in the same way that Gesualdo distorted harmonic perspective. The attempt to found Man humanly in and on the earth seems to be foundering, and the description of the Mannerist school as victims of 'collective neurosis' is not altogether inaccurate. Interestingly, they were preoccupied with Gnosticism, hermeticism, astrology, alchemy and black as well as white magic; and although the origins of these phenomena were ancient, all represent a retreat from Renaissance Reason and Proportion. The irrational and empirical genius of Gesualdo has ousted the medieval quadrivium and even the rhetorical trivium of the Renaissance.

In passion Monteverdi is hardly less extravagant than Gesualdo; the difference is that he was strong enough to stay sane. Though his vision of man as Orpheus was short-lived, his spiritual health is manifest in his metamorphosis of the basic theme of the Mannerist Baroque. In Monteverdi's collection of *Madrigali Guerrieri ed Amorosi* published in 1638, when he was seventy-one, Gesualdo's Sex and Death become Love and War. Of course Love includes sex, as a celebration of the man-woman relationship without which human life would be impossible. Similarly, War includes death: but also the possibility of honour and courage and the power to create, out of carnage and chaos, a new order. The text of 'Hor ch'l ciel e la terra' is about this division both within and without the self: I die that I may be reborn, and the rebirth involves a marshalling of the will, emulated by the tramp of marching feet. War happens not only in the world 'out there': although its victories being destruction to some, destruction may be a point from which growth starts. Love and war, like life and death, are interdependent; we are nurtured by the 'sweet and bitter', for 'one hand both hurts and heals me'. The early madrigals discovered an equation between Nature's ephemera and the pleasure of those Arcadian young men and women. More toughly, the late madrigals find a synonym for the identity of love and death in the very morphology of creation.

The evolution of Monteverdi's theatrical music parallels that of his madrigals, though we cannot trace its course since only a fragment of one opera, *Arianna*, survives between his first venture, *L'Orfeo*, and his last, *L'Incoronazione di Poppea*, first performed in 1642 in the composer's seventy-fifth year. Monteverdi has relinquished Orphic pretentions. Facing up to the inevitable failure of humanism, he admits that human beings can never be more than momentarily heroic. They sicken, grow old, and die; even while alive, their motives, without a divine or at least extra-personal yardstick to govern human conduct, are seldom what they think they are, and may readily become a tissue of lies, treacheries, malignities and perversities. And the more complacent man becomes, the more ego-centred is his morality – nowhere more so than in the Glory that was Greece and the Grandeur that was Rome.

So, evading mythology, Monteverdi moves to history: the world as it was and is, not as it might have been or ought to be. *Poppea* is about high life in the Roman Empire, which is really seventeenth-century Venice, where Monteverdi composed and produced the opera, and where high life proves to be ethically low and there is no pretence that Empire may be equated with Honour. Monteverdi opens the piece with a Prologue sung not by the potentially divine La Musica, but by Fortuna who is blind as a bat; by Virtue, who remains abstract because unconsummated in action; and only finally by Love, invoked not grandly as a life force but modestly, as compassion for fallen humanity. This defines the psychological point of the opera: which seems to be immediately counteracted by the vacuously giddy dance music with which the Prologue ends. And Act I opens with two soldiers *on guard*, on stage, *asleep*. In the brief first scene we hear of a marriage broken by ambition and greed; in the second scene the soldiers are awakened only by disaster! Though 'the gods' are still intermittently present in *Poppea, good* usually capitulates to evil.

Most of the characters in *Poppea* are motivated by malice, lust and self-interest. What Monteverdi, who thought carefully about this as about his other libretti, seems to be asking is: given the crassness of human nature in a fallen world, is there anything to be said for being human? His answer is, of course, yes. Even if this is what we are, stripped of pretence and pretention, we may still sometimes feel honestly, may sometimes love as well as lust and may even experience remorse. So long as we are alive, we act; and if we usually act for worse rather than better, it is also true that while there is life there is hope. So the story of *Poppea* is not, after all, really viewed as history but as a tale which, although not a myth, may contain mythic truths. It is significant that the action functions on every social level; love below stairs is given parity with the high and mighty, and if the low types speak-sing ignorantly, in the style of raucous street music, they sometimes speak from the heart. The grandeur of Lords and Ladies may collapse in bathos; the comedy of servants and serving-maids may flower into pathos. Humour heals wounds, through the agency of music, in which sense *Poppea* looks beyond the heroic baroque towards Mozart. The opera is named not after the Emperor but after a young and unheroic woman who is prophetic, in her bemused fashion, of Mozart's regeneratively redemptive Pamina, as will be seen in a later chapter. Indeed although *Poppea* is not a humanist testament like Monteverdi's first opera, it is in a sense more deeply, because more democratically, humane: not merely socially, but also emotionally in that all categories of experience are valid. The suicide of Seneca, too 'good' or too conventionally proper to live in the world as it is, is followed immediately by comic interludes between servants, taking the mickey out of patrician pride.

Related to this is the sectional, almost cinematic, technique. Formally, the opera is not, like *Orfeo*, a continuous play in music but a succession of brief scenes, discontinuous because life itself is 'one

damn thing after another'. Even through the double murder plot of
Act II scene 9 the music reminds us that 'other modes of experience'
are possible. Despite our fallen natures, developed coloratura,
ordered dance rhythms, controlled harmonies move tentatively
towards 'modern' concepts of tonality and form, succouring survival
in so doing. This is movingly evident in the final scene, despite or
because of the fact that Nero, the young Emperor, is a grotesque
parody of Orphic Man who, 'fiddling while Rome burns', destroys
instead of creating. Monteverdi's Orfeo, challenging the gods, had
heroically stormed heights; his Nero plumbs depths at the instigation
of mere whim and caprice, abolishing any law that, even in the most
trivial particular, threatens his momentary pleasure. Even as a pimply
adolescent, as he is in the opera, he has no doubt that if (and it is a big
if) heaven belongs to Jupiter, then 'del mondo terra lo scettro e mio'.
For the nonce his destiny is determined by his obsessive passion for
Poppea, a young chit of a girl with no inner resources to deal with the
bewildering jet-set society in which she finds herself. She is a seventeenth-century Marilyn Monroe whose exquisitely sensual coloratura
both arouses and responds to Nero's besotted voluptuousness. 'Non
è piu in cielo il mio destino, ma sta dei labbri tuoi nel bel rubino' cries
Nero, tossing the Heroic Ideal on to the trash-heap. By the end of the
opera his political destiny is in ruins, his world 'in peaces, all coherence
gone'. He sings a vainglorious aria boasting of his kingship and
godhead, trying to cheer himself up in the face of calamity. His
virtuosic ostentation is succeeded by silence; and when Poppea tries to
reply, her arioso can manage no more than faltering confusion. Yet if
she cannot convincingly act the Queen and Empress, she learns her
own kind of courage, singing an aria, or rather an air, which is also a
lullaby and passacaglia, the ground bass of which, as so often in
Monteverdi, ballasts her fortitude.

Becoming a duet, the passacaglia also involves Nero in her dream,
which turns out to be a kind of reality. He says that the Sun, the
Glorious Orb of Empire (meaning himself) has now sunk into her
eyes, which are those of a simple young woman. A sudden intrusion of
trumpeted Coronation Music serves only to remind us of the illusory
pomp of Empire, which seems trivial in comparison with the lullaby's
tender truth. For this love duet is as devoid of ostentation, almost as
childish, as the duet of the adolescent servant-lovers in the second act.
Indeed the two love duets are thematically related, and both spring
from a recognition of the vulnerability which, beneath the pride, is the

heart of the human condition. Becoming as little children, or as lowly servants, even emperors may love again: momentarily, of course, for we are mutable as well as mortal. So this is far from being a conventional happy ending. If monstrous crimes are apparently discounted, this is not to pretend that they have not been committed, and will not be committed again. Our final view of the lovers is as babes in the wood, as the duet winds down, slower and slower, in infinite wistfulness.* Yet although such bliss can be true only for the moment, it *is* true, while it briefly lasts.

Its truth is a paradox, as is most of the work of this wondrous composer. If it seems odd that so grandly epic an opera should end so intimately we come to realise, as we listen, that the lullaby metamorphoses the confusion from which Poppea had started into (at least potential) 'con-fusion': an incipiently democratic fusing of contradictions that deserves to be accorded rights, if not equal rights. Monteverdi did not know that he was writing a revolutionary opera, though he did know that he was dealing with the common heart of humanity. Love, affection and care, if nearly impotent in a world dominated by self-interest, are not totally discountable. The startling modernity of *Poppea* is further evidence that Monteverdi is not merely a great composer, but is also one of the supreme 'makers' of, as well as in, European history.

Most opera contemporary with late Monteverdi is modern in a more discreditable sense, though it fascinates in being so like us. Through seventeenth-century Italy, especially in dazzling Venice, there was frenetic excitment over opera, which was becoming not so much a court entertainment and humanist ritual as a public commodity. Opera-houses were built recklessly; operas were thrown together with no less insouciance. This is one reason why they are difficult to perform nowadays. Only the shortest of short scores was written down; libretti and music were strung together empirically, even chaotically, details being filled in *ad hoc* by tribes of assistants. What mattered, in a rapidly changing world, was vibrant response to emotional and perhaps intellectual turmoil.

The seventeenth century, like our own, was a period of violent

---

* I find it difficult to credit the scholarly case, made in 1974, that the final love duet is an addition by another hand. Who could have been capable of so supremely relevant a stroke of genius, even allowing that he was bright enough to base it on the servants' duet in the second act?

change in which the scientific revolution transformed man's destiny. People were bemused by what was happening, just as we goggle in fascinated incomprehension at the prospects revealed by the electronic shattering of time and space. Monteverdi was unique in seeing and hearing, beneath the flux, the shape of things to come. The representative composer of the seventeenth century had no choice but to accept the flux, responding seismographically to its exciting if alarming vagaries. Francesco Cavalli (1602–1676) was *maestro di cappella* at St Mark's, Venice, in which capacity he produced quantities of church music. But the traditions of the Church were not what, in the appropriate modern phrase, made him 'tick'; he found time to churn out around forty operas between 1637 and 1666. They take place in a limbo between the mythology of Monteverdi's *Orfeo* and the modern history of his *Poppea*. If their backdrop is Arcadian, the age they celebrate is hardly golden, but rather a hurly-burly that bears a startling resemblance to that of our televisual supermen and of science fiction. One of his most successful operas, *La Calisto* (first produced in 1651) has been successfully revived in our own day, and it is not difficult to understand why. Here the ideality of the masque degenerates into a whirlwind of mistaken identities; no one knows who or what he/she/it is, whether male or female, human or divine. Our own obsession with transvestism springs from a comparable confusion over identity. We do not have the sensuous beauty of Cavalli's music to pour oil on our troubled waters, though we do have stage engines and complex scenic devices, especially in the electrified forms of the media, to complement the gimmicks – descendents of the less mechanically efficient if no less ambitious contraptions of the court masque – that enraptured Cavalli's public. Neither for him nor for us do these mechanical devices clarify life's confusion.

La Calisto begins in a world laid waste by Jove's thunderbolt, deputising for a nuclear bomb. The point is serious enough, for although nuclear physics had not been discovered people were all too aware that, in a wavery world undirected by God and mismanaged by men, anything might happen. In such a world the identity of divine and human creatures may be confused, often by disguise. The love story of divine Jove and human Calisto overlaps with that of Endymion and Diana, and we cannot simply say that the divine is our upward aspiration, the human our downward dissipation – in more senses than one. We live in our uncertainties, in a tentatively hopeful-hopeless muddle. The jokes in drag reach lunatic proportions when

Jove gets entangled with Diana, both disguised as someone of the opposite sex. Reversals of situation and identity are complemented by ironic juxtapositions of mood, as in the collocation of the 'low' anti-masque of Furies with Juno's exquisite and potentially heroic *bel canto* aria 'Raccaonsolate e page'. The jokes are outrageous, existing, televisually, in a dream within a dream: the sexual disguises and reversals, the thugs' 'comic' torture scene and the like are instantly recognisable, almost cosily familiar, to us, brought up on the *Rocky Horror Picture Show*, not to mention a 1980s piece such as Caryl Churchill's *Cloud 9*, in which an African explorer seduces his friend's wife (portrayed by a man), his school-age son (portrayed by a woman), and his black servent (portrayed by a white), before marrying his governess (a lesbian)! The difference between Cavalli and us is that although his world was chaos, his Arcadian ideal at least existed within living memory. His transitions between farouche action, the ecstasy of *bel canto* song and the lilt of triple-rhythmed dance occur spontaneously, leaving an undercurrent of pathos that stirs the heart. However arbitrarily dire the events, the music offers delicious alleviation. Even in this unheroic opera, as in *Poppea*, Mercury is still present, travelling between worlds. It is pertinent to note that Mercury's ambiguity was also sexual; he was often presented as an androgyne.

Not surprisingly, Cavalli's technique is even more televisual than that of *Poppea*, since it is more empirically random. The music veers between instrumental dances, usually for humanely civilised strings, wherein he created euphony as in the Golden Age masque, and recitative sublimated into arioso when people sing of the passions that drive them in the heady present. Whereas the dance music, incorporating public values, is fairly fully notated, the private life of recitative is restricted to vocal line and bass, with the harmonies to be filled in on harpsichord, lute, harp or organ, in the moment. Thus the music reflects the precarious contemporaneity of the experience: arioso is feeling acting itself out; aria is its transcendence, the human voice elevated by *bel canto* to 'higher' expressivity. In Cavalli, transcendence is infrequent, and when arioso flowers into aria it does not last long, since in the conditions of the mundane world man-made, dance-dominated order cannot be expected to survive efficaciously. Significantly enough, extended arias in Cavalli usually occur in the moment of death. In *L'Ormindo* (1644) the heroine Evisha expires in lithe melodic lines over a triple-rhythmed ground which, like our previous instances of ostinato basses in Monteverdi, overrides Time. Even so,

Evisha's death turns out to be only a pretence; in the action, if not here in the music, Cavalli evades death along with sin and guilt, using forms which are as open-ended as life itself. Only Monteverdi discovered, within chaos, new possibilities for order. Out of that strength Orpheus, having been momentarily crestfallen, is to be resurrected. This process may be approached by way of the St Cecilian odes that became fashionable during the second half of the seventeenth century.

The Orpheus story, as has been noted, is Janus-faced, being interpretable either as an attempt of fallen man to rediscover himself in reattaining the One, or as man's vainglorious attempt to arrogate to himself God's properties. Monteverdi's *Orfeo* attempts to do both at the same time, and perhaps owes its richness to its confusion. After *Orfeo*, the bemused seventeenth century equivocated between the two interpretations but came down heavily on the side of humanistic vainglory. Literary parallels are helpful in this context. Throughout Shakespeare's plays – which are contemporary with Monteverdi's *Orfeo* but considerably antedate *Poppea* – music is valued as a manifestation of human passion, as when Mariana at the Moated Grange in *Measure for Measure* uses the anonymous boy's song as an Orphic means of assuaging her frustrated desire. But the point lies in the assuagement: *musica humana* puts her in touch with *musica mundana*, the Music of the Spheres, which helps her to go on living. Similarly Lear's 'restoration' music is passion music in more than one sense: a string fancy which starts from human passion yet dissolves its harmonic suffering into the benediction of quasi-vocal polyphony. The act of incarnation may lead to revelation, the Flesh becoming Word. Like sixteenth-century musical technique itself, this was an equivocation that could not be long sustained. Shakespeare and Byrd could only have occurred at this time, when a potent apprehension of human sensuality and (complementarily) mortality could be reconciled with an awareness of divine grace. Yet some such equilibrium remained an ideal well into the heyday of the Classical Baroque. This may be why, during the later seventeenth century, a pronouncedly elegiac tone enters thinking about music. Milton's *At a Solemn Musick* is a magnificent example of this here in England.

He opens by referring to Voice and Verse as a 'blest pair of Sirens, Pledges of Heav'ns Joy', who are 'Sphear-born', harmonious and divine. Although he is thinking of Verse as being part of the Word, the traditional music of the Church (if not *his* church), he none the less presents the 'wedding' of Voice and Verse as an Orphic experience. They will employ their 'mixt power' in order to 'pierce dead things with inbreath'd sense'. Their force will be baroquely 'affective', influencing human behaviour. From that point, however, the elegiac flavour in Milton's poem takes over, for their 'high-rais'd phantasie' proves to be not life as it is, but a vision of life as it once was and ought, in Milton's view, to be again. Music ought to evoke that 'undisturbed Song of pure concent' such as is sung in heaven and was sung on earth in our prelapsarian state. We have to be reminded of the Music of the Spheres in order that

we on Earth with undiscording voice
May rightly answer that melodious noyse
As once we did, till disproportion'd sin
Jarr'd against Nature's chime, and with harsh din
Broke the fair musick that all creatures made
To their great Lord, whose love their motion sway'd
In perfect Diapason, whilst they stood
In first obdience, and their state of good.

What Milton is asking for in his 'perfect Diapason' – the oneness of the octave between God and Man – is a return to the old monody and to medieval organum. But of course he could not admit to that and would not, in his heart, have wanted to; for he knew that the 'pain of consciousness' or, in theological terms, the consequences of the Fall, cannot be evaded by wishful thinking. So he ends with a prophecy:

O may we soon again renew that Song,
And keep in tune with Heav'n, till God ere long
To his celestial consort us unite,
To live with him, and sing in endless morn of light.

The lingering rhythm of the final line reinforces the wistfulness inherent in the passage; and the wistfulness remains, whether we interpret the line in personal terms, implying that we will be fulfilled only when dead, or whether we think of it as a prophecy about the destiny of the human race. The whole of Milton's work proves that he knew that, if ever the prophecy were fulfilled, it could not be in the form of a return to the past, since Paradise once Lost is lost forever; or at least can be Regained, as in Milton's late epic, only by becoming something different.

The balance between regression and progression in Milton's verses is mirrored in the music of his friend Henry Lawes who, like Milton, lived through a period of civil dissent, a conflict of forces material and spiritual: between the old Faith and the new, between Court and Country. Henry Lawes was admired by Cavalier poets such as Carew and Cartwright, whom he set, as well as by Charles I himself. Yet his allegiances were divided as were those of most people in this gentlemen's war. He was also a close friend of Puritan Milton, who addressed a sonnet to 'Harry, whose tuneful and well-measur'd Song First taught our English music how to span Words with just note and accent'. Lawes is praised because he does for English music what the Italian monodists did for theirs; he 'humours' our tongue with his 'smooth airs', so that 'Dante shall give Fame leave to set thee higher Then his Casella, whom he woo'd to sing Met in the milder shades of Purgatory'. Lawes effected the most intimate alliance known between words and music because his melodic lines are not merely, like Dowland's, triggered by verse but are, to the most meticulous detail, shaped by it.

Appropriately enough, Lawes demonstrates this in composing a 'Hymn of Orpheus' in which the Orphic magic lies in the fact that declaimed words became music in through-composed style, the technique stemming from the English ayre but absorbing the lesson of Monteverdian recitative. Music 'summons Heaven and Hell' as the vocal line leaps and plunges; 'shakes the world' as the line oscillates; responds with affective melodic contours, rhythmic gestures and harmonic tensions to the words' thundering, freezing, burning, frying and melting. Though all this may happen in examples of the earlier madrigalian idiom, it is not so physically projected into action. Here musical stylisation is itself becoming theatre (as is still more evident in three 'dialogues' by Henry's more musically audacious brother, William). These too are overtly Orphic, the first, 'Charon, O Charon', being a conversation between Charon and a lover (Amintor) who is trying to persuade the guardian of Hades to allow him to expire. In the second dialogue, 'Charon, O gentle Charon, let me woe thee', a nightingale plays Persephone in appealing to Charon for comparable release; while in the third Orpheus himself appears and, urged on by Alecto, succeeds (though his 'harpe is out of tune'), in summoning Eurydice from the shades. The dialogue ends with all three singing in consort, because 'true love makes a heaven of hell'. Clearly Orpheus's tragedy is defused. The arioso is brilliantly physical – and 'theatrical'. In the charmed circle of the Caroline court, whose modes and manners, inspired by Henrietta Maria, were French and Italian, such music is punningly 'played' and acted to the extent that it

may be latently or patently comic. The final ensemble in the
nightingale song, for instance, expresses the conceit that the tears of
love are in danger of drowning the Stygian ferry in wailing chromatics
not notably distinct from the ludicrous caterwaulings in 'The Catts as
other creatures doe' – an 'in joke' about specific courtiers that is none
the less powerfully naturalistic! Interestingly, an entirely serious
elegy, 'Musicke, the Master of thy Art is dead', composed in memory
of John Tomkins (brother of the more famous Thomas), makes a
comparably equivocal effect since the dissonant suspensions and false
relations (prompted by 'strange grief') and the wailing chromatics on
'Let's howle sad notes' are so extravagant as to be grotesque. It does
not follow that because sorrow is thus play-acted it must be insincere,
though one might say – and this is true of William Lawes' most
adventurous string music also – that it implies a specialised, self-
enclosed audience.

The gamey physical enactment in this music by the brothers Lawes
is a stage towards the presentation of dramatic action in inherently
musical terms, but is only the first stage; the Lawes do not invent the
musical stylisations whereby Orpheus becomes a High Baroque
composer of operas. How that happens is revealed in the music-hym-
ning odes of Dryden, Purcell and Handel. Ultimately, the new order
they represent negates Milton's view of art as revelation, and
discounts the compromise between the physical and metaphysical
implicit in Monteverdi's *Orfeo*.

It is not an accident that this second great revolution in musical
history complements the final acceptance of the Copernican system
and the launching of the Scientific Revolution. As long as the earth
was believed to be the centre of a divinely-appointed universe Man
and God could be intimate. Once the First Cause had been shifted into
the physical body of the sun, from which all things derive life, man's
relationship to God became too complex to be humanly apprehensible. In the resultant bemusement – as Monteverdi's *Poppea* and
Cavalli's *La Calisto* had suggested – it seemed easier, as well as more
logical, to envisage God not as a mystical entity but rather as geometry
relatable to the new science; and to concentrate on man's ability to
explain away, through his intellect, the mechanical processes of
Nature. At the same time man may rejoice in his power to appreciate,
understand, and therefore control, his sensual passions. A Cavalli,
immediately responsive to the process of change, does not get far with
the reordering; yet from his very confusion emerged the necessity for

new, reformative techniques. We noted how confusion became 'confusion' at the end of Monteverdi's *Poppea*. That was prophecy such as only genius was capable of.

Dryden's odes to St Cecilia were written only about forty years later than Milton's *At a Solemn Musick*, yet they are as 'modern' as Milton's poem was outmoded. The original St Cecilia was a Roman martyr of the third century whose existence is not much more than legendary, though martyrs associated with her seem to have been historical figures. She became the patron saint of music in the sixteenth century, largely because – according to the Oxford Dictionary of Saints – an Antiphon taken from her Acts tells us that 'as the organs (at her wedding feast) were playing, Cecilia sung (in her heart) to the Lord, saying: may my heart remain unsullied, so that I be not confounded'. At the founding of the Academy of Music in Rome in 1584 Cecilia was nominated its patroness, at the same time becoming a female, Christianised, Orpheus. In the legend she converts her husband and brother to Christianity, and all three are martyred: a rather grim perversion of the Orpheus-Aristeus-Euridice triangle. In his Ode, first performed in 1687, Dryden brings in the organ as Cecilia's sacred instrument, to deputise for the lute-lyre; but the baroque organ is essentially a polyphony-harmonic sustaining instrument, adept at playing the sensually harmonic music the Baroque age specialised in. By this date the English monarchy was restored, and St Cecilian Odes were designed to celebrate that mundanely magnificent event.

So in Dryden's poem it turns out that the breach of civil war had been healed not so much by divine dispensation as by man's command of a mechanical view of Nature:

From Harmony, from Heav'nly Harmony
This Universal Frame began:
When Nature underneath a heap
Of Jarring Atoms lay,
And could not heave her Head,
The tuneful Voice was heard from high:
'Arise, ye more than dead'.
Then cold, and hot, and moist, and dry,
In order to their stations leap,
And Musick's pow'r obey.

The force of music may be called heavenly in that it is the First Cause; but once the jarring atoms have cohered gravitationally to make the Newtonian universe, music's power is to be valued only for its human effects. These are twofold. Music's order is a social analogy, for the disruptive tensions of harmony (remember the speech of Monteverdi's Messenger and Gesualdo's fragmented chromatics) must bow to public ceremonial dance and to the evolving scheme of tonality related to it, just as the individual must be suberservient to the State if chaos is to be evaded. But music's function is Orphic too, and a properly-ordered social Whole makes for the fullest expression of the Parts. Thus music is to be valued for its direct effect on human conduct. The trumpet's loud clangour excites us to arms; the double double beat of the thundering drum makes us yet more bellicose; the warbling flute renders us more amorous; the ever serviceable violin may induce friskiness or languishment as occasion offers. The universal order is dedicated only to the fulfilment of man's sensual nature. Though 'from Heavenly Harmony this Universal Frame began' it runs through 'all the Compass of the Notes' in order that the diapason may 'close full in *Man*'. Milton deplored the loss of the perfect diapason that was man's oneness with God; for Dryden the octave is synonymous with Man himself, who is thus the object of creation. Nervousness over the dubiety of merely human reason, typical of the earlier years of the seventeenth century, hardens – and it would not be altogether inaccurate to think of this as in part a sexual metaphor – into supreme self-confidence, which may sometimes be indistinguishable from complacency. Through his enjoyment of his senses, command of his Reason and hopeful power over Nature, Man has taken God's place.

This is the fulfilment of the Renaissance's sensual-material ostentation so revered by that *humanitor novi temporis* Francis Bacon: a fulfilment made feasible only by the scientific revolution and the economic development of a mercantile society. The Renaissance had, indeed, anticipatorily symbolised the deification of man in the ceremony of the King's Two Bodies – his mortal body which was carried to its last resting place and to dusty disintegration and his garishly coloured effigy, made of relatively durable *material*, which represented his pretend-eternal divinity as a terrestrial institution. It is therefore not surprising that the divine or mystical aspects of music, associated with St Cecilia and the organ, are mentioned in Dryden's poem only perfunctorily, among the art's other affective attributes: having a beatific vision is one among the many varieties of experience, like making love or enjoying a good dinner. Orpheus, Dryden says, could transport savages, beasts, and even trees into states of ecstasy;

complementarily, Cecilia can make angels mistake earth for heaven. This is precisely what men of the heroic world, believing so potently in man's glory that they could imagine an earthly paradise was feasible, not merely hoped for, but expected.

Henry Purcell, the leading composer of England Restored even as Dryden was its laureate poet, retains, even when writing man-glorifying St Cecilia odes, far more of Milton's elegiac ambiguity than does his literary peer. This was partly because his was a genius of finer strain but also, perhaps, simply because he was a musician, conservatively rooted in old-style choral polyphony and in the string fancy which was its instrumental complement. Though he did not set Dryden's famous Ode – the prototype of many turned out by hack poets for state-magnifying performance on St Cecilia's birthday – the burden of his several St Cecilian odes is very close to Dryden's. He is, however, far more tentative in 'mistaking Earth for Heav'n'. Significantly the first Ode, *Welcome to All the Pleasures*, composed in 1683 and unpretentiously scored for solo voices, small chorus and strings, does not entirely abandon ecclesiastical polyphony though it is conceived in a convention – that of the verse anthem – which permutes operatic stylisations to church use.

Ostensibly it is, like Dryden's grander ode, designed to celebrate the humanist's paradise – a riot of sensual pleasures revelled in so unthinkingly that they may seem to be oblivious of Time. Yet the opening is unexpected: although it is, conventionally enough, a masque or opera overture in the French manner, with a slow section in duple time followed by a quick triple-rhythmed fugato, it attains a linear-harmonic texture that plumbs deeper than social ceremony, and maybe hints at qualities beyond the terrestial. The ripe harmonies of the slow section express the humanist's sensual heaven while dissonantly telling us that, as human nature since the Fall is no longer innocent nor indeed 'natural', pain is inherent in pleasure. Sexual consummation, being subject to time, is a still a 'dying', as it had been for Monteverdi and Gesualdo. Love hurts as it is desired, which is why Purcell's lush harmonic textures are pierced with dis-cord and why his preoccupation with *false* relation – to which we first referred as far back as Dufay's *Ave Regina* and saw to be epitomised in that crucial arioso of Monteverdi's Messenger – becomes in Purcell almost obsessive, stressing the illusion that lies within the joys of the flesh.

The ripeness of the harmony in this Prelude depends on the fact that each line desires independence. Suspended ninth or eleventh chords occur because inner parts are seeking melodic identity; multiple false relations appear because decorative figurations are sung in contours that tug against the harmonic progression. It is significant that this small overture should remind us of a much greater, more sustained piece in the same key – the opening chorus of Bach's St Matthew Passion. In Bach too each line is a singing voice that carries intense harmonic potential: consequently the concourse of voices has tremendous interior energy; lyrical affirmation flows out of harmonic anguish. Bach is a man of faith as Purcell is not, so his music, though chromatic, is less riddled than Purcell's with harmonic ambiguities and false relations. None the less Purcell and Bach, in moments like this, have profound affinities. Both are 'Mercurian' in starting from an immediate apprehension of the life of the senses, recognising that sensual consummation is subject to Time and inextricably linked with pain: hence the dissonance of their harmony. Both tell us, through the singing lines of their harmonic polyphony, that out of the flesh's joyful suffering may spring a lyrical affirmation of the spirit.

The overture is the heart of *Welcome to all the Pleasures*. The rest of the work follows from, but simplifies, its mystical humanism. When the voices enter they welcome 'all the Pleasures that delight Of ev'ry Sense, the grateful Appetite' in triadic formations which do not, however, avoid grinding suspensions. A countertenor solo invokes 'the god of Music, and of Love' in an Orphic aria over a ground bass. Human love ought to combine with divine music (in the old, Shakesperean, sense) to absolve the pain inherent in loving. Although the Italianate cantilena is sensuous, with pathetically drooping tritones, the passion of the overture is lulled by the cooling vocal melody and by the ground bass which, because it continues unchangingly, illusorily seems to be outside time.

This states explicitly what is implicit in the overture: music 'incarnates' sensuality and at the same time escapes from it, Purcell's Orpheus figure being still a Mercurian messenger. A bass solo invites us to use our voices, 'those Organs of Nature', because singing will 'charm the troubled and amorous Creature'. The chorus that follows is a round dance in triple rhythm, simple in texture but still chromatic. Troubled amorousness proves, if melancholy, to be also delicious; the overture's tension between declining chromatics and linear independence is abandoned until the final false relation on 'soft charms' is a swoon. But melancholy gains ascendency over deliciousness in the following tenor solo: an exquisite dance-air in which he invites love-become-music to 'temper the heat of desire' with its 'innocent fire'. This air, in two twelve-bar periods with a modulation from E minor to the relative major, is of heart-easing simplicity. It tames the passions, like Orpheus-as-Apollo; yet does so with a wistful-ness on the brink of tears (listen to the dissonant melodic note on the word 'innocent' itself, or the upward-yearning appoggiatura on the word 'lute'). It is as though in saying farewell to the senses we are losing all we can hope to know of reality.

The final chorus, in which we venerate 'holy Cecilia' in a round dance in old-fashioned fugato, bears this out. From this most of the chromaticisms and all the false relations have evaporated, leaving only diatonic concords in the tonic major. The key of E major is not common in seventeenth-century music, which may help to make the music sound unreal as compared with the reality of the E minor overture. The work does not, after all, end in sonorous splendour. Gradually, the rejoicing dies away, one part after another fading out, insubstantial as a dream, until only the bass is left. Once more, the chorus works in Mercurian fashion: it seems to invoke a world 'beyond' the humanist's here and now; at the same time it says that if you take music out of the context of human living and dying it is no more than a fairy tale. This is an early example of Purcell's association of the major key with illusion, the minor – with its more varied harmonic possibilities – with reality. Later, E major, the sharpest major key in common use, is to become the High Baroque composer's paradisal key, as F minor, the flattest minor key in common use, is to become his deathly and infernal tonality. Purcell's earthly paradise here proves as frail as the masque's 'insubstantial pageant' to which Shakespeare's Prospero refers in his valedictory address. This is backhanded evidence that Purcell was more in touch with a heavenly paradise than any High Baroque composer (with the supreme excep-tion of Bach) wanted or needed to be.

'Functional' tonality – which may or may not be symbolic in the sense suggested above – was one of the means whereby the classical baroque idiom aimed to consummate music's humane purposes. Monteverdi's *Orfeo* is a play in music, underlining sublimated speech with harmony and interspersing dances as social interludes in the personal drama; his *Poppea* is more tonally organised, but is still episodic, like life itself, in its 'cinematic' technique. Purcell had, by the 1680s, evolved arioso techniques that have harmonic direction, even though *Welcome to all the Pleasures* does not accept corporeal fulfilment as man's 'be all and end all'. Less than ten years later, however, in the last of his St Cecilian odes (composed in 1692), he sets ceremonial verses which are of no great distinction but close to Dryden's heroic prototype, and creates music that is fully-fledged theatrical action, yet musically self-subsistent. Dance had stood for the Public Life in the theatre music of Monteverdi, and still more in the operas and ballets of Lully, state composer to the *Roi Soleil* at Versailles. Purcell, learning from both, displays in the dances and the large-scale overture to the 1692 Ode a new potency in handling tonality. The by now conventional relationships of tonic, dominant, subdominant and relative minor are enriched by sequential transitions. Theoretically, though not often in fact, the two 'halves' of binary form answer one another like mirrors. Fugato is exploited as a principle of unity defined by and fitting into the key scheme since tonality, and the harmony it controls, incarnate the public weal. Musical is identified with social and political order. Purcell's sectional scoring, for strings, woodwind and brass, is both architecturally deployed and dramatic in impact.

At the same time Purcell allows scope, within this public organisation, for the drama of the personal life, as we may hear in the weeping appoggiaturas and languishing chromatics of the slow sections that interrupt the celebrative grandeur of the overture itself. This personal passion within the public whole finds vent in solo arioso, an acting *out* of inner psychological stress, harking back to Monteverdi but looking forward, in tonal organisation and disciplined virtuosity, to Handel. The famous countertenor arioso 'Tis Nature's voice', said to have been sung 'with incredible graces by Mr Purcell' himself, opens with Nature's accoustic fact of the triad but makes it flower, through sobbing appoggiaturas and illustrative roulades, into an apotheosis of personal feeling. Far more physically than the arioso of Monteverdi's Orphic Messenger, this music enacts the heart of *human* nature, as distinct from the Nature we come from. It can hardly be sung without the gestures of arms and hands: through a 'physical' technique no more than hinted at in Lawes's *Hymn of Orpheus*, Purcell achieves man's Orphic deification. The Orphic presence survives when, in the succeeding monumental, incipiently Handelian chorus, 'Soul of the World', the 'jarring atoms' are majestically marshalled by man's intellect and will. Though Paradise may have been lost, Milton's Satan is in part a hero, his Eve a redeemer. Through them Purcell, Milton's heir, has learned to *impose* order on time and space.

Between the extremes of public dance and private arioso stands aria: wherein a solo voice sings of the personal life in a form disciplined by harmony and by dance metre in the interests of the Whole. What was once subservient to the will of God is now subservient to the laws of the State. The philosophical and political concepts of Hobbes, also hatched during our civil war, argued that since fallen man is irredeemably vile he cannot be trusted to act morally except under dictatorial absolutism. The English were congenitally averse to so uncompromising a position, which may be why Purcell, despite a flame of genius stronger than that of Louis XIV's state composer, failed to establish a 'classical' English operatic tradition to complement that of Lully in France. Purcell's airs, significantly, are usually short, or, if long, are based on the rudimentary technique of ground bass, the general import of which has been discussed in reference to Monteverdi. In the 1692 Ode he uses ground bass with telling effect in hymning that 'wonderous Machine', the organ: a man-made contraption which can contain a universe of sound. The regular clicking of the quavers sounds oddly machine-like, apposite to the mechanistic Newtonian world. The effect, in contrast with the exuberantly expressive coloration of 'Tis Nature's voice', is not far from ironic, and very different from that of the ground bass aria, 'Music for a while', which Purcell introduces into a play on the Oedipus story in which music Orphically heals the lacerated mind. Mental anguish and physical pain are embodied in the sobbing appoggiaturas, plopping tears and undulating snakes of the vocal line, while its lyricism abets the ostinato bass to dispense calm and balm. Interestingly, the ground modulates; the piece has beginning, middle and end as Orpehus the man summons divinely efficacious music. Not for nothing was Purcell dubbed Orpheus Britannicus, as Dowland had been called the English Orpheus.

In his late work, however, Purcell does not restrict his arias to the ground bass convention, but calls on *bel canto* vocalism in Italianate binary and ternary forms to deal with those basic postulates of Love and War. Instrumentally, in the 1692 Ode, amorous lament is acted out in the cooing of recorders, airy frivolity in the caperings of violins, bellicose aggression in the blaring of trumpets and thundering of drums, 'physical' experience being at the same time categorised and controlled. Though he did not himself create a mature convention of *opera seria*, he magnificently deploys in this Ode all the techniques essential to it. Handel, in the palmier days of Augustan England, is himself to set Dryden's most celebrated *Ode to St Cecilia* in a manner indebted to Purcell, though more classically precise. The wildness that lurked beneath Purcell's retrospective elegiacs is banished. Handel brings to fruition what Purcell prophesied, and the process entails both loss and gain.

The forty-odd years between Purcell's 1692 setting of the Dryden-style St Cecilian Ode and Handel's 1739 setting of the real thing make as much difference, despite Purcell's expert refashioning of baroque vocal and instrumental conventions, as does the similar age gap between Milton's and Dryden's poems. Purcell's setting, rooted in arioso, is open-ended, to a degree unpredictable; barriers between sacred and profane are crossed, if not as frequently as they were in the early *Welcome to all the Pleasures*. Handel's setting betrays no such ambiguities. Man as social being is triumphant, Orphic in being responsible for his own passions and in control of those of his fellows. His overture is on the French pattern, with pompous double dots and ceremonially shooting scales, though it modifies precedent in that its slow section is in triple instead of duple time, its quick fugue in four time instead of three. The key is straight diatonic D major, now established as key of Pomp and Circumstance because it is the key of natural trumpets and congenial to strings of the violin family. The tonality presses optimistically sharpwards to the dominant. The quick section is not an embryonic fugato but a fully-developed fugue on a sprightly dance tune; the counterpart fits into, and musically and socially conforms with, the harmony and tonality instead of, as with Purcell and Bach, sometimes thrusting against them. A gracious minuet, most fashionable dance of the moment, rounds off the overture, vicariously if not actively involving those 'gathered together' in the terpsichorean revel.

Against this public affirmation Handel sets Dryden's mechanistic view of creation from the 'heap of Jarring Atoms'. Chaos is naturally equated with the chord of the diminished seventh, considered 'horrendous' because, consisting of two interlocked and rootless tritones, it undermines classical tonality. The cold, moist, hot and dry elements are summoned from fragmentation to coherence by Cecilia-Orpheus, the recitative being accompanied by a machine-like hammering of semiquavers. Coherence is stabilised in a D major chorus, massively homophonic, though with illustrative rising and falling scales as music 'runs through all the Compass of the Notes';

sepulchral slow repeated notes make the Diapason 'close full in *Man*. Tonally, the chorus covers the conventional baroque hierarchy of tonic, dominant, subdominant and relative minor, with the 'optimistic' dominant dominating.

The music for solo voices favours formal aria rather than Purcell's embryonic arioso. 'What passions cannot music raise and quell' is explicitly Orphic, with obbligato cello deputising for the lyre as 'Jubal struck the chorded Shell'. A *da capo* aria in the relatively passive subdominant, it is serene in its arpeggiated contours, sensuous in sonority. Man-woman-Orpheus elevates him-her-self to Godhead without need of metaphysical sanction; and the tenor aria 'The trumpet's loud clangour' caps the previous aria's love and loveliness with pride and presumption. The ringingly heroic tenor, in a bounding 6/8 metre suggesting the chase, is of course ballasted by obbligato trumpet and drums and is soon reinforced by the 'public' chorus, since war is a communal activity. Arias of the 'soft complaining flute' and 'sharp violins' likewise juxtapose contradictory but complementary realms of feeling, this time in personal terms: the flute warbles lovingly in B minor (D major's tragic relative), while the violins nag and snap with the pangs of jealousy and the desperation it induces. The elegant formality and lucid textures safeguard love from self-indulgence and envy from despair. The final pair of arias feature Orpheus directly, first disguised as St Cecilia, singing a hymnic melody in F major, flat submediant to the perky A major of the violins' aria, with Handel himself improvising prelude and postlude on the Saint's organ; and secondly in his own person, leading the 'savage race' in an exuberant hornpipe, the violins enacting the beasts' cavortings as they bound in syncopation across the barlines. The barlines are, however, the arbiter; this very earthy Orpheus steers a clear path through them, carrying the aria back from the beasts' D minor to Cecilia's blissful F major. It is interesting that Orpheus, despite his corporeality in this context, is personified by a soprano – a legacy from the *opera seria* convention whereby heroes are sung by castrated males, whose trumpet-like tones are ironically presumed to sound larger than life.

As in Dryden's poems, Cecilia's divine pretentions are given short shrift. She is allowed no aria, only a briefly intense accompanied recitative, in which to mistake earth for heaven. That it is in fact no mistake is spelled out in Dryden's epilogic stanza:

As from the pow'r of Sacred Lays
The Spheres began to move,
And sung the Great Creator's praise
To all the Bless'd above;
So when the last and dreadful Hour
This crumbling Pageant shall devour;
The Trumpet shall be heard in high, —
The Dead shall live, the Living die,
And Musick shall untune the Sky.

So at the end the trumpet no longer excites to vainglorious expression of a power that is in the last resort self-love; becoming the Last Trump, it reminds us that we are to be snuffed out like a candle. As John Hollander has pointed out, music inverts its traditional function; instead of recalling the divine purpose, let along wafting us into a presumptive afterlife, it 'untunes' heaven itself. Mundane music, in the modern sense, has defeated *musica mundana*, the Music of the Spheres; and Heroic Man has had the courage to take it.

As does Handel in his final chorus, by far the most substantial movement in the work. The metre is firmly duple as solo soprano Opheus carols antiphonally with the homophonic chorus, resonantly in D major, if momentarily disturbed by Neapolitan chromatics at the 'last and dreadful hour'. The solo trumpet's last trump, however, sweeps aside all *frissons* of fear to pay tribute to the glorious present of Augustan monarchy. *Musica humana* untunes the sky in a regular-rhythmed fugue with plenty of tonal movement as well as corporeal energy, though with no threat to the baroque tonal hierarchy except for a fleeting touch of the dominant of the dominant of the relative. Unexpectedly, the final peroration faintly qualifies human euphoria by being a plagal 'Amen' instead of a dominant-tonic cadence. This may be a way of saying 'God willing'; Handel clearly thinks he will be!

Handel also set Dryden's longer St Cecilian Ode, *Alexander's Feast*, treating it as a cross between an Augustan public ceremony and a heroic opera. This was possible because Alexander the Great was a historical personage who became a myth; and always was one in his own estimation since he believed, or affected to believe, that he was sired by no mere mortal but by Jove. One could hardly say of him, as Hardy said in funerary tribute to his Giles Winterborne, 'you was a good man and you did good things'; but the sentence would be on the mark if one substituted 'great' for good. Dryden's poem is about this inflation of human ego, on the whole approvingly, though with ironic undercurrents. The 'argument' of the poem is a feast given in honour of the Conquering Hero by Timotheus, identified with Orpheus by singing praise songs to the accompaniment of his lyre. Handel, in 1736, makes the praise the more imposing by scoring the piece for what was a large orchestra by contemporary standards, and by producing a 'French' overture still grander than that to the other Ode.

Timotheus's invocatory aria, skittishly dancing in 2/2 with dotted rhythms and brilliant parallel thirds, presents the Hero feasting with Thais, his 'blooming bride', at his side; the positives of Love and War (related to Sex and Death) run in harness, as usual. The brisk A major solo is answered by a chorus in twining thirds, hymning the happy pair. If the aria is vainly self-congratulatory, the chorus is vacuously rapturous, as 'the people' hope to share in the hero's renown. Timotheus-Orpheus, in accompanied arioso, tells the story of Alexander's putative divine descent, to which the chorus responds in open-eared wonderment, their tentative repeated notes punctuating the strings' lyre-like arpeggios until, in resonant homophony, they pay homage to 'a *present* Deity'. In a trumpet-style *da capo* aria Alexander hears 'with ravish'd ears', 'Assumes the God, Affects to Nod, and seems to shake the Spheres'. Dryden's sly 'affects' and 'seems' are mirrored in the extravagance of Handel's coloratura; and it cannot be an accident that as climax to this idiot self-satisfaction Timotheus-Orpheus invokes Bacchus, who will bring to the soldier pleasure (but also amnesia) after pain. The touch of F minor for the pain hardly sullies the F major euphoria. It is so formal that it sounds like and – the fray having been left behind – probably is no more than a game.

At this point a conscious irony, far from those Bacchic revels in the 1480 *Orfeo*, becomes latent in Dryden's poem and patent in Handel's setting. Alexander has been so transported by self-esteem, by the community's flattery and finally by vinous excess that he grotesquely replays, re-enacts, his triumphs: 'thrice He routed all his foes; and thrice he slew the slain'. So Timotheus-Orpheus finds it advisable to temper frenzy with caution. A self-deified eighteenth-century man ought not to eschew the Reason to which he owes his supremacy: if he does, he must be reminded of the vanity of human wishes. Chosing 'a mournful muse', Timotheus recounts the tale of the Emperor Darius, whose martial triumphs turned to dust through treachery and betrayal. Such may be our alternative lot, if grandiosity and grandiloquence get the better of us. The Darius music, in flat keys around E flat, is genuinely affecting and noble, and it too is echoed by the chorus, for even in adversity the private life cannot be independent of that of society. In an A minor aria War is almost dismissed as 'toil and trouble', and Alexander is encouraged to be thankful for small(er) mercies; to 'take the Good the Gods provide', namely the 'Lovely Thais' enthroned beside him. The public chorus takes up the cry in the celestial key of E major, a semitone higher than Darius's E flat, claiming that Orpheus-inspired music has occasioned this victory for human feeling, as distinct from vainglory.

Yet is seems that music has not, after all, finally 'won the Cause'; for in Part II Timotheus-Orpheus 'strikes the Golden Lyre' again, rousing Alexander from blissful sleep with his bride, and inspiring him to revenge on his enemies in the famous trumpet aria. Thais herself leads him on his bellicose way to 'light another Helen, fire another Troy'. So Heroic Man does not learn by experience, and his stupidity is inseparable from his (blind) courage. Alexander's destiny is to fulfil his sensuality and sexuality by loving more, drinking more, fighting more and weeping more than any ordinary mortal. Only at the end of Dryden's poem is St Cecilia brought in, somewhat apologetically, to 'share a crown' with Timotheus/Orpheus, because he 'rais'd a Mortal to the Skies, She drew an Angel down'. Handel writes a massive double figure for their collaboration, thus making it more substantial than it is in Dryden. Even so, he too considers Timotheus's achievement the more impressive. To raise a mortal to the skies is the goal of heroic man's endeavour. In this context at least, man's bravery outweighs his stupidity.

It is only to be expected that Handel, along with Mozart the supreme humanist of European music, should be a theatre composer, concerned with the imitation of human action in social contexts. *Alexander's Feast* is public ceremonial on the way to being opera; and the dubiety latent beneath its homage to the man-god is usually the theme of his operas and oratorios (which are heroic operas on biblical subjects, usually without stage action). During the years of his Italian apprenticeship in the first years of the eighteenth century he wrote operas which imposed the order of integrated recitative, arioso, aria and dance on Cavallian confusion, the artistic clarification reflecting social and philosophical needs. It is interesting in this respect to compare his *Agrippina* with Monteverdi's *Poppea*, which deals with a closely-related theme. Whereas Monteverdi's Emperor is adolescent, even infantile, Handel's Emperor Claudius is the authentic man-god of the heroic world, played by a bass of gargantuan range. He is capable of singing a magnificently passionate aria to his Poppea who,

like Monteverdi's, is both tender and feckless. At the same time his
godhead is presented ironically, even satirically, as is Alexander's;
while Nero, his son, is not only adolescent but peevishly petulant. That
he is played by a castrato, contrasted with his father's reverberating
bass, surely suggests that Handel was aware of the element of deceit,
as well as irony, latent in the convention whereby supermen were
played by half-men.

Handel's exceptional intelligence encouraged him to acknowledge,
even in youth, the ironies buried beneath his heroic themes; it is to the
point that in this early opera interest is centred not so much on the
would-be heroic men as on the women. Agrippina is matriarchal
virago, scheming serpent and luxurious lover, the contradictions
making a warp and woof of fallible flesh and blood. His Poppea, like
Monteverdi's, combines the seductiveness of a Marilyn Monroe with
a sharp-edged vivacity, whirling her into stratospheric coloratura with
a cherubic triumph thinly disguising nervous apprehension. We can
hear why everyone falls for her, causing her to be enmeshed in
political chicanery of which she knows little and cares less. But
whereas in Monteverdi the girl and her emperor lover, though not
'good' characters, earn our sympathy, that being the profoundly
modern point of the opera, in Handel's *Agrippina* the only good
character is Ottone, who acts as moral yardstick to adjudicate between
human frailties. Unjustly accused of treachery, he is a tragic victim
who is given the opera's only extended arioso and its most profound
aria. It is relevant to note that Handel composed this male part not for
a castrato but for a woman. A Good Man ought to be larger than life
and free of the contagion of the flesh, yet Handel, unable to bring
himself to achieve this the hard way, compromises on a woman
simulating a man: obviously different (and higher) in range and
timbre, yet more palpably human than a trumpeting castrato.
Ottone's great arioso and aria momentarily transform the palace
garden into a *hortus conclusus* wherein not only a good man as
scapegoat but even the craftiest courtier might glimpse the possibility
of redemption, on the wings of Orphic song. Yet Ottone, unlike
Monteverdi's Nero and Poppea, is peripheral to the central action; for
although Handel saw through the fallacy of the heroic ideal he
couldn't at this stage fully realise its human implications.

He discovered what it meant when he relinquished *opera seria* in its
own right and, having settled in England, transformed it into English
oratorio, finding his stories in the Old Testament, the one book

concerned with failed heroes which the increasingly powerful British
middle classes knew 'inside out'. Among Handel's oratorios *Saul*
(composed in 1738, about three decades later than *Agrippina* and
around the same time as his Cecilian odes), touches on our theme by
way of David, singing poet and lyre-player traditionally equated with
Orpheus. Way back in the Middle Ages Alfonso X, garnering his
cantigas, had compared himself to King David, seeking through his
songs an Eternal Return to the wellsprings of life. Handel, at the apex
of the heroic age, is more interested in Orphically raising than in
quelling passion, though we have seen that he was ironically doubtful
about Alexander the Great's manic egotism. In *Saul* he remembers the
'two-way' nature of the Mercurian theme, for the Hero is also the
Villain. The oratorio asks what happens when the Leader, who is not
in fact God however god-like his powers, is subject to human infirma-
ties. Jealousy may overthrow reason; madness may bring ruin not
only to himself but also to the State for which he is responsible. This is
why the chorus – in the oratories but not operas – becomes a central
protagonist. Handel's humanity is nowhere more evident than in his
realisation that the public life embraces the destinies of private
people.

So *Saul* is an *opera seria* without (or possibly with) stage action, in
which there are two related themes, one personal, one epic. After an
expansive overture which, like Purcell's 'Simphony' to the 1692 Ode,
states the postulates, we enter the fray with an Epicinion or Song of
Triumph, such as is offered to Alexander. What is being celebrated,
with trumpet fanfares and martial rhythms, is the defeat of the
'baddies' (Goliath and the Philistines) by the 'goodies', in a resonantly
public C major. Everybody, especially the adolescent girls, praises
David the pop-star hero who in slaying the foul fiend has released us
from bondage. Only Saul, the King and Wise Man who made the
laws, has doubts, though he offers his elder daughter Merab to David
as a bride, and (maybe) bribe. The compliment is double-edged, for
Merab is a prissy prop of the Establishment whose rigorous *da capo*
aria displays more patrician pride than human heart.

But if Merab is the dead side of Saul – the letter of the law – his other
children tell us what he once was. The younger sister Michal is all
tenderness and light, and loves David with virginal passion; her
brother Jonathan also loves David with a love (as we all know) passing
the love of women. The central characters have now been introduced,
and a lapse of time is indicated by a rustically merry song of welcome,

scored for carillon. Its innocence is barbed, because inane: for when the carolling girls rashly claim that David has slain ten thousand of the enemy to Saul's one thousand, the flames of jealousy, already smouldering in Saul, flare to the surface. In dark arioso – the reality of experience intensified – he tries to murder David by hurling a javelin at him; shooting scales depict the weapon's flight. Even in evil he fails, missing the target; and his aria of rage sunders convention by stopping in midstream, without the conservative assurance of a *da capo*. Impotent himself, he commissions his own son Jonathan to slay David; and Jonathan sings a superb arioso and aria debating the battle between personal feeling (friendship) and filial duty (respect for the Law). He decides – at this date we cannot readily understand how courageous this is – in favour of common humanity.

The second act opens with a chorus enacting the chaos that human fallibility lets loose in the world. In chromatics and remote modulations – opposed to tonal relationships socially accredited and understood – virtue 'sickens in blackest night'. Jonathan appeals to his father to relent. Saul pretends to acquiesce, offering Michal, to her delight, to David as a bonus, since Merab will have no truck with him as he is a commoner. But Saul reveals his dark heart in (Purcellian) arioso which ironically reflects on the dreamy wedding music; the ultimate climax comes when he accuses his son of disloyalty and attempts to murder *him*, as well as David. The Leader who should be the Law is anti-Law; chaos is come again. From this point Saul-Othello turns into Saul-Macbeth. 'From crime to crime he blindly' (and chromatically) 'goes. No end but with his own destruction knows.' In Act III Saul recognises, in his famous 'lost' arioso, that he is author of his own ruin. Since Heaven has deserted him – he is unable to pray – he appeals to Hell, seeking out the Witch of Endor – in F minor, the traditionally infernal key which Purcell had used for his *scena* on the story. The witch offers scant consolation. He is finished: though the reason she gives is not that through rage, envy and madness he has denied his humanity, but that he has disobeyed God's impervious Law in failing to slay the accursed Amalekite. The situation is itself an irony: intensified when David, the new Hero, *doesn't* spare the Amalekite, but acts too late, when he has already finished off the wounded Saul and Jonathan, fighting at bay. The ethics are confused. Perhaps the irony indicates that Handel found them as monstrous as we do.

That such is the case is suggested by the fact that at this point the oratorio achieves its sublimely Orphean consummation in the Elegy which, centred on C major and therefore balancing the initial Epicinion, is a victory for compassion. The Dead March reasserts Saul's human grandeur, reminding us that he had once been a hero; in the context the simply triadic C major sounds more solemnly funereal than the most doleful minor key since it reminds us of hopes unfulfilled. David's aria reviews the positive aspects of Saul's and David's lives and deaths a third higher in the key of E major, usually reserved by Handel, as by most baroque composers, for seraphic moments. The gentle repeated crotchets of the theme are both a caress and an affirmation, and the musical images for 'sweetest harmony' and 'bravely died' are as poignant as they are simple. When the chorus, we the People, joins in the *da capo* in universal consolation, the orchestra appends, in cellos and basses, a regeneratively rising semiquaver scale.

Meanwhile David (again a soprano, emulating a semi-divine castrato) interjects reminiscences, in the tonic *minor*, of his personal love and loss. This is one of the supreme moments in Handel, and is really the end of the personal tragedy of youth versus age and of the public epic of a threatened civilisation. A coda is added, however, returning us to Augustan England and the beginning of imperialist expansion. We have to learn again and again that imperial might cannot be independent of individualised qualities of love, justice and reason. In some form the story, like that of Monteverdi's *Orfeo*, will happen again – perhaps even, as has been hinted in the Amalekite incident, to David. In the threnody in *Saul* Orpheus is no longer a puff to our pride but rather a stirrer of the bowels of compassion: as is still more profoundly evident in the one Handel oratorio that takes its texts not only from the Old Testament (especially Isaiah) but also from the New (especially the Gospels of Luke, Matthew and John and St Paul's epistles to the Corinthians and Romans), and from versions of the Psalms that figure in the Book of Common Prayer.

Messiah is the most popular of Handel's works because it is a repository of common sentiment: the values on which not only Augustan civilisation but also the more democratic society to come hoped to be founded. Though in *Messiah* common man's lot is seen and heard in the light of Christ's story, it is about Man before it is about God. The 'vision' Handel said he saw may have been 'spiritual', but its significance lay in its relation to a moral code: he hoped and believed that his music would make people 'better'. So the French

overture now celebrates *our* potential heroism, rather than that of a
God-King. The double dots and dissonances suggest a toughly human
fortitude which the animation of the fugue turns into celebration. The
texture is sinewy, the tonality E minor; but the bounding leaps of the
lines, the thrust of the rhythms and rising chromatic bass generate an
élan the more powerful because it does not deny the pain of the
introduction. The vigour and unity of fugue, overriding contrarieties,
can thus lead to *comfort,* and even to *exaltation.* For the tenor arioso
the key changes to seraphic E major; the pulsing rhythm, regular as a
heart-beat, the sustained notes, the symmetrical sequences, all promote certitude, the comfort of assured belonging. Though the music
is not religious in Bach's sense, it is certainly an expression of faith,
Orpheus-induced, in human postulates. So arioso burgeons into aria,
wherein 'every valley' may be 'exalted'. The aria adds to regular
rhythm and symmetrical groupings exuberantly operatic virtuosity:
an assertion of pride that is also, in its literalism, an expression of
common humanity. We are asked to look, listen and to experience
how, in this melodic line we have made 'the crooked places straight
and the rough places plain'. There it is, made straight instead of curly;
and that we hear birds chirruping in the orchestra affirms our place in
ubiquitous Nature, rather than in court or marketplace.

Against this exaltation consider the opening to Part II: which faces
the apparently irremediable facts of evil and death. 'Behold the Lamb
of God that taketh away the sins of the world' is set to music not in the
least transcendent, nor even lamb-like. In tragic G minor, and in tight
dotted rhythm sounding fierce rather than heroic, it is concerned
more with our sinfulness than with its divine alleviation. Again, the
piece is about fortitude: ours, though the hammered repeated notes,
even as they threaten us like the Wrath of God, might also be a rock we
could hopefully cling to. If they are a Rock, it is because we have made
them so, by way of our courage. Then, in 'He was despised', Christ
himself appears as scapegoat for you and me. He is an outcast as we all
are, but also a man, who brings balm in the key of E flat major, flat
submediant to G minor – a tonal relationship that in baroque and
classical music usually promotes relaxation. The vocal line of this aria
has the immediacy of arioso: listen to the 'screwed up' diminished
fourths, the fragmented rhythms, the expectant silences, and the
gut-disturbing tension of the Neapolitan chromatics. Yet although in
this arioso-like line we are borne through the guilt and pain man may
suffer subjectively within the mind, the anguish is 'contained' within

the objective formality of a *da capo* aria – which embraces within its
middle section a shift from metaphysical to physical agony, as man's
inhumanity to man becomes incarnate in a ferocious 'smiting'
rhythm. This aria is one of the most tragic utterances in music; Orphic
in simultaneously raising and quelling the depths and heights of
feeling. And it is typical of Handel's humanity that the middle
section's physical rhythm takes over, engulfing the succeeding chorus
which, in the 'evil' key of F minor, equates Christ's suffering with
ours. Surely he hath borne our griefs; and he does so, physically, in
the fast fugal chorus 'And with his stripes', with its diminished-
seventh-punctuated theme and its remorseless duple rhythm. Physical suffering wilfully makes whole that which was broken.

Yet the psychological depth of Handel's conception is revealed only
in the transition from this fugue to the more homophonic 'All we like
sheep', in a fatuous F major tune, with idiotic semiquaver scurryings
as we wander blithely 'astray', not even realising that our merry
gambols are as inane as the repeated notes in which we individually
insist on following each his own way. That our folly is inseparable
from our suffering is revealed in the sublime adagio postlude, when
the music returns to a chromaticised F minor no longer evil but
purgatorial, as the Lord lays on Christ 'the iniquity of *our* sins'. Only
from Handel's genius could we accept such devastating honesty about
our fallen selves. Evil and death are not, after all, irremediable.

This is why the rebirth celebrated in the exquisite Nativity music –
in which Handel seems to have preferred a boy treble to his habitual
adultly operatic female soprano – can prelude the faculty to rejoice,
even in our fallen world. The most famous example of such jubilation
is the Hallelujah chorus, in which Handel's heavenly vision is
identified with that of Augustan England redeemed and fulfilled. The
Kingdom of this world is indeed, as the text tells us, become the
Kingdom of the Lord, as the glory of the English Baroque resonates in
D trumpets, military timpani, homophonic antiphony, and in
marshalled sequences that habitually thrust sharpwards. No wonder
George III rose to his feet in awed response to this assertion of our
pride in being human, paying homage to Handel as composing mortal, to himself as King, and vicariously to God as creator of monarch
and composer. In reference to an empire-building potentate it cannot
of course be literally true that 'he shall reign for ever and ever'. None
the less, it is with some such wishful thinking that we rise to it; and
Handel can persuade us to do so because – as 'He was despised' and

the still more heart-rending arioso 'Thy rebuke hath broken his heart' abuntantly prove – he knew most that was knowable about human suffering, as well as pride. Alone among Handel's oratorios *Messiah* is not an opera since it is centred on the chorus of the People, its soloists are not 'characters' and it tells no story, though that of Christ is enclosed within it. Yet in a sense it is the greatest of all heroic operas, since it envisages the apotheosis of the theme: its Hero and Heroine are you and I. Humanity may attain its own divinity, without presumptuously elevating itself to godhead; and in saying 'So be it' to that Handel concludes with an Amen chorus that in contrapuntal scope, splendour and intensity challenges Bach himself.

When Bach touches on the Orpheus theme it is, as we might expect from a man whose religious faith was simultaneously physical and metaphysical, with a profound apprehension of its Mercurian implications. There is a sublime passage in the *St John Passion* which begins with the crowd's murderously homophonic yelling for the blood of Christ – they are here unredeemed, more bestial than human – and then briefly but shatteringly depicts the scourging of Christ in an arioso that rhythmically mimics the gestures of lashing, and in sharp dissonance makes manifest Christ's (and vicariously our) pain. With scarcely a pause the music sinks from tragic G minor to its flat submediant, E flat major, with – as in the Handel example referred to above – magically assuaging effect. A solo bass sings an arioso, harmonically 'earthed' on long pedal notes and slowly drooping chromatics, yet generating from spread chords, arching upwards through minor sevenths, a wondrous release. Despite incidental dissonances the lines, floated across the beat of Time, dispense balm as the words tell us of the redemptive significance of Christ's pain. It cannot be fortuitous that for this movement only Bach introduces an obbligato lute, reverting to the medieval identification of Christ as man-god with lute or lyre playing Orpheus, who attempted to conquer sin and death through the power of music. Bach's Passions have the inestimable advantage of being heroic operas about a man who not only pretended to be, but in fact was, God. Christ, being Very God as well as Man, succeeded where Orpheus failed. His triumph is auralised in the aria which the arioso introduces.

The key of the aria, C minor, is lower mediant to and relative of the arioso's balm-dispensing E flat major. The intertwining of the solo tenor with two obbligato instruments and a melodic-harmonic bass creates both rhythmic animation and harmonic stress: while the theme with which the melody instruments – archaic viole d'amore or love-viols – prelude the tenor's entry is *identical* with the scourging motif of the recitative! Yet Bach's music makes a psychological and theological point in that these manifestations of pain are transcended in the continuity of the lines, which float in immense paragraphs of 12/8, a time-signature usually associated by Bach with celestial matters. The scourging motif, sung by the dulcet love-viols, spirally flowers in dialogue with the Orphic tenor, musically mirroring the rainbow which, the text tells us, promises peace after storm. So the sequence of recitative, arioso and aria enacts a miracle: an Orphic rebirth whereby a crown of thorns has been alchemised into a rainbow halo. Though melodic contours, harmonic tensions and rhythmic interlacings have all evolved from the corporeal movements of the scourging, they become, in these winging lines, *dis*embodied. Time ceases as we prophetically envisage Christ in heaven. The great length of the piece, chronologically considered, is part of the point: though a strict *da capo* aria, it is a million light years from the baroque opera-house.

The same may be said of the 'Cross' aria sung, in the *St Matthew Passion*, when another apparition of Orpheus appears as prelude to the Crucifixion. The soloist is a bass, Orpheus as both man and God; his vocal line combines the healing properties of the Cross (it flows in spacious clauses) with its lacerating pain (the cantilena is pierced with dissonant appoggiaturas). The obbligato instrument is a viola da gamba: again an archaic instrument, more 'spiritual' than the voluptuous violin, yet more scrawnily attenuated than the ethereal love-viols of the St John 'rainbow' aria. Again, the gamba line fuses agony with balm since it mingles the sharp dotted rhythm in which Bach delineates lashing with cascades of demisemiquavers that lyrically anneal as they twine around the voice. The accompaniment incorporates lute-like plucked strings. If this hints at Orphic associations, they become irresistible when we learn that Bach wrote an alternative part for lute or lute-harpsichord, should one be available. Like the rainbow aria, the effect of this strict *da capo* piece is disembodied: the tone pallid, the inner dissonance harsh, though the flow of the cantilena, for both voice and instrument, is lyrically compulsive. The strained line and texture seem to enact a Cross-hung death, from and by which the soul is liberated. The key is D minor – minor complement to D major, baroque key of worldly power. In the seventeenth century Charpentier had described D minor as 'grave et dévot'; in the later eighteenth century it became dramatic, a negative pole to positive passion, as in the 'demonic' elements of Mozart's *Don Giovanni* and D minor piano concerto. Both aspects are relevant to this aria.

In these examples Bach's remaking of the Orpheus story, though sublime, is also peripheral: a consummation of the medieval attitude, if medieval man could have overcome his fear of the physical. In Bach's day the central theme of opera and oratorio was, as we noted in the supreme case of Handel, the hope that Man-Orpheus might deputise *for* God. Since this hope could not be validated, even the earthiest humanists tended to revert to Monteverdi's cheat of transubstantiation, introducing a *deus ex machina* to set right, in some unrealised and probably unrealisable future, the mess made by blundering mortals. A further development of this theme could occur only when aristocratic autocracy was in abeyance and a new world, which we now call democratic, was emerging. The centre of this evolution was France, where Revolution was overtly to undermine the old world. Before we take up this theme, however, we must consider the winds of change in a wider context.

Chapter IV

Orpheus democratised

Scarlatti and the new birth; Vivaldi's Orphic *Four Seasons*;
From Clérambault's *Orphée* (1710) to Rameau's *Pygmalion*
(1748); Sense and sensibility: the new Adam and Eve in
Gluck's *Orfeo* (1762) or *Orphée* (1774)

Two composers – one born in the same *annus mirabilis* of 1685 as were
Bach and Handel, the other born five years earlier – foreshadow the
shape of things to come. Both were Italian by birth, though one lived
most of his life away from that focal centre of post-Renaissance
humanism: the younger man, Domenico Scarlatti, can hardly count
as an Orphic composer except in the general sense that no musician of
his time was more preoccupied with 'making it new'. To enquire into
how he made it new is helpful, perhaps necessary, if we are to
understand the mask which the next Orpheus will wear.

Domenico's father, Alessandro Scarlatti, was perhaps the greatest
and certainly the most honoured of the Italian masters of *opera seria*,
and the son was trained, during his Neapolitan apprenticeship, in that
man-glorifying tradition. His youthful vocal music, both theatrical
and ecclesiastical, offers evidence of distinguished talent and, in the
Stabat Mater, of something more than that. Even so, he came fully
into his own only when, escaping his illustrious father's shadow, he
left Naples to become music master to the young Princess of Portugal,
daughter of the splendour-loving João V, whose passion for music
was insatiable. When Scarlatti returned to Naples after ten years, his
creative energy had been liberated. Henceforth he devoted his talents
almost exclusively to his own instrument, the harpsichord: a one-man
band eminently suited to a composer who, having 'struck the father
dead', wanted to do his own thing, to use a modern tag appropriate to
an eighteenth-century modernist. Scarlatti had this opportunity
when, in 1729, Barbara Maria married the heir to the Spanish throne
and invited the composing harpsichordist to accompany her to Mad-
rid as household musician. He stayed in Spain for twenty-five years,
becoming more Spanish than most contemporary Spaniards, with the

possible exception of his younger colleague Antonio Soler. At the Spanish court his duties were not those of a state composer but of a private tutor. So when he began to compose yet more copiously it was for his own satisfaction as much as for that of his royal mistress and of the glamorous court in which he lived, alongside Farinelli – the most astonishing vocal virtuoso in European history. Scarlatti was a hardly less phenomenal virtuoso, whose instrument lay beneath his agile fingers. Unlike Farinelli, however, he used his virtuosity in the interests of original creation of extraordinary audacity. Free to experiment, he was the New Man who discovered the future within present and past.

All Scarlatti's six hundred-odd sonatas appear to be in orthodox binary form and are not sonatas in the Viennese sense. No composer demonstrates more potently, however, how dubiously formal absolutes are relevant to created music; there is no systematic formula even in his most classical-baroque sonatas, while most of them, at least after his early Neapolitan period, move towards the 'Viennese' conception. Binary form becomes 'open'; the second 'halves', introducing increasingly varied material and abstruse modulations, grow longer than the first halves. Growth through permutation and contradiction becomes self-discovery: a search for identity which Beethoven, a far more desperate loner, was to consummate. Even in the Neapolitan sonatas composed after Scarlatti's first Lisbon visit one can hear the winds of change and chance. A piece like the D major sonata K119 is densely-populated, big city music, reflecting the mercantile energy as well as the artistic traditions of the community; the sounds, sights and even smells of city streets are auralised in breath-taking keyboard acrobatics. There is a gamin-like abandon in the chunkily percussive chords and whirling scales and arpeggios; while the companion sonata K120 – throughout his life Scarlatti grouped his sonatas in pairs – evokes a street mountebank juggling in cross-handed capers.

Such perilous cross-hand music excites, but at a fairly superficial level. The genuine revolutionary and adventurer emerges in Scarlatti's second phase, after he had settled at the Spanish court. Sonata K261 has no hint of aristocratic panache but a tootling, footling street tune, teetering into crazy repeated notes. After the double bar the atmosphere changes dramatically, even melodramatically. Sonority darkens, the repeated notes are suddenly minatory. Modulations, or rather shifts to remote keys, are 'barbarous and licentious', as the genteel Dr Burney put it; the bass growls percussively, instead of

providing a stable harmonic fundament. The return to the original
motives is uneasy, as one might expect, since democratic man's
experience is of its nature open-ended. Yet although such startlement
may be Scarlatti's prime characteristic, his range is democratically
wide. Alongside the many obstreperous sonatas we light on a piece
like the E major sonata K206. The tempo is slow, the sonority
plangent, twanging and whining like a street beggar's guitar, with
abrupt contrasts of texture, now thin and bell-like, then suddenly
massive and dissonantly reverberant. The music stops and starts, like
life itself. The common man, even a gypsy beggar, finds his voice,
which may be tender, pathetic, desperate, as well as aggressive. Not
for nothing does the end sound unexpectedly grand: heroes are no
longer restricted to the upper classes. Such intrusions of low into high
life proliferate in the late sonatas – K450 in G minor, for instance, is a
turbulent flamenco dance, while in K380 in E major martial rhythms
and contrasted colours evoke a street procession, stalking through
wide-ranging modulations.

In so far as such music states and at the same time undermines
precedents it is progressive, unexpected, unpredictable. This is
reflected in the empiricism of Scarlatti's technique which, despite his
classical training, allows him to revel in abrupt changes of gear to
remote keys, guitar-like percussive dissonances ignorant of orthodox
musical grammar, inner parts that arbitrarily come and go as whim or
the lie of the fingers dictate. The sonata in C K513 is a particularly
interesting case in that, though far from being the most audacious of
Scarlatti's sonatas, it might be said to 'about' the end of the old world.
Its first section is naively and archaically pastoral in 6/8, with a
folk-like tune repeated, however, in a foreign key. This may be a
retrospect of Scarlatti's Neapolitan childhood: which abruptly shifts
from Nativity-like innocence to a riotously bucolic dance, with
thumping beat, blaring bagpipes and wheezing hurdygurdy, reflecting the street and village music the composer heard around him. The
two apparently distinct sections are repeated; never coalesce; but are
uproariously routed by a whirlwind presto coda, taking the breath
away like a helter-skelter. What's to come is still (very) unsure.

After Renaissance man's Orphic deification in Monteverdi's opera
there was, we observed, a disillusioned disintegration of technique
both musical and theatrical in composers such as Gesualdo and
Cavalli. After Baroque man's deificiation in the odes and operas of
Handel there is a comparable disintegration in Scarlatti: with the

significant difference that Scarlatti's technical licence, unlike that of
Gesualdo, is on behalf of life, not against it. He breaks the 'rules'
because he finds them to be no longer relevant. In so doing he
produces music that is life-affirming, yet also *dangerous* in that, being
tinged with irony, it recognises 'other modes of experience that may
be possible'. Like Monteverdi before him, Scarlatti reminds us that
the word 'experience', deriving from the Latin *ex periculo,* means
'from and out of peril'. Only Beethoven will bring this home to us
more alarmingly.

Scarlatti 'makes it new' more radically than his contemporary
Vivaldi, though the latter has the more immediate relationship to the
changing world, and embraces faint premonitions of a new Orpheus.
Whereas Scarlatti was a private composer whose adventurous disposition profited from his privacy, Vivaldi was a public composer who
produced music in any convention asked for, his inspiration being,
given the level of his productivity, fitful. A red-haired and improbable
priest, Vivaldi counted among his many civic and ecclesiastical offices
the directorship of music at a Venetian *ospidale* for young ladies, many
of them bastard offspring of the nobility and of classy state-sponsored
courtezans. That his music was written for these young women conditions its nature. Himself a formidable virtuoso on the violin, he uses
the classical concerto form of Corelli in a manner less purely Roman,
more demotically varied and ebullient. Into the interlaced traditions
of eighteenth-century Venice Vivaldi brings a breath of airy
innocence, renewing the tangled past. So much ancient pomp and
circumstance, such sumptuousness of light and art, exist now in a
polyglot, mercantile, even middle-classical present. The paradox is
piquant, and with Vivaldi Mercurian two-way traffic between spirit
and flesh assumes a practical, naturalistic guise: some of the girls at
the *ospidale* became nuns; more were marriageable ladies of fashion.

Vivaldi probably regarded his many works in concerto form as
ephemeral means of whiling away empty time, for both performers
and listeners; though they are less aware of the life-giving but alarming realities of the new world than are Scarlatti's sonatas, they belong
to that world in being thus unbashedly entertaining. He turns out
concerti for any instrument going, not eschewing those often considered impolite, such as mandolin; and treats the traditional antiphony between *soli* and *tutti* with bucolic bounce as well as with
gracious sophistication. Through his exotic or vulgar instruments he
discovers a new age. If the discovery is superficial compared with that

of Scarlatti, it is none the less real. And when Vivaldi occasionally reveals more than the *façade* it is in a significantly 'modern' way. A concerto for flute, bassoon and strings, for instance, which Vivaldi entitled 'La Notte', is one of a series in which the composer explores night as the nursery of dreams and nightmares. To cultivate the unconscious, at any level, is a step away from the conscious daylight of autocratic Establishment, wherein every man knows his place. Odd things may happen when we are asleep. The 'Fantasmi' movement is comic in the contrasted colours of its solo instruments, yet also a shade disturbing. The 'Sonno' is a slow sleep-song more folk-like than operatic; the second nightmare introduces playful little demons. Both the range of mood, from reverie to farce, and the tone colours are becoming populist rather than élitist; and the superficiality of the music is an aspect of this. A whole community of adrenalin-stimulating Scarlattis would be a bit much for average men and women to live with – Scarlatti, after all, composed even his music of low life for himself and a circle of intitiates. Vivaldi, on the other hand, offers a vast output pertinent to the experience of *hoi polloi*. This is the secret both of his popularity in his own day and of his historical importance.

Surprisingly, Vivaldi composed a number of concertos and sonatas for the lute, an instrument near-obsolete in his day. We have noted how Bach substituted baroque lute for Orpheus's lyre in those two sublime passages from the St John and the St Matthew Passions. He also wrote, or arranged, a number of works for solo lute, mostly transcribed from his solo violin and cello music, and even though he did so unskilfully, being a non-player of the instrument, he created music that is the crown of the lute tradition. We can hardly doubt that he attained these heights as lute composer because of his Orphic disposition, his equilibrium between the physical and the metaphysical. Though in this respect Vivaldi is far from Bach, it is fascinating that in his lute concertos Orpheus should make a somewhat apologetic, more democratic and demotic, appearance. In the Allegros, of course, the lute usually has a lowly role, indulging in repeated-note figures and other capers designed to please the (at this date eccentric) virtuosi for whom the works were written. The aristocratic lute sounds more like popular guitar, or even mandolin. In Vivaldi's slow movements, however, the lute comes into its Orphic own. In the Largo from the D major concerto (RV 93) the lute itself sings in the Elysian Fields, its melody slowly unwinding over sustained strings.

The music breathes the reborn innocence of Rousseau's 'child-savage', elegant in natural grace but not in conscious artifice. In the D minor concerto RV 540 the lute is partnered by a viola d'amore which, in the Largo, becomes the voice of Orpheus, accompanied by the lute in gentle arpeggios. Love-viol and lute are a pre-destined Orphic duo. In a Trio in C(RV 82) violin substitutes less etherially for viol d'amore and, in the Larghetto, chants another Elysian song, accompanied by the lute's sighs and Lombard syncopations.

The Orpheus featured in these pieces is not, like Bach's lutenist, a throwback to the past but a harbinger of the sensibility of 'enlightened' common man, whose story is soon to be dramatised by Gluck. Nor is it fanciful to detect Orpheus's shy presence in the slow movement of the C major concerto for mandolin of 1736, for Vivaldi turns to advantage the mandolin's un-Orphic inability to sustain a continuous line. Using repeated notes against a background of sombre string chords, he makes the mandolin sing with a stutter, as though timidly appealing to the powers of darkness. The briefly beautiful movement is swept aside by a bucolic finale in which the mandolin returns to a more familiarly vulgar role.

There are remote Orphic associations with Vivaldi's best known, and probably best, work, the set of four concertos named after the seasons. We noted that seasonal process entered the Orpheus myth by way of the Demeter and Persephone story: each spring is a rebirth which gives anthropomorphic dimension to the human legend. Vivaldi's 'The Four Seasons' has some such regenerative force, if we think of its realism and empiricism in relation to Corelli's classical elegance. It effects a metamorphosis of that tradition hardly less radical than that between Palestrina's High Renaissance formalism and the naturalism and chaos of the early Baroque, though its revolution, like Scarlatti's, is re-creative rather than destructive. Published in 1725, 'The Four Seasons' is not formal music for court or church but common life presented in the Theatre of Nature, with all its unpredictable alarms. He described the set of concertos as a *cimento* of Harmony and Invention. The former stands for the old virtues, with roots in the Renaissance notion of Proportion as a human revelation of divine order, while the latter represents the new life, 'invented' empirically from moment to moment by incipiently democratic men and women. Invention, in this changing world, is liable to disturb, even to destroy, Harmony, though it does so with creative zest rather than with the lunatic obsession of a Gesualdo.

The first concerto, Spring, is heralded in theatrical style with fanfares, introducing a pretend-country dance: a bourrée in rondo form, which allows the jolly tune to be interrupted by naturalistically imitated scenes and events. The key is E major, Edenic rather than paradisal, sounding blissfully hopeful yet, in mean-tone tuning, very *sharp*. The tune is low, not civilised; the human cavortings of peasants are haloed by twittering birds, babbling brooks and billowing breezes, all verbally described in the series of sonnets printed with the score. The imitative passages are carefully specified, with directions as to the new bowing technique needed for their realisation. A modest storm, with shooting scales and tremolos, forms another episode in the Rondo, without being seriously disruptive at this pristine season. None the less the birds' twittering, resumed after the storm, is less blithe and more chromatic than it was initially. Even in spring there may be intimations of mortality; one is not sure whether the pedal bourdon, emulating bagpipes, is a comfort or a threat.

The slow movement again carries us beyond the daylight of eighteenth-century society into sleep and dream. A young shepherd's slumber is lulled in a rustle of leaves, while a viola soloist, loud and harsh, simulates his barking dog. Dogs may be Fidos, appropriate to faithful shepherds and their silly sheep; but their bark may be faintly minatory, the more so since this one barks in regular periodicity, measuring time like a clock, opposed to the timelessness of unconscious sleep. Again, other modes of experience may be possible, in a mutable world. Even in the Finale, a 12/8 siciliano to which happy young folk dance in an Arcadian landscape, there is an intrusion of raucous bagpipe or hurdy-gurdy, and a solo violin scrawnily imitates a peasant's kit-fiddle. The final solo is darkened by a minor-keyed episode, with ponderous pedal note and fluttery chromatics: evidence that Spring is transitory.

It is followed, in the second concerto, by Summer: which in Venice is not all a bed of roses. At the outset of the concerto disarray is palpable. The G minor tonality is flat instead of sharp – it is a wonderfully appropriate coincidence that the key-relationship of the two concertos, E major to G minor, echoes those crucial triads in the oration of Monteverdi's Messenger, recounting Euridice's death. The opening melody is disjunct in motion, with awkward octave displacements; rhythms are fragmentary; 'horrendous' diminished sevenths and Neapolitan chromatics abound. The human dialogue in this sultry heat is again interrupted by avian chirpings, more distraught than those in the Spring concerto. Cuckoos are fierce, as befits a cheating bird; the cooing of turtle doves sounds slightly sinister. Vivaldi's naturalism, like that of Scarlatti, is technically empirical; clashing major and minor seconds are not so much false relations in the traditional melodic-harmonic sense as accident(al)s that flesh is heir to. Similarly, the sectional technique is like life itself – with more reference to civilised norms than Cavalli's, yet still, like his, 'one damn thing after another'. An exhausted peasant wails in sickly chromatic sequences. When a summer storm breaks it is an Act of God that has to be reckoned with; and if the slow movement lulls us into oppressive sleep, it also torments us with gnats, mosquitos and flies, specified in the score, emulated by rasps on the G string and by ribald open fifths void of euphonious thirds. The storm of the Finale is still more violent, seething in *tonnerre* anticipatory of Rameau's theatrical tempests and of the symphonic 'steam-rollers' of the Mannheimers, who shared Rameau's patron, Le Riche de la Pouplinière. The cliché of the sequence – an eighteenth-century aural synonym for *habit* – is here used disruptively, with 'pregnant' silences during which we wonder what in heaven or on earth may be coming next. The exhibionistic virtuosity of the music is part of these shock tactics.

In Scarlatti it is Modern Man who lets loose contradiction and chaos, and relishes the excitation. In Vivaldi we have a perturbation of Nature herself since it is she, always unpredictable, who parallels human inconsequence, instead of conspiring, with Reason and Truth, to offer guidelines for human conduct. In this music, though we may *feel*, as do the birds and beasts, we are not conspicuously reasonable: nor are we when the weather has mellowed into Autumn, for this concerto, in pastoral F major, key of horns and oboes, opens with mindless low life in a merry dance that incorporates a genuine folktune. At the time of harvest, moreover, we must expect disturbances to Harmony and Proportion. Everyone is rather, some are very, drunk; the music imitates swaggering and staggering, pitfalls and pratfalls. After these naturalistic interludes the peasant dance returns, but faster, lop-sided, hiccuping, inebriated. The slow movement, in lugubrious F minor, is another *sonno*, depicting sleep after excess. Strings are muted, as in a Lullian *scène de sommeil*, but low, naturalistic elements emerge since some of the sleepers have nasty dreams. In a passage of modest empirical genius the sleepers gradually awaken, emerging from unconsciousness to consciousness in sustained string chords with which overlapping arpeggios on solo harpsichord don't

exactly fit. This impressionism is Vivaldi's most 'modern' characteristic; compared with Corelli's classical ideal, he is concerned with the
unpremeditated – with a world, not just man, in travail. In the Finale
we are again wide awake in the open air. Bounding hounds and fleeing
game make a rowdy hubbub, which we come through to domestic
comfort. Perhaps Vivaldi can embrace so much multiplicity and
disorder because of the guileless simplicity of his heart. There are
moments when one wonders if it is really possible to listen to Vivaldi
after the age of four! Immediately one admits that one can, his
childishness being a Rousseauistic rebirth from which man had to
grow anew.

The notion that Vivaldi is a little boy Orpheus is, as might be
expected, modified by the Winter concerto. It begins of course in dire
F minor, with a famous-notorious example of Vivaldian empiricism:
sharp-bowed vibrato and cuttingly unprepared secundal dissonances
that combine with piled-up fifths to freeze our sinews. Gusts of wind
accumulate into a ferocious storm until the 'freezing' music returns,
intensified with tremolando mimicking chattering teeth! The
movement blows up in a still nastier tempest.

The slow movement is peculiarly touching, for it expresses the
man-made solaces with which we try to protect ourselves from the
natural, and perhaps from the supernatural, elements. Mostly 'The
Four Seasons' is Orphic only in the anthropomorphic sense; but
Orpheus himself perhaps appears, domesticated, when we peep
through a lighted window and see-hear someone singing by the fire-
side, the cosy tune imitated by solo violin while plucked strings
provide a lute-like accompaniment in emulation of the rain splashing
on roof and pane. Occasional threat from a cloudburst on cello cannot
stifle the human music within, paying tribute to our precarious durability. In the last movement we are again in the open air, at first
nervously treading, then excitedly sliding, on ice, imitated by another
empirical technique (bowing ties) and by extravagant vibrato – always
a special effect in baroque music. Physical excitement and fear are
cunningly interwoven, as they are in life. After this the sirocco leaves
its winter quarters and the cycle starts again. We can appreciate why
'The Four Seasons' is so seminal a work. Composed at a time when
people were obsessively concerned with the formalities of social inter-
course, it celebrates 'unaccommodated' man in relation to Nature
and, in its very naïveties, points to his hopefully democratic future.
This may explain our partiality for it today. Few baroque works have

been so frequently recorded.

The demotic shocks, even jokes, in Vivaldi's music are aural complements to the revolutionary stirrings that were undermining society as the (Vivaldian) Plain Man realised that he was of consequence. Italian revolutionary activities were diverse and unfocused: that the Revolution which was to transform Europe should have happened in France may have been due to the fact that autocracy had been most deeply entrenched there; when the lid blew off, the effect was cataclysmic. During the days of *La Gloire* Louis XIV had thought of himself as a Sun so near-equated with God that Mercurian ambiguities would have been unthinkable. There is no grand dramatisation of the Orpheus story in the heyday of the French classical age, unless one counts as such the version by the Italian Luigi Rossi, which had an immense *succès d'éstime* at Versailles in 1647. The piece can hardly count, however, as an opera, at least in comparison with Monteverdi's *Orfeo*, for the mythic elements are watered down by ballets, stage spectacles and comic episodes comparable with those in the contemporary operas of Cavalli. Significantly, arias as set pieces outnumber ariosi; and although these arias are of great refinement and of a languorous beauty, they cannot compensate for the lack of a cogent libretto. This Orpheus is no longer a present experience, but a memory of things past.

Sixty years later, however, when Louis was in decline, a small, indigenous, convinced and convincing version of the tale appears in the form of a solo cantata by the highly talented Louis-Nicolas Clérambault, whose dates (1676–1749) are much the same as Vivaldi's, though he shares none of the Italian's demotic spirit. Clérambault's *Orphée* (1710) does, for all its *ancien régime* elegance, make a significant modification to the myth, the consequences of which, though far-reaching, can hardly have been foreseen by the composer.

The cantata is scored for a solo voice – again a soprano playing a man angelically larger than life – and continuo, with flute and violin as obbligato instruments. The violin, most intimately expressive of baroque instruments, represents Orphée's humanity; the flute, orginally a Dionysiac instrument but by the eighteenth century identified with Apollonian reason, stands for his 'divine', or at any rate intellectual, pretention. At first Orphée sings in recitative accompanied by continuo only, so that we are aware of him – as we were of Monteverdi's Orfeo as he reeled under the impact of the Messenger's grievous message – as a suffering human creature. When he sings, in a

dotted-rhythmed *aire tendre et piqué*, of his serpent-destroyed Euridice, he laments to the woods not in Italianate flamboyance, but in frailly
ornamented, wistful arioso, though in the middle section a more
harmonic passion mirrors his anger at the monstrousness of fate. The
echoing flute reminds him and us that, with the help of his Reason, he
might get the better of both anger and fate, though the recitative in
which he appeals to Pluto in the abode of the dead is more impassioned than reasonable, perhaps hinting at transcendence in the
restrained violence of its melodic declamation, dissonant harmony,
and wild and 'licentious' modulations, ranging as far as G sharp
minor.

But Clérambault's Orphée remains a more polished product of
civilisation than Monteverdi's Orfeo and, in the succeeding *air gai*
with obbligato on physically-lilting violin, he boasts of how it is his
human courage, even his social decorum, that makes possible his
confrontation with death. The end, however, is ambivalent. The *air
fort tendre et fort lent* which he sings in the infernal regions invokes his
heavenly aspirations as the son of Apollo, god of Light, the voice and
flute floating in luminous thirds, with lute-like pluckings on harpsichord. This is a sublimated, exquisitely ornamented *air de cour*,
harking back, perhaps, to the refinements of the earlier age of Louis
XIII. He shakes himself into the present, however, to end his appeal
with a *minuet fort lentement*, elegant but genuinely strong (*fort*). Such
remnants of Orphic magic as survive in this music are no threat to
civilisation. On the contrary, the courtly minuet suggests that social
refinement is itself a kind of magic which helps us to survive life's
barbarities: as, indeed, it does. It is worth recalling the 'difficulty' of
the minuet as a dance, with its duple-rhythmed steps that have to be
accommodated to the triple rhythmed music. Civilised man has much
to be proud of: enough to make Pluto hand over Euridice to her
husband. He warns Orphée against confusing the light of her eyes
with that of God – 'mistaking Earth for Heav'n', in the words of
Dryden's poem. Yet that is precisely what Orphée does, for at this
point Clérambault curtails the story. There is no fallible back-look-
ing, no 'fault', no sin for a Heroic Man so superbly adjusted in mind
and senses. Orphée rounds off the cantata with another *air gai*, in the
rhythms of a Corellian gigue, more Italianate in contour and
decoration, briskly appraising love's victory. Violin and flute, body
and mind, are now in tandem.

Clérambault simply stops before he would have had to admit that man, being human, must inevitably fail at trying to be God. He pays homage to the courage man has developed with the help of his laboriously-acquired civilisation, and leaves it at that. A further development could occur only when aristocratic autocracy had made way for democratic principle. This has been commented on in the earlier account of Vivaldi; its further evolution we may trace in the career of Jean-Philippe Rameau who, although born as early as 1683, did not become a fully-professional composer until he was fifty, and was still creative during his seventies. Spiritually, he belongs to the age of Enlightenment and the Encyclopaedists; technically, he complements the progressive elements referred to in Vivaldi, though Rameau's equipment is far more sophisticated.

Interestingly, Rameau's early reputation was as a music theorist who prepared the ground for the new world. Although, at the end of an era, he codified classical baroque theories of the Affections and of key symbolism, he was no less interested in 'functional' tonality, without which the sonata principle could not have come to fruition. To his harmonic system he gave pseudo-scientific backing, based on unqualified acceptance of equal temperament; and allied his theory with the tenets of Enlightenment, professing to find in harmonic rules a guide to human conduct. The empiricism of Scarlatti and Vivaldi is abandoned, but the 'rules' are refashioned to accord with the needs of the 'modern' world. The newness lies in the fact that the laws are laid down not by God or State, but by process of our own rational minds.

Like Lully, Rameau became an opera composer because he believed that music had public functions that mattered. That he did not, in the cycle of operas that brought fame in his early fifties, adhere to the traditional theme or to Lullian convention, and that none of his opera libretti convinces, follows from his transitional position. His sense of discovery was dependent on his lack of a stable convention, as Purcell's had been fifty years earlier. This is manifest even in *Hippolyte et Aricie*, his first opera and the one closest to the heroic model. It also has his best libretto: a permutation of Racine's version of the story of Phèdre who, like Lully's Armide and Purcell's Dido, is a tragic *heroine* who embraces both positive and negative emotions. There are many elements in Rameau's score which draw on Lullian tradition, though Rameau toughens Lully's grandeur with more populist vigour, as we can hear in the overture. The concluding chaconne is still a ceremonial exit-dance but, through the sequence of its variations on the ground, encompasses contrasts of mood and manner as well as texture. Such democratic 'plurality' extends to the scoring, which mingles aristocratic finesse with low virility: whereas Lully's peasants and comedians had been introduced in a sophisticated game, Rameau's chaconne accepts them for real, as its grandiose swing becomes a jaunty swagger. The opposite process occurs in the nightingale song in the last act. Though bliss is reinstated in a reversion to the old *air de cour*, this happens in a dream rather than in an Arcadian court, and the dream is embedded in a Rousseaistic vision of Nature. Technical virtuosity merges into naturalistic empiricism, as it does in the Nature-noises of Vivaldi's 'Four Seasons.'

Other techniques Rameau exploits are unambiguously 'progress-ive'. His recitative, rooted in Lully and in French heroic tragedy, acquires denser musical substance, both in lyricism and in harmonic implication. Arioso becomes more prevalent; indeed it is the normal condition of music drama in Rameau, as it is Purcell, since both are concerned with life as it happens, especially in moments of crisis. Moreover it is difficult to draw a line between Rameau's arioso and aria, for even Phaedra's magnificent address to the gods, though a full-scale Italian *aria da capo*, is dramatically immediate, not reflection after the event, as was typical in *opera sera*. Rameau writes of and in a world in process and progress.

Allied to this is the fact that Rameau, unlike the classical composers of *tragédie lyrique* and of *opera seria*, makes frequent use of the ensemble number. Societies are changed by people in consort and conflict; duos and trios occur as people hopefully, or sometimes hopelessly, co-exist. Occasionally conflicts are precipitated by super-natural events, which are now objectifications of the psychological pressures that cause people to act as they do. The most famous examples are the two trios 'des Parques' from *Hippolyte*. This is a specifically Orphic episode in which proud man confronts the fates and challenges death, descending to the netherworld. But Rameau's presentation of the supernatural is Enlightened, in that the three Fates sing in a style that, far from recalling Monteverdi or even Lully, anticipates the severe homophony of Gluck and of Mozart's Masonic musics, and even one of the choral manners of Beethoven.

The second trio, however, introduces another dimension, though it is one latent in Mozart's Masonry in so far as that was mystical as well humane. Masonry was Free in being beyond the bounds of the Church and in some ways hostile to the State. Rameau's extraordinary trio lets the revolutionary cat out of the bag, being homophonic but

also wildly enharmonic. It is thus a denial of those codified tonal
relationships which Rameau, on behalf of his age, had worked so hard
to define. The trio was excised from later productions because the
chorus couldn't sing it; none the less, Rameau had written it, defying
law and authority to create chaos as he set the indeed fateful words:
'*Hell is within yourself*'. He hardly grasped the relationship of this hell
to the self-confident view of man he advocated, though his genius did
not refuse conflict between the rational and the irrational. Gluck takes
up the theme from him, effecting a link with Mozart. Beethoven,
Mozart's successor, is to seize Fate, and hell with it, by the scruff of
the neck, convinced that 'it shall never wholly subdue me'.

Although *Hippolyte et Aricie* is probably Rameau's greatest work in
that its fine music complements a tolerable libretto on the classical
theme, it is not surprising that, preoccupied with the birth of the new,
he gravitated towards hybrid forms between opera, ballet, *divertissement* and musical comedy. His most representative piece may well be
Les Indes Galantes, first produced in 1735, for this is overtly about the
interaction of worlds old and new, and of the savage with the civilised
state. In exotic Peru, Phani – an Inca Princess – falls in love with a
Spanish conquistador, an 'old' European bent on conquest of a New
World which, in being primitive, is even older than he is. Huscar,
High Priest of the Sun, affianced to Phani, exerts his powers to thwart
their union. He sings a respendent arioso and aria to the Sun, and it
would not have escaped Rameau's audience, either at the court of
Louis XV or in the public theatre, that this Sun God is very different
from France's *Roi Soleil*, defunct Louis XIV. The Incas join in,
creating a new kind of ceremonial music: not in the least Indian but so
energetic that we can see and hear the contempuous discarding of frills
and furbelows, ruffs and perukes. Though his aria is very grand, it
owes its grandeur to its thrusting vigour. Huscar may be a savage in
relation to Rameau's hyper-civilisation, yet his blazingly scored
music, often angular in line and asymmetrical in rhythm, has qualities
that any New World has need of.

He uses his priestly powers to invoke an Act of God, as he sees it.
The human ritual music is interrupted by an erupting volcano and
attendant earthquake. He says this is evidence of his god's displeasure; and if we think of the earthquake as a physical manifestation
of the impending destruction of the Ancien Regime we will not find it
surprising that it contains Rameau's most startling revolutionary
music – though it is not so deeply subversive as that second *Trio des*

Parques, which frightened Rameau himself! The earthquake's naturalism resembles Vivaldi's tempests: whirring scales, throbbing repeated notes, screeching piccolos and growling bassoons provide the aural accountrements of eighteenth and nineteenth-century operatic storms. Originally this was the kind of music made by the Mannheim orchestras promoted, as noted, by Rameau's patron Le Riche de la Pouplinière, who was significantly not an aristocrat but a tax-tycoon. Both theatrically and musically, Rameau's earthquake is far more trenchant: powerful enough, indeed, to impart ferocity to the vocal exchange between the lovers. The Savage, having maintained that Phani must be sacrificed to appease his gods, becomes emotionally bemused, as were the characters of Cavalli during their revolution a hundred years earlier. Whether mollified by True Love, in superstitious awe of the supernatural, or in despair at the seemingly irreversible march of Civilisation, he proves a Noble Savage after all, handing the girl over to her European lover, with whom she may or may not live happily ever after. Huscar immolates himself by leaping into the volcano's crater. The point seems to be that though a rediscovered primitivism may be necessary to, it must be relinquished for, the making of a New World. The end of the scene is a tragic music of love and loss, and the change in the human dimension has been provoked by the revolutionary elements in the orchestral music, which anticipates not only Gluck, but also Beethoven and Berlioz.

This makes sense if the earthquake is also the Revolution, which Rameau did not live to experience and of which he would have intellectually, if not imaginatively, disapproved. Years later Rameau added another scene to his theatrical parable of *Les Indes Galantes,* explicitly calling it *Les Sauvages.* This takes place in an American forest near the French-Spanish colonies where Zima, an Indian, is wooed by *two* Europeans, a French and a Spanish Officer. Whereas Phani, after Huscar's suicide, is free to marry her *conquistador,* Zima rejects both Europeans and remains in the dark forest. Though one cannot assume that Rameau is himself spurning Civilisation, one can detect a certain queasiness in his attitude to it in his old age. Heroic vision merges into pastoral dream and into overt satire: which is latent in the one-act piece *Pygmalion* (1748), a legend closely related to the Orpheus story.

Pygmalion, as Rameau presents it, is an end to the myth of humanism since its point is that the Orphic artist-hero – a sculptor who falls in love with the woman he chips from stone – displays the self-love to which humanism, carried to its ultimate, obliges us. Vainglory is an ego-booster that may turn a shade comic: as we can hear in the brilliantly-scored, effervescently-rhythmed, lyrically-bounding overture, with its repeated note figures that imitate the chisel's tapping on the stone. Deservedly, the overture, which is Italianate and a far cry from Lullian formality, became famous, for its energy carried people on the crest of a wave. It made them feel good, and still does as much for us: the more pointedly because of its differentiation from the heroic manner of Pygmalion's first arioso. Here, in impassioned melodically-inflected, harmonically-fraught arioso, he bewails the agony occasioned by his infatuation for the statue which, in so far as it is his creation, is himself. Céphise, his real girl-friend in the real world, not unnaturally deplores his abasement before cold stone, singing arioso like his, but tenderer, without his all too self-conscious heroics. Pygmalion has no counter to her humane argument except that his destiny is inescapable. She ends the scene by rejecting him and praying that the gods will punish his 'barbare coeur'.

The next scene is palpably Orphean, for Pygmalion, man as artist, singing to his statue, warms her to life. Harmonious flutes initiate the metamorphosis; instruments of eighteenth-century Sensibility and Enlightenment exert their new-fangled magic. Pygmalion knows that the magic is a dream: 'par quelle intelligence Un songe a-t'il séduit mes sens?' Complementarily the statue, living and breathing, recog-nises that she is a narcissistic projection of her lover: 'tous ce que je connais de moi, C'est que je vous adore'. The music of their duologue is heart-felt: not ostentatious, but instinct with the wonder of cre-ation, in the sense that any artistic 'making' is an Orphic act. L'Amour makes precisely this point when she comes to congratulate Pygma-lion, whose talents have earned a just reward – that of being 'à jamais heureux!'. Her aria is *highly* ostentatious; human pride in creative achievement cascades in twiddles and trills as human voice and sera-phic flute flutter in union and communion. The mode is that of rococo affectation rather than that of baroque grandiosity, as befits the new world; Rameau calls her lengthy song an 'ariette vive et gracieuse'. Les Graces, Les Ris and Les Jeux enter dancing, to seal the nuptials of man and his artefact.

The rest of the piece moves self-congratulation into a social context. Man triumphant must create public perfection, symbolised in dances in which men and women gather together in ordered grace. Not for nothing is Rameau the liveliest of all composers for the dance: as we may hear in the sequence of piquantly-scored numbers – *Gavotte Gracieuse, Minuet, Gavotte Gaie, Chaconne Vive, Loure, Passepied* animated statue to execute. All these dances except the sarabande are animated Statue to execute. All these dances except the sarabande are sprightly, as befits the new, relatively demotic world. The sarabande is given to the statue, perhaps because there is a lot of the past frozen into her, perhaps because she is feeling her way, tentatively, into the future. In any case it is at this point that public implications become patent; 'le Peuple' take up the song and dance, chorically, with surpassing zest. In the final scene Pygmalion addresses the People, telling them, in music drunk with vainglory, how 'L'Amour triomphe'. His arabesques derive from the old world but are carried to an apex of pride and presumption; lyrical roulades swagger, rhythms sexily thrust. His air is treated 'en rondeau', each stanza being separated by a dance of the People around the Statue. Private fulfilment, it seems, matters mainly for its public effects, and the tamborin-like lowness of the dances complements Pygmalion's brash bravery, for the new world, like the Statue, is to be made in his image. The final *contredanse* substitutes euphoric revel, vulgar in the strict sense, for the ceremonial chaconne.

But what, we may ask, of poor Céphise, Pygmalion's real love out there in the world before he made one out of himself? We hear no more of her; she vanishes; and Rameau does not suggest that Céphise's hope that the new gods will 'punish' Pygmalion will be gratified. So the fate of the flesh and blood woman, whom Pygmalion had ditched in his self-deceit, can only be pathetic, if not tragic. Inevitably, there must be cruelties in the destruction of past values; and the ironies are complex, because if in one sense Céphise is an old-fashioned girl sacrificed on the altar of Enlightened advancement and materiality, from another angle she will become the downtrodden proletariat who will eventually seek revenge on dictatorial (traditionally male) ego. In another work of his old age Rameau explores further this double-edged cruelty.

Rameau described *Platée* as a *ballet bouffon* and gave precise instructions to his librettist Autran – who being a nonagenerian probably needed them – as to how to refurbish aristocratic clichés in the spirit of *commedia dell'arte* and of demotic street theatre. The piece comes out as a deliberate deflation of the Heroic, the satire being directed impartially against the gods (the King and nobility), minor supernatural being (the courtiers), and mere humans (the People).

The impartiality implies that in a changing world social hierarchies are muddled. If Cavalli's bemusement reflected the disintegration of Renaissance man's Orphic potential, in Rameau we have the disintegration of the more socially stable autocracy of the eighteenth century. In *Platée* Jupiter the God-King is cross because his Juno is behaving with less than divine dignity. In pique he decides to have an affair with a low marsh-nymph who has also flouted social decorum by loving a (mortal) king, carrying on as though she were a heroine of high tragedy. The marsh-nymph Platée is a Lord-Lady of Misrule, leader of the Antimasque. As vacuously vain as she is grotesquely ugly, she spurns the king who has responded tepidly to her uncouth advances. Jupiter's pretend-wooing initiates a series of ironic reversals, and we are encouraged to relish the discomfiture of the muddy marsh-nymph, jokily 'married' to the God of Gods.

In his grand operas Rameau had shown that even kings and queens have a Platée within them; being human means recognising her existence and learning how to deal with her. But in the *ballet bouffon* that bears her name he says in effect: there she is, as large as life, perhaps a bit larger; *our* civilised lives, however, depend on laughing her to scorn, banishing her from the *fête champêtre*, just as Pygmalion's Céphise was abandoned by his vainglory, though she, far from being ugly, was pretty as a picture of a Boucher pretend-shepherdess. As in *Pygmalion*, it is the new instrumental music in *Platée* that is sharpest in satirical impact: satirical in the modern sense, as well as being the creation of the goatish satyrs described in the Prologue about the birth of Comedy. The chaconne guys heroic pomposity; the busy repeated notes, ungainly leaps and bird and animal noises of the overture discredit the expressive line and rich harmony of which Rameau was master, relying on rhythm and on sensational instrumental devices in the new, middleclassical manner. Similarly the sexual inversions in the vocal roles become grotesque. Platée's is a travesti part, a woman sung by a man, like a pantomime dame, instead of an Orphic man personified by a woman. Her ornamentation parodies baroque coloratura; subtler effects are achieved by playing off the grandeur of her words against her farouche appearance. She is presented in vividly physical terms, warts and all; yet she is allowed her moments of pathos, in, for instance, her tearful distress at Jupiter's false appearances as owl and donkey. Her proud, if idiot, heart is bruised, as male Pygmalion's cannot be.

Platée is stronger as well as funnier than the pastoral dream; and

one of the things that make the piece enlivening is that Platée's duet
with King Cithéron (in which the word 'quoi' becomes the barking
frogs of her marshes), and even her final humiliation by Juno, are
hilarious. The denunciation is too comical for bitterness, which gives
a new dimension to the mythical world itself, presented at once
humourously and nostalgically. To pass to Platée's buffonery from
the luscious sevenths and ninths of the divertissement's chorus to
Hymen, from the lyrical allure of Folly's virtuosic ariettes, or from the
ebullient or languid rhythms and glowing orchestral colours of the
dances, gives a jolt to the nervous system. The jolt must have been still
more disturbing when, in 1745, this tale of an ugly duckling who goes
through a mock-marriage with a man-god was first staged at the
wedding of the Dauphin to Maria Theresa of Spain: a young woman
who was an aristocrat maybe, but notoriously unglamorous.

On the crest of the humanist's pride Clérambault, in his cantata
Orphée, had simply omitted reference to its negative consequences,
unless a certain rarefied wistfulness counts as such. Several decades
later Rameau, in *Pygmalion*, gave human euphoria a fresh gloss but
implied, without stating, something of the price to be paid for
excessive self-confidence; these negative emotions bubble to the
marshy surface in *Platée*. Clearly the time was ripe for a renovated
version of the Orpheus myth, relevant to a changing world. Just as
Monteverdi appeared to meet that need in the early seventeenth
century, so in the late eighteenth century appeared Christoph
Wilhelm Gluck, significantly an international figure, trained equally
in Italian opera, in Austrian symphonic music, and in French theatre,
embracing both opera and ballet. He lived successively in Vienna and
Paris and his work, produced in several languages, had a European
reputation.

His gravitation towards Paris bears on his desire to 'reform' *opera
seria* not by revolutionising its principles, but rather by imbuing them
with renewed moral relevance. He moved to Paris where the political
revolution was to be decisive because the heritage of French tragedy
offered an art, rooted in classical antiquity, which dealt with human
conflicts in what we would call psychological terms ('Hell is within
you'). Moreover France was the home of Diderot and the Encylopae-
dists Voltaire and Rousseau, who synthesised the cult of Nature and
Sensibility with a quasi-scientific enlightenment. Gluck's first operatic success was a version of the Orpheus story, for which Calzabigi
produced a noble and economical libretto.

In 1762 Gluck first composed his *Orfeo* in Italian, writing the name part, in heroic tradition, for a presumptively heroic alto castrato. Settled in Paris, he made in 1774 another version in French, with Orphée sung by a heroic tenor; a 'real' man apposite to a newly-real world. Newness is immediately apparent in the overture or Sinfonia, which is not baroque at all, but rococo symphonic music, bustling in rhythmic energy, with tunes affiliated, even more than those of Rameau's overtures, to the tunes of the streets. The key is white C major, for Gluck the key of Enlightenment, as it was later to be for Haydn, Mozart and Beethoven (who in the titanic inner conflict of the Fifth Symphony transforms the C minor battle for Light and a world restored into the triumph of C major unsullied). When Gluck embarks on the drama he follows Clérambaut in starting after Euridice's death. We are not even told in the opera – only in a read or possibly spoken prologue – of the serpent's bite, and are offered no preludial vision of a golden age of married bliss. The Sinfonia, being a dramatically argued sonata movement, has already hinted that the opera concerns no status quo but rather the forging of futures: which process must begin with a confrontation of the inescapable fact of death.

Against a severe classical decor 'nymphs and shepherds' join with Orfeo to bewail his lot. Nature – woods, fields and streams – is, they Rousseaustically suggest, paradisal, but man is at odds with it. It is too late for communal complacency, and fortune would seem to be as malignant as she is blind. This sombre, even gloomy, view is audible in the choral music which owes something to the legacy of French operatic tragedy from Lully to Rameau but is more symmetrically homophonic, with diatonic melodies harmonised mostly in plain triads in root position. The key is C minor (dark complement to C major's light), soon to become Beethoven's key of conflict. The consolatory manner anticipates Mozart's Masonic musics more directly than does Rameau's first *Trio des Parques*, and the link is yet more patent in the hymn-like Pantomime in E flat major, C minor's relative and, with its three flats, a basic Masonic tonality. Not surprisingly, Gluck was himself a Mason, finding in the new-old religion distrusted by the Established Church a humanitarian ethic that could embrace psychological truth.

Orfeo sings of his loss, communing with Nature in pastoral F major, to which Nature echoingly responds. In the rondo-air the strophic refrains are separated by couplets of arioso, much more impassioned and usually in 'lugubrious' F minor. Horrendous diminished sevenths abound, and the duality between the 'reality' of the arioso and the dreamy pastoralism of the refrains is sharp. Duality is, of course, typical of sonata music; Gluck's music-drama, as distinct from the overture, starts from this obvious, even crude, duality and develops, through the acts, towards the *inner* contradictions of sonata itself. Here the refrains are not so much dream as vision – the ideal as distinct from the life-like fragmentation of the arioso; such ideality is in a sense also real because it embodies the human values of Reason, Truth and Nature on which emergent democracy will be hopefully built. However overwhelmed by sorrow, Orfeo knows that an Enlightened man must bear pain manfully; and although, like Monteverdi's hero, he sings out his grief to the hills rather than to Society, he does so in datonic melodies arching in gently balanced phrases in 3/8, with tenderly sighing, rather than sobbing, appoggiaturas. Though the ariosi are vehement, the refrains, to which he recurrently returns, are ordered: not intellectually, nor with the refinements of sensibility that Clérambault was proud of, but 'reasonably' because he has, or seems to have, achieved an equilibrium wherewith to face a pointlessly inimical destiny. His dedication to Sense and Sensibility, in personal rather than public terms, links with the Rousseauistic dedication to Nature since it is in relation to her, rather than to the moral contrivances of civilisation, that man may be most honestly and honourably himself.

It is not an accident that the reforms Gluck introduced into opera paralleled those which Rouseau himself, an amateur composer more ideologically successful than his musical talents warranted, explored in his own theatre pieces, notably *Le Devin du Village*. Rousseau, it is true, did not assay tragedy and carried naturalism to the point of resorting to speech, whereas Gluck sublimated all speech into song. Both, however, aimed at the paradox of a 'natural' stylisation that could momentarily seem true. Gluck was the more successful, partly for a technical reason – transitions between spoken and sung drama inevitably introduce different levels of reality which work against the naturalism they seek for – but mostly because of superior talents. It is interesting, however, that Gluck's triumph was dependent on an element of amateurism in his technique. Handel's gibe that Gluck had no more counterpoint than his (Handel's) cook was – given the possibility that Handel's cook may have been no mean contrapuntist – a fair comment from a composer belonging to a long-established, highly-professional tradition. But it was not a comment relevant to Gluck, who had as much counterpoint as he needed. Experiential discovery is also technical exploration: which is why Gluck cultivated simplicity of melodic, harmonic and rhythmic speech, as against counterpoint and institutionalised rhetoric.

At the end of the first act Orfeo invites Love to succour his distress, as Rameau's Pygmalion had invited her to boost his already inflated morale. Pygmalion's Amour is herself rapturously self-congratulatory; the Amour summoned by Gluck's Orfeo is not an abstraction but a human attribute. Singing in G major, a tone higher than Orpheus's F, she agrees that he has won the right to protest to the powers of darkness since he, a human, believes Euridice's apparently inane extinction to be grossly *in*human. He may make the Furies listen because, singing and playing from the heart, he has a human dignity worthy of divine respect. In Act II he enters Hades, armed with his lyre, and confronts the Demons, who are demonic forces, not projected god-figures like Monteverdi's Charon and Pluto. They sing, after so much blandly diatonic major music, in C minor, in stark octave unisons and rigid 3/4 rhythms, strikingly anticipating the symphonic Beethoven, for their fury, like his, exists on both a public and a private level. It is within the mind, especially within the minds of men beleaguered and oppressed. Contemporary opinion found their ferocious dance too 'orribile' to be borne; so would Orfeo have done, were it not for the effect of his harp-accompanied song on their savagery. The scene is constructed, like the air to the woods and streams in Act I, rondo-wise. The Furies thunder out their rigid octaves, with horrid diminished sevenths and shivering tremolandi; Orfeo, twanging his harp in triplet arpeggios, beguiles them in E flat major, relative of their C minor and a key of Masonic benignity. Monteverdi's Orfeo appeals to death with all the senuous artifice of which Renaissance man was capable; Gluck's Ofeo seduces them with Englightened simplicity and truth.

At first, however, they yell ferocious negations to his appeal, and change his Masonic E flat major to the six-flatted darkness of E flat minor when they resume their triple-rhythmed octaves. From E flat minor they rise up the cycle of fifths to B flat minor and F minor, and as their tonality rises, so their fury subsides. None the less they land up in their traditionally infernal key, and Orpheus's last appeal, passionate in appoggiatura-laden lyricism, is itself in F minor. Eventually, though still in F minor, the Furies softly, even gently succumb.

Both the first and second-act rondo-arias embrace the dualism of sonata. Tentatively, Gluck is to demonstrate that the fight between good and evil must be fought and resolved within the mind, as Beethoven is to prove with ultimate intensity. We have a hint of this when Gluck's Furies, having apparently cadenced in sepulchral F minor, change their final chord to major, and abruptly shift to D minor for their final fling: sonata-style dance music of unprecedented violence which knocked people flat, and does so still. This appears only in the French version; and Gluck purloined the dance from his own ballet on that savagely tragi-comic iconoclast Don Juan. He thus offers a harbinger of Mozart's operatic *Don Giovanni*, also basically in D minor which, as relative to F major the key of Nature, is the dark side of the same coin. Its association with daemonic forces extends beyond the opera to Mozart's immediately contemporary Piano Concerto in D minor K466 – not to mention Beethoven's opus 31, and parts of the Ninth Symphony.

So Orfeo passes through the gates of Hell, singing. Hades is the kingdom of the dead but Euridice, far from being in hell, is in the limbo of the Elysian Fields where she deserves to be, being wise and good. None the less it is consistent with Gluck's humanitarian ethic that Orfeo wishes to restore her from apparent bliss to our vale of tears, and that she wants to come. Not surprisingly, the Elysian Fields music is Orfeo's own kind of serenely-blanced, harmonically-euphonious song idealised. Accompanied by harp simulating lyre, the famous Elysian song (another addition for the Parisian version) is played on a Dionysiac folk instrument the chalumeau, for which in modern performance an oboe is usually substituted. The melody is garlanded with flutes and violins Rousseauistically emulating twittering birds and prattling brooks, the effect being pastoral but no longer in any sense Pan-ic. The Orphic quest has become an idealised fulfilment of the Rights of Man, liberated from public pomposity and private folly. Man has achieved, through personal sensibility rather than through social sanctions, a balance between himself and Nature – that very harmony which, in the first scene, he had lacked. Both in technique and intention the exquisitely orchestrated music is comparable with Beethoven's Pastoral Symphony. If its unsullied diatonic C major and its softly sensuous parallel thirds sound more dreamily irreal, that may be because we are still invited to respond to Orfeo's Nature-song within a social context, whereas Beethoven's has become an imaginative statement, distilled from his own experience, about Man and Nature.

When a chorus of Blessed Spirits conducts Orfeo to meet Euridice their music, in his pastoral F major and lilting 3/8, is again Masonic, though more lyrically open than their initial funereal laments. The meeting of the lovers and their retreat, at the beginning of Act III, from Hades differ crucially from Monteverdi's version. Gluck's Orpheus and Euridice *both* fail, simply because each is human. He, as in all the versions, is understandably anxious; she cannot comprehend why he, obeying the vow, refuses to look at her, his restored love. It must be because he doesn't care; maybe he has found another woman; or thinks she is too old. Orpheus grits his teeth, thinking this kind of fortitude idiotic, which it is. To bear the slings and arrows of outrageous fortune, to face unexpected and inexplicable death, is one thing; to have to torture oneself and someone one loves because of a silly promise is another thing, at which it is 'only human' to rebel. Democratic man and woman can no longer stomach the 'blindness' of any god's decree; Orfeo says that he scarcely knows how to trust *himself*, with the implication that this is the most a real (enlightened) man may hope for. So their arioso is the most energetically dramatic music in the opera so far; and it leads to a duet of incomprehension in developed sonata style, wherein, through conflict and duality, they seek mutually renewed identity.

The simple, dualistic opposition of the first scene has thus become musical-dramatic evolution. Significantly, the first part of the duet begins in blithe dotted rhythm and in the same key (G major) as Monteverdi's lovers return to. But it soon modulates rapidly, embarking on sonata-style development, while the second and wilder part of the duet is in C minor, the Furies' key which Orfeo has to encompass in growing up to accept Euridice in her own right – in contrast to Monteverdi's version, from which woman has to be liquidated. So the opera, like much sonata music, is about learning by experience: which is why when, after their mutual reproaches, Euridice dies again as her lover looks back, it proves to be no death after all. Though he draws his sword, threatening to kill himself in remorse, Love appears in the nick of time, to save both him and Euridice. Their new awareness of what love means makes it possible not only for them to survive, but also to initiate a happy ending. Gluck gives the new psychological justification for the optimism that Clérambault, five decades earlier, embraced but could not comprehend.

So it turns out that the gods of Enlightenment, far from being irremediably other, are indeed made in man's image. Love has been submitted to a trial and test; because Orpheus and Euridice both respond to it with deep sincerity they may pass through the fire and be reunited *here on earth*. No transubstantiation, either sexless or sexual, is necessary. Since there has been no death, the lovers can enjoy the rewards of constancy and truth, and may share in the public rejoicing with which the piece concludes. Though this is a ballet-masque of pastoral bliss comparable with the Elysian scenes, and also a triumph aria and chorus resolutely in 'white' C major, the real triumph has been the real music of the duet. The rest is jolly social pretence and rococo gallantry, not exactly a wish-fulfilment as in Monteverdi, but a temporary panacea well earned. That it is temporary is self-evident; the text's assertion that they will celebrate their bliss 'for ever' is palpable nonsense, and metaphysical consolation is neither offered nor asked for.

But it is interesting that the exit-chaconne seems to admit to an element of deceit in the 'realistic' euphoria, for it unexpectedly shifts the key up from Enlightened C major to pompous and circumstantial D major, the old key of Baroque Glory. Although the music has the energy of the new rather than the grandeur of the old world, the lurch to the tonality makes it seem 'out of *this* world'. The old illusions cannot be altogether dispelled; perhaps Gluck was not totally convinced that he wanted them to be.

Chapter V

Orpheus enlightened and illuminated

The light of intellectual day in Haydn's *Creation* (1798);
Orphic man–woman as agent of regeneration and
redemption in Mozart's *Die Zauberflöte* (1791); Beethoven –
Orpheus as the dayspring from on high

If Rameau had found that hell is within ourselves, Gluck capped that
with the discovery that that is where truth is to be found also. This
becomes the burden of the sonata music that succeeds him, and is
given theatrical projection in many works concerned, like Gluck's
Orfeo, with a trial of human endeavour and endurance. Freemasonry,
so central if subversive a strand in the religious thought of the later
eighteenth century, combined the notion of a trial with Orphic
elements inherent in the Eleusian Mysteries, renewing the Mercurian motif in that the injunction to 'Know Thyself' can be a god-like
realisation of human potential, but can also allow for a visitation from
the dayspring on high. Gluck, we have seen, was a Mason; so were
Haydn and Mozart, while Beethoven, if not formally a member since
he was no party ticket holder in anything, was influenced by Masonic
thought.

When Haydn said that in his opus 33 string quartets he had explored
a new way of composing he meant, among other things, that he had
realised what sonata was: an embryonic approach to form whereby
one thing grows into another, contradictions being reconciled in the
process. From that point – the late 1770s – onwards Haydn's music
celebrates the Enlightenment's discovery of Man through the 'becoming' which is sonata. For his efforts he was venerated by fairly
common people everywhere, his success being because of rather than
in spite of his music's intense authenticity; 'common' people recognised, perhaps more readily than the declining aristocrats, that
Haydn's musical exploration helped them to discover their own
identities. Everyone, in a democratic society, may modestly become
his own Orpheus; Haydn's commercial success, which enabled him to
become a freelance musician, is thus inseparable from the spiritual

victory manifest in the Apollonian classicism of his last years. It is
interesting that when Haydn was admitted to a Masonic Order in
1785 Holzmeister, Grand Master of the Lodge, praised him for
'inventing a new order of things in the orchestra, for if every instrument did not considerably diminish its volume in order not to damage
the utterance of its companions, the end, which is beauty, could not
be attained.' The orchestra, as used by Haydn, is a musical metaphor
for democracy.

The last of the great symphonic cycle, no. 104 in D major, may
serve as instance. It opens with a slow introduction in the *minor*:
which, with its noble fourths and fifths, its double dots and its
fanfare-like figures separated by dramatic pauses, consciously recalls
the old Heroic overture. Yet if the grandeur is still apprehensible, the
sighing appoggiaturas, in the 'pathetic' manner of C. P. E. Bach, a
'modern' composer of enlightened sensibility, seems also to hint at,
and not entirely to regret, its loss. Certainly when, with an irony as
grand as it is profound, the introduction is metamorphosed into a
major-keyed allegro, the old world is banished by the new: which
discovers its own heroism, that of democratic man. The tune, balancing stepwise movement with quiet repeated notes, is hymn-like,
despite its vivacity; and if Haydn ensures cohesion by having no real
second subject, this is because all the movement has become development. The second subject grows from, even if it seems to contradict,
the first; the codetta theme comments on the second subject; and the
codetta carries us into the development proper. Such far-reaching
unity gives an assurance one might almost call religious to music that
does not surrender an iota of sonata's urgent humanism.

The main theme has a hymnic quality; the tune of the slow
movement is a *domestic* hymn that, far from being an operatic aria,
would be homely were it not sublime. None the less, tranquillity
hides an inner drama, for the form is a developing sonata-rondo in
which the theme is varied each time it returns. Mystery is revealed
within the heart of humanity, as the music wanders from G to D flat
major(!), returning home enharmonically by way of C sharp minor
and F sharp minor and major. The final statement of the 'hymn', after
a Neapolitan transition, silences, and diminished sevenths, sounds
like an ultimate affirmation; and so can lead into a minuet and trio
which, having no specific relation to court or marketplace, have
transcended past and present. The music's jubilation is the power
within common humanity; and the bucolic trio, in the 'passive' flat

submediant, evokes the Elysian Fields, lighted on, here and now.

Something of this timelessness survives into the finale, for although this is a sonata allegro related to the first movement, it embraces a real Croation folk tune over a bagpipe drone, recalling, from the European citizenship and fame of Haydn's old age, his childhood spent in rural Bavaria. Characteristically, he retrospects in order to leap forward: the codetta theme is extended in the development, and again in the coda, bolstered by ebulliently rising scales. The New Man sings and dances in Apollonian fulfilment, as he does in the final series of string quartets, opus 71, 74, 76 and 77. Except by Beethoven, no more inwardly dramatic music has been created than the first allegros of these quartets, and no more sublimely hymn-like melodies have been made than those of the slow movements. In the case of the C major quartet from opus 76 the tune has in fact become a hymn – a national anthem so noble that it almost validates patriotism, which Haydn's sage contemporary Samuel Johnson considered the refuge of scoundrels.

Haydn visited England not long after Johnson's death, and heard, with admiration, oratorios and masques of Handel. It was for and in England that he gestated his last opera, specifically on the Orpheus story, but given a significant subtitle, *L'anima del philosofo* (1791). The piece was bedevilled with misfortunes in the production stage, never saw the light of day, and perhaps is not revivable, since its enlightenedly philosophical libretto is a dead-weight. None the less it contains magnificent music effecting a compromise between High Baroque opera, English oratorio, and Mozartian sonata music, with more than a hint of middle period, not just early, Beethoven. By this time, however, the elaborate social machinery of classical opera thwarted rather than succoured Haydn's Orphic instincts; the wondrous opening of the 'Sunrise' quartet from opus 76, in which the first violin soars untrammeled into the heavens, is on Haydn's premises a more magically Orphic moment than anything in his opera. The big choral and orchestral pieces of his old age, directly inspired by English choral tradition, are also more deeply revealing of Hydn's renewed Orphism, if only because they are not only rationally philosophical but also domestic.

For *The Creation* of 1798 and *The Seasons* of 1801 Haydn transmutes Handel's 'heroic' recitative, arioso and aria into unabashedly domestic terms, while Handel's ceremonial choruses become ethical prayer, comparable with Gluck's choral movements, and with his own hymn for the Emperor. To translate heroism into domesticity is not to deprive it of drama, nor even of grandeur. On the contrary, it may deepen conflict in recognising that it is no longer mainly a matter of class distinctions and divided loyalties, but is a search for unity within the mind itself. In a democratic society each person – like each member of the orchestra – must be responsible for his own destiny *and* for the common-weal. Whirlwinds will ravage his sensibility, as they will violate Nature; but although he cannot control their incidence, he may momentarily triumph over them, just as dawn succeeds night and calm follows storm.

Thus *The Seasons* opens with a magnificent tempest which, unlike Vivalid's fortuitous eruptions, is a fully developed sonata movement. Spring banishes Winter; and democratic man's courage anneals the chaos of a distracted mind. Nor does this physiological-psychological allegory apply only to moments of exceptional frenzy or rapture. In the village pump and kitchen arias of *The Seasons*, as in the Clock Symphony's *andante*, the peasant simplicity of the tunes is nourished by the habituation of the ticking timepiece, while the kettle simmers on the hob and puss purrs by the hearth. Yet the contentment satisfies deeply as well as cosily since it may accommodate tonal surprise and enharmonic pun, disturbing silence and startling metrical ellipsis, or a suddenly savage episode in the minor. To be a democratic man, even a peasant, is not to be a cabbage. Storms within teacups are not necessarily more trivial – as Haydn's contemporary Jane Austen proved – than those that afflict the blasted heath. We have referred to seasonal process as a 'universal' dimension of the Orpheus story. Haydn reveals its socially domestic, rather than anthropological, implications. He was justified in believing that his music might be 'a spring from which the careworn may draw a few moments' rest and refreshment'.

If Orphic implications are buried deep in *The Seasons* they are near the surface in *The Creation*, for which Baron von Swieten produced as text a rehash of a rehash by Linley of Milton's *Paradise Lost*. The verse is utterly un-Miltonic in that it divests God of spirituality and man of the sense of sin. 'An object must be found', said the Baron, 'for music which, by its fervour, its universal sufficiency and perspicuity, may take the place of the Pious Emotions of former days': so he turned God into a working mechanic and the story of the creation into a Masonic parable; 'Now vanish before thy holy beams the spirits of the ancient Night'. Light triumphs through Reason, but what makes the victory significant is mankind's 'fervour, universal sufficiency and perspicuity'. Here Haydn stood for Mankind; his audience received his evocation of Light in amazement, as though he were indeed a New Orpheus.

The work begins with an auralisation of Order emergent from Chaos, as the lucidity of white C major is painfully stabilised through chains of dissonant suspensions and tonality-veiling diminished sevenths. The symbols for disorder are, of course, themselves stylised; yet the interlacing of strings and woodwind creates sonorities prophetic of romanticism and even a hint of Wagnerian sequestial chromatics. Only because Hayn's re-newal of convention was thus radical could the famous blaze of C major at the words 'Let there be Light' have had so cataclysmic an effect upon contemporary audiences, for the juxtaposition of minor and major triads was not in itself new. Likewise, the realistic portrayal of Nature in the second Part is an extension of Vivaldi's naïve presentation of Nature as a backcloth to human society. In the third Part of *The Creation* it is spelled out that the agent of social redemption is human love, as manifest in the personal life. Haydn and the Enlightenment inherited the Christian doctrine of redemption while believing that the catalyst was man become God, not God become man. The humanism of the High Baroque was basically physical, sensual and emotional. Haydn's humanism is all that, but is primarily ethical, moralistic and intellectual. The alternation of Darkness and Light is perpetual and, for better and/or worse, man is responsible for it.

Haydn did not attend many Masonic meetings, perhaps more because he was old and geographically ill-placed than because he lacked zeal for the cause. None the less, in addition to the explicit cases of his 'English' choral works, there are Masonic references in purely instrumental pieces such as the E flat major piano sonata no. 59 and the string quartet opus 54; and the sonata principle itself, which Haydn had done more than anyone to formulate, was a musical synonym for a psychological pilgrimage, capable of Masonic interpretation. The new Emperor Francis II expressed displeasure at a devout Catholic's toying with Freemasonry. He would have had more cause for alarm in the case of Mozart, whose entry into the Order in December 1784 had encouraged Haydn's in February of the following year. For Mozart the appeal of Freemasonry was more complex. The final trinity of symphonies is the greatest possible Masonic *credo*: no. 39 in the Mason's ritual key of E flat; no. 40 in Mozart's 'tragic' G minor; and no. 41 in 'white' C major, representing the triumph of

Light, and including a synthesis of homophonic and polyphonic principles. The string quintets, perhaps the greatest of Mozart's chamber works, similarly reinterpret the social aspects of Masonry in psychological terms: the D major and C major in the spirit of the last three symphonies, the G minor as an initiation, *agon*, and rebirth. In the last, E flat major quintet – as in the cantatas and instrumental pieces composed specifically, and often in that key, for Masonic rites in the composer's last year – we find a new idiom: luminously transparent, letting light *through*, seemingly of folk-like or childish innocence, yet fraught with *lacrimae rerum*. The last piano concerto, K 595, after Masonic echoes, ends with a child's ditty about Spring; similarly the tragic pain of the G minor quintet dissolves in a major apotheosis that reminds us of Papageno.

Mozart's singspiel *Die Zauberflöte* brings us directly in touch with the Orphic theme, revealing how Masonic initiates could, evoking the Eleusian Mysteries, reintroduce mystical transcendence into humanitarian ethics. It was written in 1791, Mozart's last year, for a vaudeville theatre; embraced a diversity of manners from grand opera to popular song; and seems confused because it reflects a world in transition. Indeed the confusion is so extreme that some commentators, notably Brigid Brophy in her brilliant book *Mozart the Dramatist*, have maintained that the libretto, concocted by Schikaneder, the owner of the theatre and himself a Mason, embraces two distinct story-myths interchanged in mid-stream. The original source – from sundry fictional rehashes of classical themes – was an adaptation to Masonic ritual of the Orpheus and Euridice story. In this version the Queen of Night, far from being nocturnally evil, is an earth-goddess with magical powers: none other than Demeter and/or Isis, perhaps with overtones of the Christian Virgin Queen. This explains why she has as daughter the 'good' heroine Pamina, and has in her service three Ladies who perform charitable acts, such as rescuing heroes from dragons. The daughter is stolen by a wizard who imprisons her, appointing as her guardian his blackly degenerate underling. The parallel so far – it is very close – is with the Persephone story. The Queen is Isis-Demeter; Pamina is Persephone; Sarastro the wizard is Pluto, Prince of Darkness, who steals her and shrouds her in the earth; Monostatos the underling is Charon, the black servant of Death.

In the second layer of the story Tamino is Orpheus, who descends to the netherworld to conquer darkness – not by the wavery and

obsolete light of mysticism, but by the Light of Intellectual Day,
ousting ignorant superstition. At this point the story was changed:
possibly because self-consciously secret Masons thought that overt
reference to an Eleusian descent would be letting a dangerous cat out
of the Masonic bag, possibly because the implicit feminism of the tale
offended Masonic patriarchalism. Values are reversed, the Queen
becoming a force of evil and, in social-political context, the Roman
Church, while Sarastro becomes the White Priest of Masonic
Enlightenment. The heart of the story is now Tamino's trials by fire
and water whereby, as Enlightened Man seeking perfection, he
restores buried Persephone-Pamina to the light. Pamina too suffers
trials; and there is reason to think that this twist may have been
Mozart's. Certainly it is she who finally leads *him* from darkness to
light, and who sings the opera's ultimately consummatory aria.

How the two stories were joined and the complexity of the
anomalies that remain are discussed in Brophy's book, to which the
reader is referred. For us what matters is that the contradictions and
confusions are both Mozartian and profound. Mozart was himself, as
befitted his time, an ambivalent character: a Roman Catholic who
sends his lecherous Don Giovanni, tragicomic symbol of modern
untrammelled libido, to Hell; but also a Mason dedicated to
Enlightenment through reason, education and social benevolence. He
could not – and his Shakesperean stature depends on this – passively
accord with an either-or view of the human condition. Both rational
and irrational belief had their truth. Like Blake, his near-contemporary, Mozart knew that 'without Contraries, there is no Progression';
like another near-contemporary, Goya, he knew that 'mere' reason
could not obliterate the nameless horrors that lurk in the psyche's
depths. Though the more direct parallel may be between Goya and
Beethoven, Mozart too nurtured a daemon and demons beneath his
civilised decorum.

So psychologically, if not intellectually, it makes sense that in *Die
Zauberflöte* the high priest of Reason, who sings noble Masonic
hymnody, should be allied to an apostle of darkness who sings *buffo*
popular songs – Monostatos, whose very name indicates his solitary,
asocial state, and whose lubricious heart is even blacker than his skin.
Complementarily it makes sense that the earth-goddess-queen should
embrace darkness along with light in her coloratura arias – old-fashioned
in their heroic grandeur, yet fierily modern in the lightning-like
scintillation of their arabesques, prophesying storm. Most of all it is

Mozart who, through his music, makes the Queen's daughter Pamina, originally a minor figure, the heart of the drama. Tamino is given the flute by the Three Ladies, servants of Pamina's mother, the Queen of the Night, presumably in her original benevolent guise. The regenerative flute is thus associated with the female principle which, although it may be 'subconsciously' nocturnal, is not necessarily malign. On the contrary, the gift of the flute is prophetic of Tamino's eventual union with Pamina as redemptive Eve; and the flute, if rationally Apollonian in Tamino's eighteenth century hands, preserves too its ancestral magic by way of its female donors. The libretto possibly, Mozart's music certainly, tells us that enlightened reason is inoperative without intuitive magic, the two being associated with the male and female principles respectively.

So the opera is not so much about the conflict between Darkness and Light as about the 'new' man and woman who are moulded by it. When the Masonic vow of silence forbids Tamino to speak to his Pamina, her anguish is equated with that occasioned by Orpheus's vow not to look back. But Pamina does not just 'fade away' of her sorrow, like Euridice; she sings what is perhaps the most sublime aria even Mozart ever wrote – in G minor, of course, and in a slow 6/8 rhythm, as though the pulse is dying of inanition. Yet the arching melody drops balm; the Neapolitan progressions and German sixths of the harmony at once hurt and alleviate. Spiritually, if not in the superfices of technique, the air, fusing operatic aria, folk-song and hymn, is the most Bach-like music Mozart wrote – certainly more so than the somewhat self-conscious imitation of Bachian fugue he experimented with in the C minor work for string quartet or piano duet.

Since Pamina, apparently rejected, feels spiritually dead already, she contemplates suicide; but is prevented by the three magic 'boys' who complement the Queen of the Night's three magic Ladies. With their help she is able to embark, a woman in consort with male Tamino, on joint trials by fire and water, such as were common to the Eleusian mysteries and to Masonic initiations. As their Trial begins, three mysterious 'Knights in Armour', support the lovers with the *Christian* sanction of a Lutheran chorale, embroidered with coolly impassioned chromatic fugato that gives further evidence of Mozart's Bach studies; in being Lutheran, if Christian, the chorale is itself to a degree subversive. *At Pamina's instigation* Tamino plays his flute – previously used only for perfunctory parleying with the creatures – to

lead them, in a childish little march in a very white C major, through
their test. ('Wir wandeln durch des Tones Macht froh durch des
Todes düst're Nacht.') Full chorus and orchestra append a resonant
coda, making their personal victory a public event.

So Pamina, not Tamino, has become the agent of redemption in
'eternal' love between a man and woman. Their redemption is
comically echoed in the subplot of Papageno and Papagena. He, a
bird-catcher, is man in a state of Nature before Nurture – an
unregenerate, to complement Tamino's intellectually conscious,
Orpheus. He impudently tootles Dionysos's pipes, making Pan-ic
melody, while his bells parody Apollo's lyre; non-parodistically we
may also relate them to the musical glasses that figure in one of
Mozart's last Masonic compositions. Rousseau's 'noble savage' is
fused with Nature's bird and with the innocent child; and although
this is not itself regeneration, it is a point from which rebirth may
begin. Papageno's Edenic music, which we have related to the finales
of the G minor quintet and of the last piano concerto, gives a deeper
meaning to Gluck's piping in the Elysian Fields: as we may hear when
Papageno experiences a mini-rebirth, immediately after that of
Pamina. Early in the opera she had sung a duet with him emphasising
their kinship; now he too undergoes, if he does not exactly suffer, a
trial, since he is, by Sarastro's Masonic-Puritan ethic, denied the
simple fulfilment of the appetites (for food and sex) which define his
nature. Having had his identically bird-like mate Papagena whisked
from him because he is not yet spiritually ready for love, he sings a
brisk street or perhaps bucolic ditty, trying to cheer himself up with
tootles on his pipe. He decides – with a shift from a pert G major to a G
minor reminiscent of Pamina's 'suicide' aria, including its Neapolitan
intensities – to hang himself. He, as was she, is prevented by an
intrusion of the three Boys, who advise him to resort to his magic
bells. As he tinkles them, Papagena is restored to him 'alive and well'.
These bird-innocents will not graduate to Light with Tamino and
Pamina, but their smaller rebirth is not trivial and it is Pamina,
catalyst between intellect and intuition, who has made it possible.
Like Persephone, in being herself restored to life she restores the
world. Day and Night, Man and Woman, Reason and Love are
united, mutually and magically incarnate.

The orthodox morality of the Enlightenment adhered, as has been
noted, to the well-illuminated notion of God as Master-Mechanic or as
First Architect and Mason. Even though the mystery within the

pilgrimage appealed to the Enligtenment's cult of Hellenism and also,
by way of Persian Zoroastrian rites, to its sense of the exotic, rational
man could only blench at the irrationalism thus revealed. None the
less the truly great artists were such precisely because they did *not*
blench. It is not fortuitous that Mozart's last works were, despite their
light-giving sociability, profoundly death-haunted: one thinks of the
Clarinet Concerto and of the mysteriously 'commissioned' Requiem,
not to mention the irrational pluralism of *Die Zauberflöte* which
embraces that very descent to the dark labyrinth that Gluck's Orphic
opera had approached but then evaded. Mozart neither evades nor
cheats. Beneath the two poles of Sarastro's noble harmonic sobriety
and Papageno's instinctual piping lurk forces darkly primeval.
Though less explicit than Gluck's opera in referring to the lost Eternal
Beloved, Mozart's Masonic opera is the more religious, as well as the
more psychologically complex, work. Not surprisingly, the psychological and sociological implications of *Die Zauberflöte*'s regeneration
and redemption theme persist throughout the operatic mythology of
the nineteenth century.

   Beethoven's torment-and-rescue opera *Fidelio* is indeed *Die
Zauberflöte*'s direct successor, giving a more naturalistic, though not
less psychologically profound, relevance to the times' revolutionary
turmoil. By way of Weber's *Der Freischütz* the trial and redemption
theme is overtly linked with the quest for the Eternal Beloved, and the
two motives move in tandem towards their apex in Wagner's *Flying
Dutchman, Tannhäuser, Lohengrin, The Ring, Tristan* and *Parsifal*: by
which time the Mercurian process has become mainly internalised. A
still more sublime instance of this process had already occurred,
however, in Beethoven's *Missa Solemnis*, wherein the composer treats
the Eucharist as a trial as well as a sacrifice. He admired *Die Zauberflöte* above all Mozart's operas; his liturgical music consummates the
religious implications of Mozart's Masonic humanism.

   More than any of the Viennese masters Beethoven is an Orphic
composer in using sonata to seek order through metamorphosis. Even
in his early years he transforms public values in terms of the private
life, since the struggle for the self has to be fought and won before it
can have social relevance. 'They' may have thought that the destiny of
Europe was being decided on the battlefields of Waterloo; Beethoven
knew that it was in fact being waged within his mind. In his first
period he started from the public assumptions and musical conventions of the late eighteenth century, but stressed their subversive at

the expense of their stabilising elements, with effects often as scarily comic as they are belligerently dramatic. In his second period, however, he does something that no composer had done previously, though Haydn and Mozart had hinted at it: his forms become themselves 'morphological'. Whereas the opus 18 string quartets are intelligible in relation to eighteenth-century tradition though they often alarmingly defeat eighteenth-century expectations, the opus 59 quartets are a new kind of music. The first movement of the F major quartet looks forward to the future not only superficially in its sonority but deeply in that, beginning with a spacious lyrical theme that would seem to comfort without encouraging complacency, it submits that song to radical metamorphosis. It does not move through a temporal process towards resolution of its contradictions, as does a Haydn or Mozart symphony; it rather offers several alternative futures which remain open-ended. Its coda is even longer than its development, since it can be content with no preordained end or easy options. This richly complex movement is followed by a scherzo whose rhythmic motif is announced in several different, unrelated keys, each statement leading to a different extension. Many alternative possibilities are thrown at us: a folk-style variation, an upward-spurting, downward-peetering permutation, a mysterious fugato, distraught syncopations, hectic whirligigs. This sounds like modern music: which it is, being 'news that *stays* news', as Ezra Pound put it.

If we think that these scary instabilities are to be annealed in the sublime Adagio – a cross between hymn and sonata prophetic of the Adagio of the Ninth Symphony – we are in for another shock: for in a thrill-garlanded cadenza the adagio is metamorphosed into the finale, which begins amiably as a dance. But the dance is, as Beethoven tells us, 'Russian': potentially dangerous as well as outlandish, as we may hear when the music garners fright as well as excitation. The coda is extraordinary: an apparently arbitrary succession of moods in turn jolly, hectic, sentimental, expectant, ending with what might be called a shrug of the shoulders. The old world is demolished. Alternative futures are adumbrated in multiple endings which are no end. Beethoven said of this work that it was not for his own day but for the future; it is still true that only he himself, in his third period music, has followed through its disturbing implications.

Such music is Orphic, though the god does not appear. Perhaps he is present in an almost immediately contemporary piece – the wondrous slow movement from the G major Piano Concerto opus 58.

The orchestra opens the movement, fiercely and rigidly declaiming a dotted rhythmed theme in unison octaves, the key being E minor, relative of the concerto's basic G major. The piano soloist fulfils an Orphic function when he plays, unaccompanied, a serene song, harmonised at first in Gluck-like diatonic concords, though with nobly weeping appoggiaturas, later extended into anguished diminished sevenths and Neapolitan progressions. It was Liszt who first suggested that the strings' octave unisons and the piano's song must have been inspired by the approach of Gluck's Orpheus to the Furies. Though there is no direct evidence of this, the effect is psychologically parallel; and it is difficult to believe that Beethoven was unaware of it when, as the soloist's entries grow longer, harmonically richer and more expressively ornamented, the orchestra's dotted-rhythmed mutterings, like those of Gluck's Furies, grow progressively softer as well as shorter. Finally they are silenced by the soloist's chromatically deliquescent cadenza. As coda they relinquish their dotted rhythm, except for a *ppp* murmur on cellos and basses and a cadence in sustained string harmony suggestive of Orpheus's own song. He plays a slowly arpeggiated tonic triad on his piano-lyre, with a lingering appoggiatura that, merging into the finale, returns to benedictory G major. This finale is a song-dance rondo of folk-like geniality, as though Papageno has grown up without losing his bird-like innocence.

Orpheus may also be present in a still more sublime slow movement: the 'Heiliger Dankgesang eines Genesenen an die Gottheit' from the A minor string quartet opus 132. The Lydian hymn – the mode being traditionally associated with healing – recurs in rondo form several times, each more celestially embroidered. It instigates life in the faster, wide-leaping episodes in D major, appropriately the key of power and glory. Here Orpheus has returned, 'subjectively', to his medieval meaning, for he is not so much Man-become-God as the Mercurian Messenger through whom the holy spirit may visit and revitalise us. This is what happens in the *Missa Solemnis*, which Beethoven believed to be his greatest creation.

The Christian Eucharist enacts part of Orpheus's story: Christ, a slain god, descends into the dark labyrinth in order to be born again, in a process related to the seasonal cycle. Beethoven depicts this, in psychological terms, in the Benedictus of his Mass. The movement is introduced by a purely orchestral Praeludium. There is precedent for this in the improvised or composed organ music that was traditionally played, 'with a rather grave and sweet sound', during the mystical moment of the elevation of the Host. Such music, created by a Frescobaldi, a de Grigny or a Couperin, was slow, soft, polyphonic, close-textured, chromatic: so is Beethoven's Praeludium, which introversively deepens the holy silence and darkness already generated by the Sanctus. Although its theme of rising second and fourth leading into a descending scale harks back to the Kyrie, it here sounds embryonic. The hushed fugato, swinging in slow triple pulse, in warm harmony mysteriously scored for low flutes, low strings, bassoons and organ pedal, evokes the half-lights of a forest; and suggests, in its horizontal and vertical dimensions, a Gothic cathedral – itself a stylisation of a 'lofty forest glade'. The dark texture is *labyrinthine*, enacting a Persephean and Orphean descent below consciousness. When at last the music 'earths' itself – Beethoven said 'I am electrical by nature' – on dominant and tonic pedals, diminished sevenths and dominant ninths throb over the ostinati. The music 'introspects itself' in its convoluting chromatics, and it is significant that this supernatural moment should be prophetic not so much of early romanticism as of its end.

If we may crudely think of the relationship between soloist and *tutti* in a classical concerto as parallel to that between the self and the world, we may hear in the slow movement of Beethoven's Fourth Piano Concerto a harbinger of romaticism. In the Praeludium to the Benedictus of the *Missa Solemnis*, however, there is no longer a separation from, let alone a hostility between, the self and whatever is other to it. Introversion is completed in the overlapping sevenths and ninths, the enveloping texture, the darkly sumptuous scoring. Like Wagner in *Tristan* and *Parsifal*, or Mahler in the Adagietto of his Fifth Symphony (in which a harp deputises for Orpheus's lyre), Beethoven, as high priest of the romatic ego, has discovered that the only way to find the self is to lose it. The parallel with Blake's Innocence and Experience is striking, for Beethoven, who was Blake's exact contemporary, really was Blake's Bard who 'present, Past and Future sees'. Again like Blake, Beethoven thought of himself as a Seer who had heard Jehovah speaking to Adam in the Garden. In his Mass he calls on the 'lapsed soul' to regain the self, surrendered when man adopted the 'starry pole' of Reason in place of the Imagination. The Earth, which is fallen man, will 'arise from out the slumbrous mass' when the Human Imagination reanimates the 'starry Floor' of Reason, the 'dewy grass' of sense impressions, and the 'watery shore' of the 'Sea of

Time and Space' (the material world). Beethoven, like Blake, exhorts us not to 'turn away'. If we don't, 'fallen, fallen light' may be renewed. This light is not, for Beethoven and Blake, the Enlightenment's Intellectual Day.

Renewal occurs when, from the Persephone-like descent of the Praeludium, a shaft of light is born. A high C major chord in second inversion shines on two flutes and solo violin; inevitably we recall the same chord and sonority, but in E flat, at the end of the Credo. Then it had been hopeful prophecy; now it is revealed truth: for the solo violin as Holy Ghost floats down from the heights in a swinging 12/8 – a time signature associated by Beethoven, as by Bach, with angelic matters. Beethoven had anticipated the lofty solo violin, the swaying 12/8 metre and the gently throbbing accompaniment in the E major slow movement of the E minor quartet from opus 59; according to Czerny, Beethoven conceived it while contemplating the starry heavens and meditating on the Music of the Spheres. In the Benedictus this celestial serenity is vastly expanded, the unearthly effect deriving from the gentle pulse breathing in stepwise moving quavers; from the dissolution of accent since the falling scales are frequently tied across the beats; and from the diaphanous scoring, with solo violin posed over interlacing woodwind. The polyphonies are often supported by pizzicato strings, echoing Orpheus's lyre, and by soft trombones, recalling the sacral brass of the dead. In the Praeludium the polyphony had veiled the harmony, just as Eleusian and in imitation Masonic initiates were veiled in preparation for descent to the underworld. Now the veiled figurations become translucent. Light filters through, and when the horns enter on a dominant pedal, the basses softly intone the plainchant Benedictus, Orphically reborn from the hint of it in the Praeludium's rising second.

The Orphic qualities of this music are reinforced by the fact that, despite the Christian connotations of the plainsong quotations and the canonic polyphony, its atmosphere is Hellenistic. Persephone, recovered to life and light, sings in no — not even in Kant's Invisible – Church, but in the forest glade a cathedral may represent, or in a pastoral landscape similar to that painted by Gluck in comparable orchestral colours. Beethoven, however, has freed his music from that 'Sea of Time and Space' in which Gluck's Orpheus and Euridice were happy to be reunited. The exfoliating violin, haloed by flutes, is at once spiritual (shedding the illumination of the Holy Ghost) and sensuous (embodying the loveliness of Persephone, 'gathering flowers, from gloomy Dis restor'd'). Thus the Benedictus becomes the new kind of 'cantique ecclesiastique' that Beethoven hoped to create in a 'choric ode on the victory of the Cross' which he spoke of not long before his death, and which may have emerged as the C sharp minor string quartet.

So Beethoven heals the breach between sundered Dionysos and Apollo, creating a mandala within the mind. But his achievement was exceptional, indeed unique: in which respect he was and is the most crucially 'modern' of all composers. The Benedictus's equilibrium between man and god is neither 'classical' nor 'romantic', since it is timeless and placeless. It has no direct successors in the nineteenth century, when Orpheus's story is glamorously romanticised – or debunked.

Chapter VI

Orpheus romanticised and debunked

Schubert's Eden and the Orphic dream in the C major string
quintet (1828); Liszt as Orphic actor: the Piano Sonata (1853)
and *Orpheus* (1854); Tchaikovsky's mimed dream of the
Orphic prince and the Sleeping Beauty (1889); Orpheus
debunked, and happy in Hell: Offenbach's *Orfée aux Enfers*
(1858)

The romanticising of Orpheus may already be discerned in the later
works of Beethoven's younger contemporary, Franz Schubert. When
he was born in 1797, Mozart had been dead for six years and Haydn
was at the height of his winter harvest, while Beethoven was gestating
works which would overthrow the traditions he sprang from and
reversed. Sonata, depending on tension between the public and the
private life, was itself a revolutionary, and incipiently romantic,
principle of composition. Mozart attained a poise technically
incarnate in his balance between lyrically vocal, operatic melody and
the instrumental drama of sonata. Beethoven, primarily an instrumental composer, emphasised the re-creative aspects of the new music
while still believing, at least until his last years, that his private rebirth
was an agent working for public – for social and even political – good.

By Schubert's time, however, corruption within Viennese society
could be disguised neither by the tawdry triviality of the degenerating
aristocracy nor by the industry, piety and sentimentality of the rising
middle class, to which Schubert's parents belonged. As a man
Schubert was, like Beethoven, conscious of political oppression in
Austria; unlike Beethoven, he did not think it possible, or perhaps
even desirable, to do anything about it. As a musician, he revered
Beethoven with self-obliterating fanaticism, while deploring what he
called his 'eccentricity' which drives a man to distraction, instead of
resolving him in love'. His own music seems to be created simultaneously out of conflict with the world as it was (the Beethovenian,
dynamic aspect of his work) and out of yearning for Viennese civilisation as he imagined it had once been (the early Mozartian, lyrically
vocal aspect of his work). From the one point of view he, like
Beethoven, heroically protests; from the other he seeks in his music to

resolve frustration in love, creating an art wherein ideals are not corrupted by human malice or rapacity. Schubert composed neither for the established Church, though he produced a quantity of ecclesiastical music, nor for the State, though he made abortive attempts at opera. His quintessential music was created not for institutions in which he could no longer fully believe, but for a communion of friends and lovers. Beethoven's third period music became a discovery of paradise within the psyche; Schubert's music, especially in the doom-haunted last years of his brief life, became a search for a vanished Eden.

This is nowhere more evident than in his last major work, the String Quintet in C, surely one of the high points of European music; significantly Orpheus, romanticised and perhaps domesticated, appears in its slow movement. The first sonata allegro is cast on a large scale, the second cello helping to promote a quasi-orchestral resonance. The initial theme is song-like, with a quasi-operatic turn, but lyricism proves Protean in emotional implication. Bounding arpeggiated motives, generating energy, alternate with repeated-note figures that promote mystery, as they remotely modulate, even during the exposition. The harmonic texture is warmly spaced. The second subject complements the first nostalgically, for it droops rather than rises, and begins not in the conventional dominant, but in the flat mediant (E flat). Both subjects are developed within the exposition in that the figurations, interacting, change their emotional identities – a more sensuously expansive, less intellectually wrought, version of Beethoven's Mercurian processes. A further twist occurs in the codetta theme, which alchemises the stepwise movement of the second subject into a dotted rhythm prophetic of the minatory military motives that, in the symphonies of Schubert's successor Mahler, herald Europe's twilight.

Such multifarious material necessitates spacious development whereby themes that had been songful become, in fluctuating modulation, wild, or those that had been heroic become a sigh of regret. The recapitulation must likewise be expatriated on, for what has been refashioned must be reheard. The second subject, now in Schubert's favourite, sensuously passive flat submediant, sings of ineffable mutability: 'Schöne Welt, wo bist du'. The coda introduces a dark chromatic descent beneath the original yearning song. One might almost say that the two final tonic triads – the first loudly dynamic, the second warmly enveloping in middle register – epitomise the movement's progression from reality to dream.

The slow movement transports us abruptly to the upper mediant, heavenly E major, associated by Schubert, as is explicit in the texts of many of his songs, with Eden. Here Schubert, an Orpheus romantically resuscitated, very slowly sings the lyrical tune, harmonised in diatonic triads over a lyre-like pizzicato bass; a counterpoint on first violin sounds like a remote echo of the military motif of the first movement, tamed by Orphic therapy. The dream-like quality of the sustained song is thereby emphasised: which makes it the more surprising, yet not entirely unexpected, when the dream is sundered by a middle section that leaps from heaven to hell – and from blissful E major to its Neapolitan flat supertonic, F minor, which we have seen to be no less traditionally a key of the infernal regions. Orpheus's song does not pacify the Furies; on the contrary, they tear him to pieces as he day-dreams in Eden. In panting syncopations, with grinding triplets, a more operatic theme ranges through enharmonic modulations so extravagant they anticipate the mature music of Wagner. These furies are more frentically introverted than those that growl at Gluck's Orfeo, and perhaps more incipiently paranoid (and expressionistically romantic) than those Beethoven had fought and conquered. Schubert's Orpheus does not entirely subdue them, even though he sings his radiant song again, *da capo*; for throughout the song the Furies' triplets persist, delicately transformed and no longer ferocious, yet ambivalent in that they tend to submerge the song's serene homophony. In the coda their F minor again momently ruffles E major tranquillity, before their murmured disgruntlement fades in a simple dominant tonic cadence in E. Psychologically, the effect is odd; terror still lurks even in Eden, and in the security of Home.

Here Schubert is the romantic child as well as Orpheus; and although the scherzo brusquely returns to earthy corporeality, being all upwards thrusting energy over a tonic pedal, with Beethovenian cross-accents, it is undermined by weird modulations. So although energy is liberated, it still seems uncertain of its direction. And just as the middle section of the slow movement opposes hellish Experience to Edenic Innocence, so the trio of this scherzo introduces within physical well-being what is in effect another slow movement of infinite mystery. Its key relationship is again that of flat supertonic to tonic – in this case D flat to C; and although it begins in (non-harmonic) unison, echoing the stepwise movement and dotted rhythm of the first movement's codetta theme, it soon modulates by way of abstruse enharmonics. These modulations are as disruptive, within the private dream, as the enharmonics of Rameau's *Trio des Parques* had been within his public domain. Schubert's trio, far from being a beer-garden daydream such as we find in the trios of Haydn, Mozart and even Beethoven, approaches Mahlerain phantasmagoria.

The *da capo* of the scherzo cannot efface the trio's mystery; nor is it really obliterated by the rondo finale, which effects to forget the tempests of Schubert's joys and sorrows in evoking the hedonistic present of Viennese café music. For the movement begins oddly in C *minor*, and ranges through several keys before establishing the major. The more jaunty the figurations, the more enigmatic the adventures of harmony and tonality. Languorous tavern lyricism is entwined with the trumpery trumpetings of militarism, as the dotted rhythms and triplets of the previous movements gather obsessive ardour. The strangest things happen when Schubert adopts the device – familiar in Rossini's operatic finales which, addressing an audience, play their own applause – of concluding the movement by whipping up the tempo. Frivolity becomes frenzy. The final section of the coda recalls both the scherzo and the first movement, the last sounds being the cryptic Neapolitan relationship of D flat to C, emphasised by the cellos' trill – directly recalling the muttering Furies of the andante, who thus have the last word, or rather, growl.

While Schubert is closer to Mozart than to any other composer, the lyrical and dramatic bases of his art are more widely separated; from the struggle to reconcile them sprang the mingle of passion and nostalgia which is his art. With Mozart, the dancing play of melodies seems the essence of mutability itself; but Schubert's singing tunes and ambiguous harmonies are his own *consciousness* of mutability, romantic in spirit, so that, despite his reverence for the past, his late music is inexhaustibly prophetic – especially of Wagner, whose *Tristan* Schubert would have lived to hear, had he been allotted his three score years and ten. Yet if we therefore feel with Schubert, as we do not with Mozart, a tragic sense of potentialities unfulfilled, it is also true that the spine-tingling beauty of his last works is inseparable from the sense of doom that hung over the composer and his world. He even anticipates the dichotomy between Art and Entertainment that has increasingly dominated European music since his day: not merely because he supported himself by making chains of waltzes, marches and polkas more distinct from his sonatas and symphonies than were the comparable pieces of Haydn, Mozart and Beethoven, but also, at a deeper level, because his mature music, notably the Quintet, teeters between dream and hedonism. Later nineteenth-century composers, such as Liszt and Offenbach, treat the Orphic theme as 'escapology' by way of play-acting dream or fear-evading frivol: alternatives we have seen to be already latent among the complex motivations of Schubert's wondrous Quintet. Schubert's greatness may consist largely in his awareness that human experience – certainly his experience – is in essence sensuous: which may be why he appeals so strongly to us who are without inherited faith. For us too, as well as for Schubert who had so little time to enjoy it, the beauty visible and tactile in the world around us, and audible in the sounds Schubert's imagination evokes, is as transient as a dream. The music is still almost before we have heard it. The dream is past that was more real than the waking life.

Schubert's reliance on his sensuous life called for formidable moral strength. Unballasted by God or State, it is easier romantically to act out a role; and it is obvious that Orpheus, being a man playing God, *can* be construed theatrically. Certainly he became an actor in many of his romantic metamorphoses, nowhere more vividly than in the music of that arch-romantic, Franz Liszt, the most 'transcendental' piano virtuoso who had ever lived. Throughout his long life Liszt exhibited himself in a variety of masks. Many of the piano works he took with him on his gladiatorial tours through Europe were based on his assumption of someone else's identity: most notably his operatic transcriptions and paraphrases which, in the days before mechanical sound reproduction, presented, as a one-man show, the operas that were the staple musical diet of his fashionable public. Although operatic arrangements for piano were a minor industry in Liszt's earlier years, his potpourris and fantasies on the operas of Mozart, Bellini, Donizetti, Meyerbeer and whomever differ from the average commodity both in their technical difficulty – they are not parlour music for amateurs – and in the necromantic quality of their imagination. They do so because Liszt, far from merely (if at all) indulging in a commercial enterprise, identified with the theatrical protagonists and re-enacted their dramas himself.

In the case of the Fantasy on Bellini's *Norma* one might say not that Liszt improves on the original, but that he refashions it in terms larger than Bellini – and perhaps larger than life. Norma is reborn when Liszt assumes her mask, as well as that of Pollione her lover. Similarly, in the great fantasy on Mozart's *Don Giovanni* Liszt identifies with the rapscallion Don, himself an actor, but also with his women and the awe-ful Stone Guest. This fantasy is no mere transcription, let alone a potpourri; it is a tone-poem which turns the piano into a one-man orchestra, creating a highly-wrought structure from the interaction of characters and motives. Liszt begins at the opera's end, with the hero's hell-bent fate imaged in whizzing scales and whirring tremolandi; places in the centre a variation set on the seduction duet 'La ci darem la mano', craftily undermining eighteenth-century *politesse* with effervescent virtuosity; recapitulates the Stone Guest episode in still more infernally chromatic frenzy; but apparently allows the Don to carry the day by ending with a dazzling excursion around the cynically hedonistic 'Champagne Song'. Whether he does in fact carry the day remains, however, a moot point, for the 'Champagne Song' turns into a *galop infernale* which teeters, in virtuosic extravagance, on the edge of hysteria. Perhaps Liszt laughed, a little uneasily: as do we.

In himself 'investing' the characters in other peoples' operas Liszt offers a prototype for what happens in his original music, in which he wears the masks successively or even simultaneously of Byronic lover, gypsy, devil and saint. In the volumes of piano pieces he called *Années de Pélerinage* Liszt aurally depicts his travels through France, Italy and Germany, translating into pianism techniques derived not only from opera, but also from folk, popular and salon musics. Formally, the pieces are not complex, favouring ternary or rondo structures; the lack of subtlety makes theatrical projection the more efficacious. They may be inspired by Nature; whether benign, as in the delightful evocations of Swiss village life, or malign, as in the spine-chilling *La Vallée d'Obermann*, wherein Liszt calls on his newly-explored pianistic resources to arouse the Awesome Sublime – an actor's *travesty* of the awe generated by the Praeludium to Beethoven's Benedictus. In each case Liszt could say, with Byron's Childe Harold, 'I live not in myself, but I become a Portion of that around me'. More accurately, perhaps, he should have said that the world 'around' vicariously becomes himself, in the same way as he 'possessed' the characters in Bellini's and Mozart's operas.

It is not surprising that the 'world' should embrace art as well as people and places. Some of Liszt's most harmonically adventurous passages occur in music inspired by works of art: for instance the relatively early *Dante Sonata*, which grotesquely equates the Divine Comedy with Liszt's attitudinising progress across the 'stage' of

earth, hell and heaven. The ardour with which Liszt as actor-Orpheus
plays the game ensures its slightly hilarious success; but an actor-
Orpheus is not identical with the real thing. This may be why the most
impressive of Liszt's smaller pieces inspired by Art is *Il Penseroso*,
which presents the artist as melancholic. Through the tenebrous
registration and deliquescent chromatics of this piece Liszt *acts out*
experience that, ten years later, is to prove cataclysmic in Wagner's
Tristan. The process is intellectually sophisticated, whether Liszt is
triggered by the cultural riches of Europe or whether, donning gaudy
(and becoming) gypsy costume, he emulates the sonorities and
rhythms of a peasant band.

At the same time Liszt, growing older, must have realised that his
multiple identities involved a deeper issue: what ultimate self was
precipitated out of the masks? Weary, too, of his round of concertis-
ing, he retired from public life and, settling in Weimar in 1848,
devoted the next decade to exploring his creative rather than executive
gifts. For the most part he relinquished his self-glorifying instrument
in favour of the relative impersonality of a symphony orchestra. Even
so, he composed during these years the one-movement Piano Sonata
in ('tragic') B minor which is his richest and most durable work both
in intrinsic musical substance and in historical significance. Here
Liszt the actor is most nearly identified with Liszt the Orphic man.

There was a precedent for the sonata in Schubert's *Wanderer Fantasy*, actually a four-movement sonata in which all the movements
have the same or closely-related thematic material derived, mask-like,
from the composer's own song. Liszt telescopes the conventional
sequence of movements into one, creating all his themes from five
interrelated motives. The introductory descending scale assumes
various metamorphoses according to its shifting modality. A theme
beginning with five assertive repeated notes is transmuted into lyrical
yearning; is twisted into a demoniacal snarl; expands into hymnic
grandeur. So while the sonata preserves links with traditional pro-
cedures such as fugure and sonata, it also explores vestigial serial
techniques prophetic of the Wagnerian leitmotif, and beyond that
Schoenbergian serialism itself. These prophecies are not merely
technical: the technique exists *because* the masks of lover, devil and
saint are now synonous, just as the actor-singers in Wagner's music-
dramas tend to be aspects of a single ego. Liszt's sonata makes of the
romantic piano a universe of sound, and of the sonata a projection of
the psyche in and for itself, with its social and religious connotations

played down. If we think of the Liszt sonata as a link between Beethoven's *Hammerklavier* Sonata and the two great piano sonatas of Charles Ives we have a notion of its strengths and limitations. The *Hammerklavier*, probing the depths of the psyche, is a marriage of Heaven and Hell, in Blake's sense; so, if more tentatively, are the two Ives sonatas. Relastively, Liszt is not bound upon King Lear's wheel of fire but consummates the marriage on stage. If the metaphor seems indelicate, so is the music, and in that lies its force. Liszt-Orpheus, subduing furies within and heaven-storming by his own extravagance, gives a thrilling performance: but performance it still is, just as the piano *Légendes* about the two St Francises (saints with Orphic attributes) are moving music which is 'religious'.

The piano sonata which contains Liszt's quintessence was composed in 1853, during the Weimar years when most of his attention was devoted to the orchestra: for which he devised, perhaps 'invented', the symphonic poem that was supposed to oust the obsolete symphony, and to a degree did so. The one-movement symphonic poems do not achieve the re-creative trenchancy manifest in Liszt's sonata perhaps because, like the operatic fantasies, they are more dependent on extra-musical dimensions. None the less, whether Liszt identifies himself with Hamlet, Prometheus, Mazeppa or whomever, he 'invents himself' in working out his heroes' destinies in symphonic terms. His greatest orchestral work, the *Faust Symphony,* is not a symphony but a triad of symphonic poems, interrelated to cover the same range of experience as the Sonata, less economically. The movements depict Faust, Gretchen and Mephistopheles: whose themes do not develop in sonata style, but are varied permutations of the same motif, since all are aspects of the same psyche, Liszt himself.

Faust is Liszt as heroic striver; his theme opens with tonally-neutral augmented fifths, apposite to mankind's perenially unanswered questions. It proliferates in related motives expressive of (in Liszt's words) unbounded strife, unfulfilled desire, audacious self-confidence, disillusioned self-disgust. In the Mephistopheles movements the same themes are parodied by chromatic distortion, linear inversion and metrical fragmentation, so that they pertain to the Devil no less than to modern man. Only Gretchen's themes remain inviolate, she being the passive paradise activist Faust hopes to win to when his divided self is healed. Liszt found a precedent for this morphological approach to form in late Beethoven, who does enter paradise in purely musical terms. Liszt is not up to that: so the consummation of the

Heavenly Chorus at the end is a wish-fulfilment, as the Arietta that
concludes Beethoven's opus 111 is not. If the Piano Sonata remains
Liszt's most formidable piece it may be because, using the same
techniques of thematic metamorphosis as the *Faust Symphony*, it
knows its own limits, notwithstanding the 'mystical' enharmonic
triads at the end. This is not to deny that the *Faust Symphony* is a great
work, relevant to all mixed-up kids, middle-aged strivers and fuddled
oldies: which covers a high percentage of the human race.

One of Liszt's symphonic poems has *Orpheus* as it subject; perhaps
it is not coincidental that he wrote it in 1854, the year after the Sonata.
It is a blessedly unpretentious piece which defines the limited scope
and depth of romantic Orphism. First performed at a festival
production of Gluck's *Orfeo*, it is a 'subjective' descendent of that
version of the story. Indeed, Liszt's verbal preface suggests that he
thought his attitude to the tale was as 'enlightened' as Gluck's; he says
that we may learn from the myth how our baser natures may be
subdued, so that Dionysiac and Bacchic furies may never again
threaten our piece of mind. The music hardly bears this out, for Liszt
is the *homme moyen sensuel* now far from *moyen*, and more concerned
with sybaritic self-indulgence than with social obligations. At the start
Orpheus plucks his lyre, for which two orchestral harps luxuriously
deputise, in arpeggios ringing through pedal notes on horns and
woodwind. The first theme, on low strings and woodwind, is in
Enlightened C major, hymn-like, ballasted by repeated notes in the
dotted rhythm of fortitude. It might be Gluck's *Orfeo* a shade vulgar-
ised, but for chromatic undulations that hint at personal eroticism.
Sensuality is enhanced in rising sequences until, with a blissful modulation to the upper mediant (heavenly E major), Orpheus sings his
love song to appease the powers of darkness. He is represented – again
in reminiscence of Gluck – by a plangent oboe or cor anglais, sometimes doubled by strings; his very operatic tune, beginning with the
repeated notes syncopated, followed by falling fifths, is accompanied
by harps and pizzicato strings as the man-god's lyre gets busier.
Chromatic passing notes, intruding into the dulcet melody, send it
winging into triplets. The lyre-chords are usually triadic but often
enharmonically related; modulation becomes almost incessant as
Orpheus's melody, now chromaticised on high strings, swells into a
sexy song of seduction. Chromatic alterations change the original
nobly perfect into pathetically diminished fifths, until the work
climaxes in sequentially rising modulations, anticipatory of Tristan's

fervour.

The triumph this results in, as the C major tune returns as a grandiose march, is not far from the Romantic Lover's sexual conquest; and this mundane magic briskly routs the furies, who wriggle and writhe in tremolando chromatics on cellos and basses. Despite Liszt's Preface, his Orpheus's erotic passion seems to be more efficacious than his enlightened sensibility, for although the sturdily diatonic march-hymn provides consummation, it is enveloped in the enharmony of the lyre-harps' arpeggios. Orpheus is left with a pathetic cor anglais solo, again more self-indulgently recalling Gluck, when the furies' tremolandi are silenced; and the final diatonic concords, usually proceeding by mediants, hint at mystic matters, as does the similar end of the Piano Sonata. This attempted sublimation of terrestrial passion in enharmonically related triads parallels the famous 'aspiration' prelude in *Lohengrin* and more tentatively anticipates the fushion of *animus* with *anima* (and of love with death) in *Tristan*. For Liszt, however, the experience is not so much apocalyptic as a post-coital daydream – another instance of his habitual, if enlivening, game-playing. It is not Liszt's fault, though one can hardly call it an accident, that the scoring reminds us of a Hollywood love scene.

This reference to cinematic illusion provides a link to another, later romantic who was also an actor, Tchaikovsky; (it is to the point that the very word 'illusion' derives from the Latin *in lusione*, in play). Liszt was Hungarian by origin, French in cultural milieu, European in status. His gypsy mask was palpably that, whereas Tchaikovsky's wildness was endemic in his birth. Born in the old White Russia, he was victim of a dying world, dedicated to the past and to the mother figure who embodied it. His homosexuality was probably related to his mother-fixation, and was certainly the impetus to the paranoid sense of guilt under which he laboured. Yet Tchaikovsky's near-psychotic state was his trigger for creation. His initial stimulus for composition coincided with his beloved mother's death when he was fourteen; the peak of his creativity occurred around the time of his disastrous marriage, entered into only in order to stifle scandal and effectively ended after its first night and his (probably consequent) suicide attempt. Given these traumatic conditions it is understandable that Tchaikovsky should have founded his art on an extreme interpretation of the romantic duality between reality and dream. This is evident in his musical proclivities. He abominated the music of his contemporary Moussorgsky who, also homosexual and (in his case alcoholically) neurotic, sought identification with real people – children, simpletons, peasants – whom he was not; nor could he comprehend heaven-and-hell-storming Beethoven. He loved the music cultivated in his family circle: the operas of Bellini, the ballets of Delibes, the valses, mazurkas and polonaises of Chopin and of the salon composers who imitated him. His idol was the Italianate Austrian Mozart, though when he attempted pastiche in 'rococo' style the music, though charming, is conspicuously un-Mozartian.

This is because Tchaikovsky's Mozart is not the Shakesperean whole man, aware of the heights and depths of experience, but a maker of eighteenth-century *contes de fées*. Connected with this is the fact that Tchaikovsky was a professional theatre composer, working for the Russian ballet wherein, in voiceless mime, patterns of exquisite lucidity may be woven out of life's tatty imperfections. Romantic ballet had its roots in French classical theatre, being what happened to the seventeenth and eighteenth-century *ballet de cour* when dance as a ritual of humanism, existent in a real court in the real world, was no longer feasible. That the centre of romantic ballet was Russia is not fortuitous, for the life of the Russian aristocracy, nurtured on French literature and Italian opera, had become an oasis of dream in the vast emptiness of the steppes, from which proletarian revolution was soon to shamble. Russian ballet is dream made visible and audible. Most of Tchaikovsky's ballets find their subjects in fairy tales, usually in an eighteenth-century permutation. The finest of them, *The Sleeping Beauty*, composed in 1889, is perhaps his most deeply representative work.

It is not difficult to understand why Perrault's seventeenth-century French version of the tale should have fired Tchaikovsky's imagination. The fairy story was not of course invented by Perrault, being a folk myth whose roots are entangled with both the Demeter-Persephone story and that of Orpheus and Eurydice. The Princess *is* beauty, childhood and innocence. She is put to sleep, a kind of death, by the prick of fortune's malice, Cararbosse's spindle being in the folk sources an initiatory menstruation myth as well as the serpent that nips Eurydice. Today, as well as in folk legend, menstruation is often called the 'curse': which Carabosse utters. Beauty's hundred-years sleep is an introverted prepartion for growing up; significantly, not only she but the entire world of the castle in which she exists seems immobilised, statue-like in silence and stillness. The labyrinth of the

Dark Forest through which the Prince has to journey in order to awaken her, is the toil and turmoil of growing up – hers, as well as the prince's. Clearly this mythic story chimed with Tchaikovsky's deepest needs. He, afraid of the adult world, was fixated in childhood and the Edenic dream, yet could grow through it by symbolic magic as the Prince's true lover's kiss redeems him in dance that is itself dream. As swaying bodies move in co-ordinated grace, Tchaikovsky's music disciplines passion in submitting to the behests of Petipa's choreography, yet swells and swings – overreaching the enchantments of Tchaikovsky's model Delibes – to become, in the Rose Adagio, comparable with the sustained *élan* and elegiac poise of Bellini, whose operatic worlds discovered grace through suffering. In mime and movement, allied with arching lyricism, love is healed of mortality and guilt; and so are you and I. The moral point is not so far from that of Gluck's and Mozart's version of the Orpheus story, though Tchaikovsky's Orphic Prince has no lyre.

Even so, the end of this greatest of ballets is musically very odd: for after a joyous mazurka in which everyone celebrates the fairy tale's happy-ever-after, Tchaikovsky appends a severely modal coda that is, in the context of his Frenchified Italianism, severely 'Russian', though not uncouth like the indigenous Moussorgsky. It *sounds* Russian because of its austere modality, though it is in fact based on a sixteenth-century French dance tune: a fact that reminds us that the ballet is supposed to be set, archaistically, in Perrault's seventeenth-century France or earlier, 'a great while since, a long, long time ago'. The effect of this minor-modal coda is distinctly chilling. A breath of cold wind from the steppes dismisses Beauty's awakening as itself a dream, or at least as no more than evanescent, for she (and we) will die again. As the theatre lights dim, theatrical illusion disperses, admitted to be such. When we emerge into the darkness of the city streets, what our eyes blink at is neither, like the Mazurka, merry nor, like the Rose Adagio, serene.

Tchaikovsky's purely instrumental music is not overtly Orphic as is *The Sleeping Beauty,* though it frequently has affinities with that seminal work. This is true of the last and best of his symphonies, the *Pathétique*, written in the same year as the ballet. In the traditionally 'suffering' key of B minor, this symphony is frankly autobiographical and is content to accept, even to rejoice in, its 'balletic' structure. Whereas Tchaikovksy had been wont to apologise for his alleged deficiencies in teutonic symphonic technique, he is now aware that his strengths are inseparable from his theatricality, whereby personal neurosis is projected into action that could be, even though it is not, danced and mimed.

The symphony has the traditional four movements, though not in the usual sequence. The first movement consists of an adagio Introduction and sonata allegro. The first sound is a cavernous undulation on solo bassoon, piercing a chromatic descent on double basses. The undulation has physical presence; we don't need to be told that Tchaikovsky is the supreme composer of the dance, at least since Rameau, to recognise in the phrase a bodily gesture. We still respond corporeally when, in the Allegro, the phrase is converted into an upward thrust followed by sighing appoggiatures: the energy of which bounces into scintillating semiquavers scored with the lucidity characteristic of Tchaikovsky's theatre music. The first subject group climaxes with the appoggiaturas, now metrically aggressive on brass; simmers to a burble of semiquavers around the dominant of the relative major; and so ushers in the second subject, a song as spaciously serene as the first subject had been frenetic. Though the second subject is related to the first, which it inverts and expands, it is emotionally at the opposite pole; if we think of it in relation to the Sleeping Beauty's Rose Adagio we will recognise that this song is love fulfilled *in dream*. Evolving spaciously, it gathers into itself the animated motives of the first group, and is repeated, more fully scored, in thrilling octaves with throbbing triplet accompaniment. Slowly, it dies to silence. The two subjects, Reality and Dream, cannot heal the emotional breach between them. Tchaikovsky makes, and needs to make, no attempt to imitate the methods of Beethoven.

The development is not accurately so described: the subsided song is merely swept away by a tornado. In explosive fortissimo the first subject's 'undulation' returns to be bandied in many keys through various sections of the orchestra, precisely fierce, scored with a clarity that still 'projects' theatrically. The Song appears only in the form of a falling scale derived from its opening tones, now sounding savagely martial rather than love-lorn. The restatement of the Song in the tonic major anneals without being final; and the coda, still in the major over a descending pizzicato bass, is calm yet not resolved, since the heart-easing song is now no more than a falling scale. The Sleeping Beauty's awakening has proved itself a dream: of which the second movement provides another instance since, a lop-sided valse in 5/4, it is unadulaterated ballet music. The key is the relative major, as is that of the first movement's Song. The stepwise-flowing tune ends in a little kick in dotted rhythm, irresistible to legs, arms and body. The trio is darker, though still in D major, over an unremitting tonic pedal. The effect is trance-like, inducive of some magical transformation, had the music a theatrical dimension.

The second movement thus releases the dualism of the first in graceful physicality. The third is also corporeal action, for it is a march, with a tune precipitated out of the kick at the end of the lop-sided valse. At first the march sounds like rapidly-flickering, Mendelssohnic fairy music, with strings diaphanously scored in eight parts, in antiphony with woodwind. But the march tune is also grotesque, incorporating a descending scale that stems from the 'savage' development of the first movement's song. Formally, the march is a rondo in which the episodes affect the recurrences of the tune. A chromatically-thrusting motif, ironically in E major, mediant to the basic C, drives the fairies crazy, turning them into gibbering hobgoblins – 'bad' fairies no doubt in the service of the malignant Carabosse. The climax blows up in whizzing scales in contrary motion and the march is recapitulated in tutti, farcically raucous, blazing in brass and bludgeoning with timpani. The celebrated scoring at the end provokes spontaneous cheers, but is scary as well as jubilant. Here Tchaikovsky's orchestral complements Liszt's pianistic virtuosity; both are necromancers as well as actors. Carried to such a theatrical extreme, however, this exhibitionism can be no more than a mad and temporary evasion of introspection: which returns in the inspissated gloom of the final Adagio Lamentoso, both structurally and thematically related to the first movement. The 'lamenting' appoggiaturas and chromatics of the first theme are again juxtaposed with a broad, stepwise-moving song in the relative major. Again the song explodes in whirling scales, but this time is interrelated to the first theme's chromatics. In the coda, over a syncopated tonic pedal, song is reduced once more to a declining scale, sinking into sepulchral depths of the orchestra, whence that bassoon undulation had originally crept.

So the Sleeping Beauty cannot be revivified in the Sixth Symphony. Repeatedly she raises her lovely head to sing her D major love-chant, but her Orpheus-Prince (Tchaikovsky himself?) cannot give her the kiss of life. Finally she subsides into muddily labyrinthine depths. The neuroticism of this quintessentially Romantic artist bears interestingly on his universal popularity. No one was more aware of the division between dream and reality, ballet and symphony, yet achieved, through technical virtuosity, so controlled an expression of their interdependence. Tchaikovsky spells out the common man's Orphic dream with a precision that neither Hollywood nor the telly can hope to match. Rachmaninov and Puccini are other 'neurotic' artists who rival Tchaikovsky in this respect, though perhaps neither has quite his archetypal punch.

It is not surprising that the theatrical elements in Tchaikovsky Sixth have overt operatic associations. The Song of the first movement resembles Don José's D flat aria from *Carmen*, an opera Tchaikovsky much admired – and envied, since it combined Mediterranean passion with lucidity in a manner that he erroneously thought to be beyond him. Similarly, the semiquaver figuration in the first movement recalls the excitation of the bedchamber scene in Verdi's *Otello*, recently first performed and vivid in Tchaikovsky's memory. If that great opera is very much about 'reality', it is also about self-deceit, and in that sense self-illusion and self-indulgence. Tchaikovsky's dreams, reanimating dead Beauty-Eurydice, implied a visual-aural imagination of exceptional acuity. More commonly, dream will come to seem a cheat, the more so as the rampant industrialism of the nineteenth century began to impose its mechanistic and mercantile values on human beings.

Tchaikovsky's ballets were mimed dreams of human perfectability here on earth, belatedly harking back to the court masques of France's *grand siècle*, when men and women kidded themselves into the belief that paradise, symbolised in the *cortesia* of their dances, was already achieved or just round the corner. That dream did not survive harsh realities, as we saw in tracing its evolution through Rameau's latent and patent ironies to Gluck's pre-Revolutionary metamorphosis into socially democratic terms. When once Revolution had happened, one of two things resulted in musical-theatrical arts: either dream as escape became a substitute *for* reality, as in the danced and musicked mime of Tchaikovsky; or human perfectability was debunked in a cult of hedonism and cynicism, as in the comic operas of Rossini. In France there is a gradual declension from the never-never-land beauties of Watteau, who live in a dream within the heart, to the saucily fleshy nymphs of Boucher, who are painted on the bedroom wall, to the Second Empire queens with their tinsel crowns and paste pearls that become the more meretricious the more they are marketable.

In Offenbach, low priest of the music theatres of the Second

Empire which was a travesty of the First, the aristocracy of money attempts to buy up paradise in what is literally a vulgarisation – a making common – of the heroic ideal. The climax to human endeavour is the justification of adultery for reasons of State: 'il faut bien que l'on s'a.nuse' or one will go mad with tedium and so bring Civilisation to ruin. The effrontery is as superb as the abandon of the music; but it springs from an awareness of the abyss. It is significant that Offenbach ended his career with a 'serious' opera – *Les Contes d'Hoffman* – about a magician who can simulate life.

Since this is an Orphic myth, we are not surprised to discover that in mid-career (1858) Offenbach made his own version of the Orpheus story, with a libretto by Hector Crémieux tuned to his age's insouciance. He inverts the classical precedents. Orpheus's lyre, the gift of Apollo the Sun-God who should encourage man's intellectual and spiritual aspiration, is, in the more crudely seductive guise of a café violin, conspicuously ineffective in the hands of his Orphée, a fashionable music teacher in Thebes. Singing self-congratulatory pyrotechnics to his facilely exhibitionistic fiddle, he bores Eurydice to distraction with his hour and a half long (café) concert(o), though he fails to 'bore the pants off her', which was undoubtedly his intention. She, in comparable inversion, is hardly ravished by Aristeus, her alternative lover (and Orphée's half-brother), though she finds him 'ravishing' in the colloquial sense and *falls* for him – also in the colloquial as well as literal sense – heavily. The serpent that bites her is a farcical revival of the old metaphor that equates sexual orgasm with dying. The minx Eurydice reveals her besotted passion – one might jollily call it lust – for Aristeus in her ludicrously ornamented *couplet* (the technical term is again an appropriate metaphor), enhanced by girlish giggles on piccolo. She doesn't know that she is indeed in love with easeful Death, though it transpires that Aristeus is Pluto in lamb's clothing: a god of death who in his disguise as bee-keeper and shepherd sings mellifluously Arcadian café music. He is the honey of corruption: literally so, if one recalls that promiscuous abandonment to the sensual-sexual moment, in the Second Empire as in any 'decadent' society, offered fertile soil for syphilitic infection. Momently, however, Eurydice is happy to 'die' in his arms. The dying is and is not metaphorical: not 'real' in so far as it is a sexual orgasm, real in so far as Aristeus is now identified with Pluto.

Orpheus, in this amoral world, himself has an alternative lover, a

shepherdess cornily called Chloe. When Eurydice goes off with Aristeus for a naughty weekend in Hades, Orpheus is not at all disturbed,
though he decides that he ought to reclaim her for forms sake; Public
Opinion, which appears recurrently in cynical travesty of the Greek
chorus, would expect as much. When he solicits Jupiter's help it
becomes apparent that the gods are the mortals writ (not very) large.
But whereas in classical antiquity this had served to boost humanity,
in Offenbach it cuts the gods down to our paltry size. It fits with the
cult of hedonism that the gods' Revolutionary Chorus is occasioned by
boredom and epicurianism; weary of ambrosia and nectar, they
demand a more varied and Parisian diet. The be-*littling* of the gods is
neatly encapsulated in Jupiter's ruse to get a peep at Eurydice, who
has proved so attractive to mere mortals: he transforms himself into a
miniscule mosquito – another creature that nips – in order to get past
John Styx, Offenbach's Charon, guardian of the underworld, and to
creep through the keyhole of her bedroom. Sexual metaphors are still
rife; and this sex seems successful, since she is as delighted with him as
is he with her. So Jupiter ensures that Orpheus will break his vow by
hurling a thunderbolt at him. Startled, Orpheus looks back; and
Eurydice has no hesitation in staying with Jupiter for a (jovial) happy-
ever-after. Orphée, *faute de mieux*, returns to his earthy Chloe. The
immoral moral is that pie in the sky should be gobbled up while it's
going. Pluto, Death himself, is given a celebration party, with a
Hymn to Bacchus more momently enlivening, though hardly less
crass, than the Bacchic revels at the end of the 1480 *Orfeo*.

   Orpheus in the Underworld comes out as a punning title, a pun being
itself an illusion. Its 'underworld' of thugs, tycoons, whores and
pimps has no supernatural dimension; indeed the plot and characters
were pointed with contemporary references which at this date cannot
easily be disentangled. The *opéra bouffe* tells us that this is the best we
can hope for, 'in this day and age', in emulating the classical
humanist's concept of man as god. Today, social conventions serve
sensual appetite; public opinion can be manufactured – and this long
before the reign of the 'media' – so that no public truth is possible;
everything is sacrificed to money. The glamour that surrounds the
apparatus of material power is mocked out of existence; and against
this mockery the only 'positive' seems to be the ultimate negation of
oblivion – a point plumbing deeper than Offenbach may have
realised. For the Charon figure, John Styx, at least once had a True
Love in Arcady: but 'that was in another country; and besides, the

wench is dead'. As compared with the champagne-quaffing, mind-lessly-fornicating denizens of High Society he is alone, and a back-number: a dim-witted, inefficient guardian of Lethe who when alive had been king of the notoriously stupid, provincially bumpkin Boe-tians. He too *boasts*, pathetically, of how 'once upon a time' he was sexually attractive; and momentarily the pathos of his air – in A major, key of youth and innocence – touches the heart. The feeling is as fleeting as must be the hedonistic excess in which everyone attempts to live; but it is real – perhaps uniquely so in this operetta – while it lasts.

Nemesis comes when, after the Hymn to Bacchus, Society dances a sedate, old-style minuet, pretending that the glamour of the court of Louis XV, if not the palmier days of Louis XIV, might be recover-able. In ultimate metamorphosis this minuet turns into a *Galop Infernale*: no Arcadian revel but a Dionysiac and Bacchic orgy that demotes Apollo in resuscitating the post-Revolutionary can-can. The commercial motif has become patent in Offenbach, who wrote for the bourgeois aristocracy whose power derived not from titular right but from high finance, and whose emergence we commented on in reference to Rameau's *Pygmalion* and *Platée*. Offenbach's theme is prostitution, in one form or another; we are merry because we are rich, melancholy because our earnings are immoral. Hell is without as well as 'within us'; we gallop into it in welcoming delirium.

Although Offenbach's *Orphée aux Enfers* would seem to be the polar opposite to Tchaikovsky's *Sleeping Beauty* in that it eschews the balletic dream for the cynical present moment, it depends on its own denial of reality. 'Up to the minute', immediately in touch with social life here and now, it generates a zest that can be indulged in only by obliterating the natural impulses of the heart: which is why the brittle shell of frivolity hides emotion both gloomy and cruel. Offenbach's strength is that although, teetering on the edge of an abyss, he was afraid in his life – he had the socialite's pathological fear of solitude – he was in his art-entertainment unafraid. Offenbach's music admits that life is not really an eternal can-can; we only have to pretend it is, if we are to survive. Whereas Tchaikovsky deals in our common dreams, Offenbach celebrates our commoner appetites; and discovers that they may be as frightening as they are powerful. This core of bitter honesty within pretence is not maintained by lesser, especially later, composers of 'light' music, among whom we may number Gilbert and Sullivan: whose zest is milder and whose dream is cosier, though the cruelty, if blunted, is still present.

Orpheus debunked left his legacy of frivolity and petulance to the increasingly machine-dominated societies of the later nineteenth and early twentieth centuries, producing ultimately a near-total severance of Art from Entertainment. Machine arts have their own resilience, enlivening as well as damping the body politic. None the less Entertainment, as separate from Art, tends to induce amnesia, which becomes almost total in today's 'Muzak'. Compensatorily, Art may get too big for its boots, attempting to take the place of religion. We noted the first stirrings of this in the Orphic theme in Beethoven, who was himself *not* too big for his boots. Wagner as Orpheus possibly was, though he was justified in regarding himself as Beethoven's successor and is, as is commonly accepted by the history books, the essential gateway from the nineteenth into the twentieth century. Musically, he discovers a new Orphic relationship between Dionysos and Apollo: whose splintered state is to be the central preoccupation of Igor Stravinsky, probably the greatest and certainly the most 'representative' composer of our time.

Chapter VII

Orpheus in the waste land

The Apollonian and the Dionysiac in the New Song of
Tristan's shepherd: Dionysos and Apollo in Stravinsky's
Petrouchka (1911), *Rite of Spring* (1913); *Soldier's Tale*
(1918), *Apollon Musagètes* (1928); *Perséphone* (1934) and
Orpheus (1948)

From his earliest years as an opera composer Wagner pursued the
theme of the Hero's quest and redemption, latent in Mozart's *Die
Zauberflote* and Beethoven's *Fidelio*; the process grows more 'inward'
through the sequence of *The Flying Dutchman*, *Tannhäuser*, *Lohengrin*, and *The Ring of the Nibelung*. By this time introversion has
become complete in the sense that the operas are a revelation of what
we would call Jungian archetypes within the psyche: to which a more
autobiographical twist is given in *Tristan* and *Parsifal*. Wagner's
music is now both an implosion and explosion in European consciousness; those very harmonic tensions which 'Europe' had evolved to
embody our consciousness of self existing in time end in time's
obliteration. The chromatic deliquesence, the creation of leitmotivic
polyphony from the 'spreading' of vertical chords, the use of the
sequence as simultaneous aspiration and frustration – all these
Tristanesque techniques are identified with the opera's mythological
theme.

Wagner took the Tristan story from Europe's Middle Ages, when
the modern world was in labour and the old in its death-throes.
Tristan's name means 'triste'; he was born out of death, suffered the
wound of duality, and died into life, ending the egotistic cycle of
humanism. *Tristan* is a climax to the punning equation between death
and sexual consummation that we have seen to dog European history,
for sexual energy is what man is left with when the trappings of
civilisation have been discarded. *Tristan's* passion-laden chromatic
harmony carries the burden of our hundreds of years of purgatorial
aspiration, suffering, strife and guilt; and returns them to unconscious nirvana. The self cannot sustain the lacerations of passion in the
conditions of the temporal world: so the light of conscious Day, which

a Gluck or a Haydn had laboured to disseminate, must be snuffed out
by unconscious Night, as the sea of orchestral harmony engulfs
Tristan and ourselves. It is worth noting that the water metaphor grew
increasingly potent through nineteenth-century romaticism, from the
arpeggiated caresss of Schumann's cradling amniotic waters to the
sensual swaying of Chopin's Venetian *Barcarolle,* from Wagner's
immense empy sea to Delius's *Sea Drift,* at the end of which the
appoggiaturas that aurally image the breaking waves irresistibly suggest a new-born infant's wail. Not for nothing are *mer* and *mère*
etymologically related.

For Wagner-Tristan the moment of truth comes when he admits to
his (and our) guilt; it was 'I myself' who brewed the portion, and we
can no longer hand over responsibility to God or State. Wagner
dramatises on a stage what had been implicit in late Beethoven's
'absolute' music: the precise moment being instigated at the opening
of *Tristan*'s third act, when the ripe swell of harmonic tensions – the
climax to the dualistic process that had begun with the 'invention' of
harmony in the Renaissance – begins to evaporate, and Tristan is
awakened from near-paralysis, as he lies prone in his gangrened,
cobwebby castle, by the *monody* of a shepherd's pipe. The cavernous
orchestral sonority, still traditionally anchored on 'infernal' F minor,
evokes the 'labyrinthine' depths to which Tristan, undergoing what
we would call a nervous breakdown, has surrendered. But the ripe
sonorities also heal the agony of the upward thrusting appoggiaturas,
while the *rising* dissonances free the higher strings so that, alchemising
chromatic tension into whole-tone and enharmonic release, they float
upwards from the dark sea into the empty air. What had been prefi-
gured in the last bars of Liszt's Piano Sonata and of his *Orpheus* is
consummated in the shepherd's solo cantillation, played on primitively wailing cor anglais, anonymously and from afar.

The tune the shepherd pipes is a horizontalised, linear version of
the interlocked perfect and imperfect fourths and fifths (traditionally
musical symbols for God and Devil) which, in the first bars of the
opera, had made Tristan's anguish incarnate. His anguish, indeed, is
human duality: which is at last released in the Shepherd's monody, at
first sounding quasi-oriental in its self-rotating chromaticism but
becoming, in his 'New Song' when Isolde's sail is finally sighted,
almost purely pentatonic. Triston's shepherd thus reverses the
Orphic myth. He is a primitively Dionysiac being who through his
primitively non-harmonic music reanimates moribund Modern Man,

promoting what we would call Freudian regeneration, from which life and consciousness are reborn. But the awakening, like that of the Sleeping Beauty, is momentary, achieved only by submission to the death instinct; and when Tristan has died Isolde, as Great Mother and *Anima*, completes the regenerative redemption Mozart's Pamina had promised to Tamino, hymning in her *Liebstod* the equation of Love and Death. The difference is that Mozart expected regeneration and redemption to become manifest in the world, which for Wagner seemed no longer possible – though he rejected Monteverdi's cheat of the Hero's stellar apotheosis.

The parable is continued in Wagner's last opera *Parisfal*, in which the wounded Amfortas is Tristan-Wagner, Kundry corresponds to Isolde as Dark Goddess, while 'young' Parsifal is the Orpheus figure and Holy Fool. Wagner regarded *Parsifal* as a Passion ceremony, however ambivalent he may be about the sexual connotations of the Grail legend's lance and cup. It is revealing to consider Bach, Beethoven and Wagner as three progressively de-dogmatised stages in the Passion of Christian Europe. For Bach, an historical Christ-Orpheus-Apollo is still incarnate in his Church, so he may present the Christian story in terms at once dramatic and liturgical, confident that his public will understand the relevance of Christ's Passion to their lives. Beethoven was a Promethean hero who lived through his passions and Passion in his music, himself becoming the Christ-Orpheus-Dionysos-Apollo whom he, like Blake, believed to be potential in every man: 'Jesus Christ *is* the Human Imagination'. His supreme greatness lies in the fact that the Second Adam is born in the 'becoming' which is his last sonatas and quartets, and the vision we glimpse through that music is the closest we are likely to get to paradise.

Wagner too, and more overtly than Beethoven, saw himself as the Modern Hero whose Passion complements Christ's. Moreover, he was not content to work out that Passion in seemingly abstract music, but must project it even more directly than did Bach into a opera-house that is also a church, and into an art form wherein poetry, having meaning within rational concepts, complements music, which has substance but no rational meaning, while the visual elements are rendered dynamic through music. Although Wagner was wrong in thinking he had created *the* art form of the future, he was genuinely prophetic, and no composer, not even Beethoven, has been more widely and deeply influential. Yet there is a paradox here:

for Wagner's Dionysiac impact celebrates a failure, however heroic. The god that he worships in his opera-house church is the human ego; and that is a god which, after long travail, had failed. Though *The Twilight of the Gods* is a rediscovery of our archetypal selves, and we may indeed be godly, the opera *is* none the less a twilight, rather than a vision – as is Beethoven's 'transcendent' Arietta from opus 111 – of a god's resurrection. Valhalla is consumed in the purgatorial flames and, like the Wagnerian sequence, returns to its source beneath the engulfing waters. Orpheus's male Will and Art are subsumed in the female generative principle, a regression which, although necessary, is not an end.

Tristan und Isolde has often been called the beginning of modern music, and is so in a deeper sense than is usually intended. For the disintegrating chromatics and the shepherd's almost-oriental sounding monody, allied with the immensely slow rhythmic-harmonic pulse of *Parsifal*, usher in the twentieth-century revival of music as magic rather than as expression and communication. Debussy's purely monodic *Syrinx* (1913) for solo flute reinstates the flute in its original Panic and Dionysiac associations before it was appropriated by eighteenth-century Enlightenment; while even in his palpably harmonic music Debussy used Wagnerian chords divorced from temporal relationships, allowing them to exist without antecedence and consequence. Between Debussy's liberation of the chord and Stravinsky's liberation of rhythm there is a deep affinity, for both deprive music of the sense of progression. It is no accident that these two profoundly 'representative' twentieth-century composers created their most seminal works just before or during that First World War that may mark the beginning of the end of Western Civilisation as we have known it.

Stravinsky takes us back to the starting point of this book, for his long life's work was based on a dichotomy of extreme violence between Dionysos and Apollo. He has been representative by turning his back on most of the assumptions that makes us what we are, thereby suggesting that we are subconsciously distrustful of the beliefs on which we have been nurtured. The Stravinskian dubiety is also ours, only his art's admission of it is more honest, less afraid, than most of us can hope to be. We live at the end of an era that, starting with the Renaissance, has been founded on man's presumed ability to control his destiny through Orphic reason and the power over nature that reason may give us. Nature includes human nature;

and post-Renaissance art has been largely based on the belief that man, through the Orphic ordering of his passions, may influence the emotions and ultimately the behaviour of other people. Stravinsky never accepted music as expression and communication in this sense, and his Russian ancestry goes some way to explain this since Russia, swinging from tribal ancestry and feudal hierarchy into the modern world, bypassed the Renaissance.

True, Stravinsky's teacher was Rimsky-Korsakov, least 'primitive' and most European of the Russian masters, and his early works, notably the *Firebird* ballet of 1909, follow Rimsky in exploring Russian fairy-tale worlds with extreme orchestral virtuosity; fabulous pre-history is reincarnated in the artifice of mime, and in the sonorous resources of a mammoth symphony orchestra. But whereas Rimsky-Korsakov never graduated beyond fairy artifice, the young Stravinsky was made of sterner metal. His reasons for leaving Russia may not have been basically artistic, but the consequences of his exile were culturally far-reaching. Settled in Paris, he unconsciously explored the relevance of White Russian primitivism to 'Europe' and the modern world. This begins to happen in *Petrouchka* (1911), which has a significant affinity with the fairground limbo of Satie's *Parade*. Stravinsky's ballet, set in a Russian peasant society brilliantly evoked in the orchestra's hurdygurdy sonorities, presents Petrouchka as a Russian Pierrot who is, like Schoenberg's lunar Pierrot of 1913, or Debussy's Pierrot *fâché avec la lune*, or the pierrots and harlequins of Picasso, a puppet Orpheus, shut out from the world he was born into, yet unable to possess new realms of consciousness. Peasant has become puppet, struggling towards a 'Western', unpeasant-like awareness through his love for the ballerina Columine who, dancing her Lanner waltzes, is the sophisticated world in decay; and he is destroyed, or perhaps saved, depending on one's point of view, by a bestially Dionysiac Moor whose music is both orgiastic and oriental. Most of the elements of Stravinsky's subsequent work are here: the time-and-place travelling between primivitism and sophistication, between East and West, the equivocation between tragedy and farce, between Nature and Nurture.

Although the Chaplinesque Puppet-Pierrot is murdered, it appears that he has an embryonic soul. Scared by his ghost, the Showman-Charlatan – a mechanised god-figure parallel to the Managers in Satie's *Parade* – nervously drops the body and scuttles off to a bitonal snarl of trumpets on triads a devilish tritone apart (C and F sharp).

Petrouchka's alienation from an insentate world is thus neatly auralised, and perhaps, as with Schoenberg's *Pierrot Lunaire,* the
'alienated' un-hero is being identified with his creator. The first stage
in the puppet's regeneration is to accept the Blackamoor's bestiality as
potentially his own, and a virtue. Dionysos must be reinstated: which
is what happens in Stravinsky's next major work, which made him an
international celebrity overnight.

Written on the eve of that First World War, Stravinsky's *Rite of
Spring* (1913) is at once a fertility rite and a sacrificial murder.
Although its savagery may be destructive, like the war, it is also
constructive in that, returning to the wellsprings of life, it hints that
the 'consciousness' that had led Europe to this pass might be dispen-
sed with, at least temporarily. So Stravinsky, using the stylised gestures of ballet mime and the paraphernalia of an enormous symphony
orchestra, itself a product of industrial technocracy and the capitalism
that had made it feasible, explores a source of strength which he, as a
Russian, possessed but which Western man had relinquished. This
was not something about which Western man could be indifferent
though he might, as the scenes at the first performance testify, be
scared to the brink of hysteria. At this point we can hear how the
destructive sadism of *The Rite of Spring* is inseparable from its
vernally Persephonean renewal. Moreover we can now see that
although Stravinsky's rite is violent whereas Debussy's music is non-
violent, these two revolutionary composers are allied both technically
and imaginatively. Both use short hypnotic phrases, often pentatonic,
in incantatory repetition; both employ static harmonies to produce
effects as much oriental as occidental. Stravinsky's rhythms are
corporeally energetic, whereas Debussy's tend to trance-inducing
passivity; yet since Stravinsky's rhythms are hypnotically repetitive,
they too destroy the temporal sense, occasionally breaking into
complex, ecstasy-inducing metres similar to those in real primitive
musics. Furthermore Stravinsky, in using the orchestra as a gigantic
percussion band that deprives individual instruments of their melodic
and harmonic identities, creates an effect analogous to Debussy's
atmospheric 'cocoon' of sound. This is true of rowdily orgiastic
passages as well as of the nocturnal interludes, such as the weirdly
wonderful piece that introduces the Persephonean dance of adolescent girls.

The blazing ferocity of Stravinsky's Rite still stuns us, though we
recognise that in being danced in a theatre and played on a symphony

orchestra it is 'true' only imaginatively. We are not in fact engaged in sacrificial murder, and would be locked up if we were – despite the mass murders about to be perpetrated in the War. In his next ballet (*The Wedding*, composed in 1914–15 *during* that war), Stravinsky tries to put death behind him and to concentrate on the life ritual of a peasant wedding, not now in 'pre-historic' but in feudal Russia. His singers simulate but do not quote real peasant tunes, while his orchestra of pianos and percussion creates the illusion of a peasant band. Even so, the visible band is attired in modern evening dress, for this wedding is not for real, any more than is the Rite's murder. We can understand why Stravinsky, like his predecessor Tchaikovsky, was throughout his life obsessed by ballet as an art of mime and mask; he in fact made a fairy ballet, called *The Fairy's Kiss*, on a theme related to *The Sleeping Beauty*, out of a ragbag of Tchaikovsky's music. Both *The Wedding* and *The Rite of Spring* are games of let's pretend: which reveal truths about ourselves we might otherwise sweep under the carpet. *The Rite*, embracing the Persephone story, contains the prospect of Spring's renewal; *The Wedding*, fusing pagan with Christian concepts, offers hope of redemption. Though it functions vocally by way of primitively incremental repetition and instrumentally by unremitting percussive metre, it attains consummation when at last the hubbub ceases and the lover, approaching his Sleeping Beauty in the silence of the night, becomes Tchaikovsky's Fairy Prince, chanting in bell-haloed pentatonic *monody*. This is one of the great Orphic moments in twentieth-century music.

But the burden of consciousness cannot be brushed aside by a mere revocation of the primitive springs of life. That Stravinsky was aware of this is indicated by a theatre-piece he wrote at the end of the war, in 1918. *The Soldier's Tale* is not a Diaghilev ballet calling on the sumptuous resources of capitalist civilisation to tell a tale that emotionally undermines the Western world that made it economically possible. It is rather conceived in the spirit of improvised street theatre, and was written in neutral Switzerland, where Stravinsky had retired 'for the duration'. Dramatically, the piece calls on several widely disseminated folk tales; specifically it fuses aspects of the Orpheus and Sleeping Beauty legends with the story of Faust which, more than any other, incarnates the myth of Western man, striving towards consciousness, and even willing to sell his soul for the power it may offer. Although Stravinsky is not 'on the side of' Faust, he no longer pretends that he can be discounted.

The story is told by a narrator who speaks and never sings, sitting outside the action. The parts of the Peasant-Soldier Faust and of the Devil are mimed and danced; the band is a septet very close in disposition to that of the New Orleans jazz band. The primitive element typical of *The Rite* and *The Wedding* is thus sophisticated into music which, although African based, was a creation of the impact of a white New World on black sources. Transitions between 'Europe' and the primitive occur spontaneously, since the New Orleans band had Africanised the snatches of Italian opera, French quadrille, Spanish tango and white American march and hymn that melled in that cosmopolitan city. To the grittily cheery sound of the New Orleans band Stravinsky gives a more astringent edge, exploiting jazz not so much for its intrinsic qualities as for its negative capabilities. This is the beginning of his turning away from primitivism, or at least from unqualified acceptance of it. In treating jazz satirically as well as satyrically he recognises that neo-primitivism, though necessary, was not enough.

At the beginning of the piece the Soldier-Faust is trudging down a country road, returning 'home' to Mother and native village. He plays his violin in jazzy vivacity to help him on his way, the double stops and syncopations having the virility of European folk fiddle as much as of Negro jazz. He meets the Devil in the guise of a butterfly-trapping lepidopteralist, the Soldier being one of the butterflies. Only at the end does the Devil appear in his own shape; mostly he wears the masks of the World and Flesh, in which neither we nor the Soldier recognise him. As usual the Devil is effectively seductive and the Soldier, lured by prospects of material gain, sells him his violin, which is his soul, in exchange for a magic book (How to Get Rich in Ten Easy Lessons) offering short-cuts to money and power. Acquiring both, the Soldier meets the Devil in the form of a vulgarly opulent cattle-dealer and a superannuated whore. His spiritual degeneration parallels his material advancement until, with the help of the Narrator who abandons his neutrality to save a soul, he deliberately loses one of those traditional card games with the Devil, regains his violin, and potentially his happiness.

He resumes his pilgrimage back home to Mother: and to a sick Princess who is also a Sleeping Beauty, like to die of the Soldier-Faust's apparent capitulation to evil. Reborn, the Soldier becomes Orpheus to this Sleeping Beauty, playing her a sequence of dances of variously ethnic character – Latin American tango, French valse or

German waltz, American ragtime, all vivacious, if dry and chippy. She recovers from her sleepy sickness; but at this stage Stravinsky abruptly dismisses the Orpheus motif as wish-fulfilment, returning to the Faustian *denouement* of damnation. The Devil reappears in a flurry of fire and brimstone, with pointed ears, cloven hoof and flailing tail. He has repossessed the soul-violin on which, himself a notorious fiddler, he scrapes a *Marche de triomphe*. The Soldier totters after him, impotent, as the music becomes anti-jazz, freezing the nerves instead of liberating the body. The nagging of the violin's open strings, which in the Soldier's initial march had had the tense virility of folk fiddle, sounds in the Devil's hands like a rattling of bones; the contractions and ellipses of metre deliver stabs to the solar plexus. At the end we are left with a long percussion cadenza: a skeltonic chitter in which both music – the violin is silenced – and the Soldier are defeated.

The Soldier's Tale comes out as a very wry piece, precipitated from the aftermath of war. Yet a nervy vitality simmers within its dehydration, and its use of the idiom of a New World, though bearing little similarity to the body-energy of real negro jazz, is far from being merely parodistic. The satiric exploitation of European conventions – especially the 'wrong note' harmonisation of Lutheran chorales – proves re-creative as well as destructive: as becomes manifest when, after his return to Paris, Stravinsky embarked on the phase of his career that came to be called neo-classic.

In 1921 T. S. Eliot, an American exile in Europe, wrote in his seminal poem *The Waste Land*: 'These fragments have I shored against my reins'. This is what Stravinsky does as a Russian exile who had become a French citizen. Pillaging fragments from the Apollonian composers of Europe's humanist heyday, he reassembles them with a personal logic relatable to Satie's unexpected collages of traditional materials, as well as to the geometrically cubist order of Picasso's abstract phase, and perhaps to the collocations of disparate cultures in the Cantos of Ezra Pound. Playing down the Dionysiac for the Apollonian, Stravinsky develops the satirical relationships to European traditions he had explored in *The Soldier's Tale* in more positive directions. He finds in Lully, Pergolesi, Bach, Handel, Haydn, Mozart, Clementi, Tchaikovsky or whomever evidence, however fragmented, of what 'Europe' had once meant. The Orphic artist's task is to remake a whole from the dismembered parts, even if he may now do so only through musical and mimetic artifice.

Beneath the time-and-space travelling of his European revocations

Stravinsky remains potently aware of his Russian, pagan primitivism, balancing his Christian heritage: as is evident in one of his greatest works, the opera-oratorio *Oedipus Rex*, composed in the mid-1920s around an uncomfortable classical myth that the hopefully self-confident Heroic Age preferred to ignore. Stravinsky makes a musical-theatrical parable indebted on the one hand to primitive Russian ritual and on the other hand to sophisticated *opera seria* and its affiliated ecclesiastical form, oratorio. The convention of *Oedipus Rex*, with a narrator in modern evening dress framing the stylised music drama set in a hieratic language, Latin, is an inflation of that of *The Soldier's Tale*, and although the latter is satirical and the former tragic, both remind us of the link between the Greek *trageodia* and the satyr. Oedipus is a Faust-figure rendered more pompous and circumstantial; as Western Man inflated to prideful delirium he is given melodies that amalgamate primitive Muscovite incantation, the liturgical chant of the Russian Church, the operatic rhetoric of Monteverdi and Handel, and even the brass-band panache, over an *oompah* bass, of early Verdi. If such music makes us startlingly aware of our bifurcated Dionysiac-Apollonian state, it is, in its energy, the reverse of depressive.

By way of its once notorious eclecticism *Oedipus Rex* makes the classical Oedipus's story ours. The primitive features of the score remind us of our Dionysiac origins; the High Baroque features recall our post-Renaissance pilgrimage towards an Apollonian deification of the Will; while shades of nineteenth-century vulgarisation, in both the strict and the metaphorical senses, hint at our decline. The *other* dimension of quasi-oriental and medieval liturgy points towards an alternative destiny. Stravinsky's genius consists in his having, as our inevitably eclectic spokesman, made sense of twentieth-century nonsense, fusion out of con-fusion. This is why the notorious double dedication of his next major work, the *Symphony of Psalms* (1930), cannot be dismissed as cynicism. The work was 'composed for the glory of God and dedicated to the Boston Symphony Orchestra': which is fair enough since without the mundane orchestra the godly sounds would be inaudible.

Its structure, embracing a toccata-prelude, a double fugue and a finale, seems to be humanistically baroque. 'Neo-baroque' would, however, be an inadequate clue to the music's nature: for in the first movement baroque toccata merges into the motor rhythms and sharp sonorities of Stravinsky's primitive phase, while the textures of the double fugue have a hard linearity that might recall Machaut rather than Bach, were they not *sui generis*. Moreover, the piece is organised in a hierachy of symbolic key relationships as rigorous as those of Bach. C major is God's key – very different in effect from the white C major of the Enlightenment, though it is possible that Stravinsky thought the parallel between whiteness and super-human purity appropriate. E flat major is man's key, and it is again appropriate that in European classical music E flat had been a key of power (the *Eroica* Symphony). Phrygian E minor serves an intercessory key of prayer, the E natural sometimes acting as major third to God's, sometimes becoming enharmonically identical with F flat as appoggiatura to man's E flat. The extraordinary self-rotating God-theme in the fugue is a horizontalised version of the 'intercessory' figuration of the Prelude, and is god-like in auralising the metaphor of the serpent swallowing its own tail. Man's theme, starting from godly fourths, *falls* in fallible chromatics, with more humanly – sometimes even Bachian – harmonic implications. The total effect is a synthesis of the corybantic fervour of pre-historic Russia, the humanism of the European Baroque, and the liturgical spirituality of the Russian Orthodox Church.

These inter-relationships become explicit in the finale, which is both a ritual invocation and a hymn. At its end, over an ostinato of fourths, swinging like an immense censer, the vocal lines become almost static, noodling around pedal points. Yet the 'added notes' in the texture create a wondrously succulent, scrunchy sound, like rising sap; and as the Psalmist's words tell us that the Lord has put a New Song into his mouth, the melodies are liberated in wide-leaping ecstasy. Along with its Christian connotations, this is a Rite of Spring; Dionysos and Apollo are mated on equal terms, and for modern man, not merely for Stravinsky as our spokesman, the primitive depths 'below' consciousness, the human force of reason, and the priestly preoccupation with musical metaphysics prove inseparable.

Thus the first movement, though it resembles a baroque toccata and *da capo* aria, behaves more like corporeal ritual music in its rhythmic energy, and more like liturgical incantation in its quasi-monodic lines. Yet it clearly is not ritual dance or ecclesiastical ceremony, for neither its physically not its spirituality is fulfilled. The motor rhythms are disrupted, the melodies caged. Similarly the double fugue is double because it is about division within the psyche; its segregated God and Man themes are complementary aspects of human consciousness, which have become dissociated, that dissociation being our modern dilemma. During the double fugue the two poles finally meet, though the marriage is not easy, as the Byzantine terror of the climax demonstrates magnificently. Never the less, the marriage is consummated: so in the finale barbaric Dionysos and civilised Appolo are one, until in the sustained lyrical periods of the coda the metre beats in a rhythm no longer motorised, but tidal like the ocean and steady as the turning earth.

During his neo-classic phase Stravinsky composed three works – two ballets and a *mélodrame* – dealing directly with the Orpheus myth. The earliest of them, *Apollon Musagètes* (1928), concerns the rediscovery of Apollo as sequel to the Dionysiac Rite and Wedding. Stravinsky uses the convention of masque as a mask, taking as his model the five-part string orchestra of Lully, state composer to Louis XIV, Sun King at the peak of European humanism. Though the music, springing from bodily movement, is physical, it is austere in its string sonorities: which were visually matched by the black and white decor. The idiom is basically French, most Apollonianly civilised of cultures, though the classical French gestures of Lully merge into the romantic (French-derived) ballet-style of Russian Tchaikovsky. The dance-ritual of humanism is Orphically metamorphosed into the religion of Art, which is simultaneously reality and illusion.

The story, in so far as there is one, recounts how Apollo, the civilising force of reason, proportion and harmony, is the necessary catalyst if man is to create art from Dionysiac instinct. The Prologue, *Nuissance d'Apollon*, is in white C major and is pervaded by the heroic dotted rhythm of the Lullian overture. The spacious phrases rise in open arpeggios, the sonority is luminous: the more so when tonality shifts, rather than modulates, to the upper mediant, heavenly E major. The arpeggiated phrases soar, though the dotted rhythm anchors them to a tonic pedal. When Apollo 'vient au monde' the ceremonial slow introduction is succeeded, according to Lullian precedent, by a rapid dance for the 'apparition des deux déesses', beginning in dorian E minor. The violin melody leaps, almost cavorts, as the arpeggios are expanded, and scale figurations bounce over a pizzicato accompaniment. Balletic Lully is here fused with the dancing Tchaikovsky, the theme anticipating the New Song in the last movement of the *Symphony of Psalms*. It sounds still more lyrically and rhythmically fulfilled when it is taken up by cellos as the goddesses greet the new-born god, crowning him with a white girdle and offering him nectar and ambrosia, the traditional food of the gods that Offenbach's materialistic divine beings had had a surfeit of. The quick middle section ends in slightly savage offbeat sforzandi, recalling Stravinsky's Dionysiac roots. The *da capo* of the ceremonial section is shortened yet still more spacious, with the original E major arpeggios over a dotted rhythmed pedal now in white C major. The texture glows. The harmony of the coda, though mainly diatonic concords, often telescopes tonic, dominant and subdominant, transforming those norms of progression in European music into timeless moments. This, more than any other technical feature, conditions the characteristic 'scrunchy' sound of neo-classic Stravinsky: at once earthy and airy.

In the second tableau Apollo assumes the role of Orpheus, personified by solo violin, playing at first unaccompanied, in free rhythm, with the vernal sonorities Stravinsky explores in his near-contemporary Violin Concerto. The solo cadenza leads into a slow dance in 2/8, starting in G minor then freely modulating. The Lullian dotted rhythm persists, though the affinity with the ballet music of Tchaikovsky is now unmistakable. Rameau is the first great composer of European dance, Tchaikovsky the second, Stravinsky the third; and Stravinsky combines Rameau's earthy zest with Tchaikovsky's sensuous ideality, as we may hear in the *pas d'action* wherein Apollo-Orpheus invokes the three muses, Calliope, Polymnie, and Terpsichore. His song-dance animates them in a hierarchy of three different tempi over an absolutely regular 2/2 pulse. The basic tonality is B flat major, and it may be that this key, a tone lower than C major, has here the associations it had for Lully and the Heroic Age, when it was both pastoral and earthy, possibly because in the Renaissance two flats had been the flattest, lowest transposition permitted in vocal modality. If this reveals the corporeality of dance, the Apollonian 'head' still dominates. The *pas d'action* ends by repeating the original material in inverse order; art is dependent on conscious intellectual discipline.

Three 'variations' follow, allotted to Calliope, Polymnie and Terpsichore respectively, each muse performing a dance appropriate to her, rigorously disciplined by the conventions of her art. Literary Calliope's dance is built on the poetic alexandrine, and Stravinsky appends a quotation from French classicist Boileau: 'Que toujours dans vos vers le sense coupant les mots Suspende l'hémistiche et marque le repos'. The 9/8 rhythm lilts through arpeggiated figures

moving from B flat minor to D minor. A brief 'middle' in D minor-
major broadens the tempo to 3/4 and Russianises classical metrics in a
'dolce cantabile' tune on cello, based on the Alexandrine of Pushkin.
Polymnie's variant veers between D, G and A majors, encapsulating
tonics, dominants and subdominants. Pattering semiquavers energise
the thinly scored music which, especially towards the end, sounds like
rarefied, intellectualised Tchaikovsky. The coda moves briefly
flatwards but cadences, after appoggiatura-trills on A sharp, in dulcet
G major. Terpsichore's variant, being that of the dancer, returns to
the heroic dotted rhythm and hints remotely at the theme of the
overture, recalling too the radiant E major of the overture's middle
section. Climax arrives with Apollo's own variant, which is rather
grand, sturdily masculine in the white lydian mode, though its string
sonority is strikingly Tchaikovskyan. Controlled direction leads
towards emotional, even romantic, afflatus when, dancing a *pas de
deux* with Terpsichore, he unites poetry with mime. The arpeggiated
melody, played con sordini, is still based on the lydian mode, which
was traditionally endowed with therapeutic properties. Art, being
music, is of its nature an Orphic enterprise.

But Orphic therapy implies the existence of Dionysiac wildness to
be tamed, and as the *pas de deux* evolves from its lucent cantilena
quivery trills and acciaccatura-bespread chitterings stir beneath the
elegant facade. Their effect, as they surface, is positive in that they
carry the music from lydian F to the glowing C major of the opening:
which shifts to E major – key of the overture's 'middle' – for the
coda-dance of Apollo with the Muses. Beginning exuberantly in 2/4
often divided into triplets, this turns into a 6/8 galop in iambic metre
over a rigid tonic pedal. The suppressed, animal-like barbarism
creates stabbing syncopations and cross accents; the ferocity of
experience is tightly controlled by Art, and the discipline is essential
because the energy is potent. At the climax the quasi-*cantus firmus* of
the dotted minims on violas, cellos and basses rings like a carillon
through the bucking syncopations of the violins. The coda is justly
marked 'agitato', the iambic phrases over the *cantus firmus* being now
chromaticised as well as fragmented. Reminiscences of previous
dances lead into the Apotheosis which, after that re-emergence of
Dionysiac darkness, ends a hyper-civilised humanist masque with the
quasi-religious ritual of a hymn, severely modal, telescoping the
tonalities of E major, G major and B minor.

Though basically concordant, the sonority embraces acute, even savage passing dissonances as the music leads into an expanded recapitulation of the arpeggiated opening of the Overture. Pedal notes on D equivocate between that key and the dominant of G. The final pages are extraordinary grand. At first resembling the 'Chime and Symphony of Nature' evoked in the closing peroration of the *Symphony of Psalms*, the music slowly swings to rest, pendulum-wise, beneath string tremolandi that seem to offer glimpses 'over the horizon'. Finally the pendulum ceases, rather than ends, on a triad of 'tragic' B minor. We cannot doubt that the sublime effect of this apothoesis is attributable to its equilibrium between Apollo and Dionysos. If Stravinsky had discovered, after his *Rite* and *Wedding*, that Dionysos was not in himself adequate, he now finds that the same is true of Apollo.

The tension within the apparently serene textures of this Apotheosis springs from the Apollonian head's imposition of order on the body's movements, reflected on stage in the artifice of mime. But the conclusion would not be so awe-inspiring were not the music still informed by darker powers, and it is to the point that in his next theatre piece Stravinsky makes an Apollonian work 'about' the Dionysiac experience itself – the descent of Persephone, daughter of Demeter the Earth Godess, beneath the earth to the kingdom of the dead, and her resurrection in the spring of the year. *Perséphone* (1934) is another *Rite of Spring*: only whereas the 1913 masterpiece presented the Dionysiac experience Dionysically, *Perséphone* presents it in Apollonian light. Its relationship to the immediately preceding *Apollo Musagètes* is significant. In that quintessentially Apollonian piece the Orphic inspiration is male: it is Apollo's head and 'spirit' that blow into the muses the breath of life. In *Perséphone*, on the other hand, the central figure, though Apollonian in grace, is an embryonic earth goddess. The Apollonian experience is viewed from a Dionysically feminine angle.

Perséphone is not, like *Apollo-Musagètes* or the later *Orpheus*, a ballet but a 'mélodrame' with a text by André Gide, theatrically performed by a singing tenor as High Priest and by Persephone as (speaking) narrator. Mixed chorus and a children's choir represent the people, gathered for the Spring festival. The orchestra is large, with triple woodwind and important parts for two harps and piano. This orchestra is, however, employed sparely; tripled brass and woodwind function the more efficaciously as harbingers of Spring because they are used soloistically, rather than in substantial tutti.

Textures are, for Stravinsky, euphonious: lyrically radiant, harmonically luminous – perhaps more so than in any other of his works.

The *mélodrame* falls into three parts. The first, *Perséphone Ravie*, is introduced by the Priest-figure who tells the tale in quasi-liturgical declamation. The modality is basically aeolian E, with lydian alterations. The two harps and piano lend an Orphic flavour to the accompaniment, while augmented intervals in the declamation suggest oriental, or perhaps pseudo-Greek, cantillation. A rocking ostinato on pentatonic minor thirds for the harps introduces women's voices singing in exquisite homophony; they plead with Persephone to stay with them, ensuring the permanence of the birds and flowers. Parallel thirds and sixths prevail, though passing seconds and fourths sometimes sound gentle as a caress. The tender modality evokes 'le premier matin du monde', recalling Ravel's 'green paradise of childish loves'. When the women sing 'tout est joyeux comme nos coeurs' the parallel triads are chromaticised, with modestly erotic effect, and the celebration of 'ivresse matinale' provokes an effervescent stutter from the voices, jazzy syncopations on piano and horns, and a sharpwards modulation to or around D. A catalogue of spring flowers from chorus and Priest creates a delirium of bliss, always ordered in Apollonian lucidity. The bubbling and sizzling of woodwind, cascading of harps and glint of string harmonics again create a 'Chime and Symphony of Nature' as succulent as that in the finale of the *Symphony of Psalms*, but far more femininely delicate. At the end of the movement the Priest resumes his declamation, now a semitone lower around E flat, announcing to 'le peuple' Persephone's inevitable, Pluto-ravished departure. Addressing Persephone, he sings 'Viens! Tu regneras sur les ombres'. Slow chromatics on low clarinets and bassoon waft her to the underworld.

Yet the second movement, *Perséphone aux enfers*, is not horrendous. The thin textures and more angular lines, often on oboes and bassoons, damp the first movement's radiance, and the nagging dotted rhythms grow tense; even so, the sacral music for the dead, traditionally scored for woodwind and brass, is based on heavenly E major, and the dotted rhythmed figures are similar to those that open *Apollon Musagètes*. The Priest's declamation, now centred on E again but with many modal alterations that are faintly oriental in flavour, is noble, in a spacious 3/2. The reason why the music is not aggressively hellish emerges as it proceeds. In the Persephone myth, human guilt is insignificant; purgation is not *necessarily* involved with the seasonal process of the year though, as we have seen, man's anthropomorphic proclivities often make it so. In this context the chorus, in meandering unison incantation, simply tell us that 'les ombres' are not in eternal, or even redeemable, torment, but merely in a state of non-being in which 'rien ne s'achève, chacun poursuit sans trève'. Now, as the bride of Pluto or Death Persephone will 'regnes sur les ombres'; the diatonic texture in triplet rhythm is as gentle as that of the first movement. Endlessness is suggested by the open ostinato patterns and pedal notes, with no murmur from furies except for a few sforzandi unisons from altos and tenors. Even so, they inform us that 'les ombres ne sont pas malheureuses, sans haine et sans amour, sans peine et sans envie'. Persephone is in hell not merely because she is ravished and imprisoned, but also because her youth and beauty may alleviate the dead's non-entity. And at this point Persephone herself becomes a female Orpheus. Sopranos and altos, returning to the triadic euphoniousness of the opening, chant in a floating 3/8 – almost in early Renaissance *discantus* style – of the young goddess's healing power. The Priest, Charon-like, leads her to the portals of hell.

Pluto is introduced with a godly rising fourth on trumpet, though there may be ironic undertones in his syncopated march rhythm and Verdian *oompah* bass. Dionysically infernal music does ensue in stammered and hammered semiquavers for low bassoons, double bassoon and tuba, with arabesques from higher woodwind and occasional stabs on strings. In a very flat A flat minor the gawky dotted rhythm of the opening of the movement recurs. Yet although this is a music of Furies, it is still impeccably lucid in scoring, ordered in metrical proportions, and, like Pluto, perhaps faintly comic in effect. Certainly it is not minatory enough to prevent the Priest and choir from evoking, in a permutation of the initial declamation, Mercury the Heavenly Messenger, who will restore Persephone to light and to the earth. In so doing, he will regenerate the seasonal cycle, so the personal, psychological theme, though present, counts for less than the 'anthropological' aspect. He 'descends' in bell-tolling scales, a *deus ex machina* who initiates a joyously syncopated jazz break! The rest of the movement is a dialogue, with Orphic harps active, between darkness and light. The tide turns in an exquisite passage for solo strings in level rhythmed crotchets, beginning in phrygian E but sinking to E flat. The Priest's lydian incantation, offering hope, is poised against the (softly) barking furies and lamenting dead. Entwined with the dotted-rhythmed figures of the *mélodrame's* opening, the Mercurian apparition leads into the last movement, *Perséphoné Renaissante*.

This begins in A major, traditionally a key of youth and renewal, and with the original dotted rhythms now elastically resurgent. These A major perorations are the only passages in the forty-five minute work to be scored for full orchestra. If their courtly grandeur recalls the High Baroque, civilised humanism does not destroy Stravinsky's earthy roots. Again the sonority is rich but succulent; and grandeur soon merges into the innocently triadic euphony of the first movement's 'premier matin du monde'. When the Priest resumes his declamation it is around his original 'node' of E, with the now familiar 'Greek' or oriental modal alterations. As he and the chorus restore Persephone to her earth-mother, 'primitive' Russian ostinati suggest a fertility rite; tonality has sunk by a semitone, but 'printemps' is heralded by a fortissimo C major chord in false relation with the basic E flats. In final chorus 'restoration' is manifest in the restored 3/8 rhythm and triadic euphony of the opening.

An extended coda begins in pentatonic G flat, two flutes twining over undulating thirds on violins. Few passages in twentieth-century music tug at the heart strings more than this, whatever Stravinsky may have said about his Apollonian impersonality. This is appropriate, since the words Persephone speaks against the music are the profound point of the *mélodrame*. 'Prends-moi', she says to the earth-people, 'je suis *ta* Perséphone. Mais bien l'épouse du ténébreux Pluton'. Life and death must be accepted as indivisible. Given that, she can say to her lover 'charmant Demophoon': 'me serrer dans tes bras Que de l'enlacement je n'échappe et sorte En dépit de l'amour et le coeur déchire Pour répondre au destin qui m'apelle. J'irai vers le monde ombrageux où je sais que l'on souffre. Crois-tu qu'impunément se penche sur le gouffre De l'enfer douloureaux un coeur ivre d'amour?' Nature-noises babble softly on woodwind while she speaks. The Priest rounds off the work with something close to his original declamation at the original pitch, accompanied by leaping figurations on strings, the bass recurrently returning to a pedal E. The chorus tell us that Persephone, eternally youthful goddess-woman who descends into the abyss, brings 'un peu d'amour' to the shades' 'détresses et malheures sans nombre'.

Perséphone is the only work in which Stravinsky gives the female principle central place in his Dionysiac-Apollonian axis. Though he composed grander and greater pieces, he has made none of deeper tenderness and beauty, and has done so in confronting the most 'archetypal' of themes. In playing down sin and guilt in dealing with the anthropological aspects of the story he has not, however, faced the Orpheus myth *head on* – to use a relevant metaphor. When, a decade or more later, he does just that in his ballet *Orpheus* (1948), he eschews feminine wiles or weakness in creating the last major work, as *Apollon Musagètes* had been the first, of his neo-classic phase. After it, he was to adopt his own permutation of the intellectualised order of serial pitches.

Like Gluck, Stravinsky begins his *Orpheus* only after Eurydice is dead. There are no preludial rejoicings in the 'real' world; the ballet opens with the irremediable fact of death, as Orpheus weeps for his lost beloved: 'dos au public, il ne bouge pas'. The music is white note, not in C major but in the aeolian mode, calmly diatonic on strings, while a drooping ostinato on harp emulates both Orpheus's lyre and plopping tears. Friends, bringing presents and condolence, dance in slow processional crotchets until, at the cadence, the aeolian minor third is sharpened to major, with unresolved flat seventh, a 'blue' note perhaps suggesting timeless continuity, as it does in jazz. When Orpheus dances solo, however, agitation succeeds calm. Tonality is screwed up initially to B flat minor, lines grow angular, rhythms jittery. This *Air de Dance* is extended, and tonally wide-ranging; the big leaps, syncopated rhythms and sparely scored, tense textures express the difficulty of Apollonian enterprise, attempting to create order from chaos.

The Angel of Death appears in the role of Monteverdi's Speranza, to escort Orpheus to Hades. His hopeful key, displacing the distraught B flat minor, is a bright A major in which unfolds a reveillé-like trumpet fanfare. As they walk or stalk into the 'ténè-bres' the melodies are broader, more open, with sacred brass reverer-ant, though the texture is still dissonantly stark. The music for the Furies is bitty, nagging, snarling. Like Gluck's furies, they are Orpheus's own agitation intensified; and he, as a twentieth-century man (at the end of a Second World War) is in more desperate plight than was Gluck's hopefully Enlightened hero. The core of Stra-vinsky's ballet, as of Gluck's and Monteverdi's operas, is the duologue between the Furies music, with its dioysiac ostinati and its teetering between keys in mediant relationship, and Orpheus's would-be con-solatory song, played on two interlaced oboes, with harp-lyre brokenly accompanying. The basic tonality is infernal F minor; in the middle section tormented souls in Hades stretch out their arms in a marvellously 'physical' phrase, imploring Orpheus to intercede on their behalf as well as his wife's. Once again, mimetic action objectifies grief: to potent effect, since the Furies are gradually tranquillised, as the keys shift between D minor and major.

Having been blindfolded by the Furies, Orpheus is reunited to Eurydice in a gentle *pas de deux*, ambiguous in tonality but veering towards F *major*. The music for their processional exit moves back to D major-minor, with viola and cello figuration rotating in nervously persistent semiquavers. Whereas Monteverdi's and Gluck's lovers had pranced, in dotted rhythms, out of hell, Stravinsky's lovers shuffle, even stumble. But as they approach the light of day, strings flow more lyrically and fluidly until, to ritualistically severe music for brass and strings with angular leaps and dotted rhythms that imply over-confidence, vainglorious Orpheus enacts his fatal looking back – or rather tears off the bandage the Furies had tied around his eyes. Immediately Eurydice dies again.

It is interesting that Orpheus can speak with the movements of his limbs but cannot, in the mute world of dance, communicate verbally. As modern man he desperately wants to be literate and visual; and is destroyed because he cannot tolerate his blindness, even when facing unknowable mysteries. He must see with the outer, not with the inner eye – whereas Stravinsky's Oedipus, like Shakespeare's Gloucester in *King Lear*, saw truth only when blinded ('I stumbled when I saw'). Stravinsky's Dionysiac revenge on failed Orpheus is terrible indeed. Monteverdi had evaded the consequences of sin and guilt by a transubstantiating wish-fulfilment. Gluck had claimed that rationally enlightened man might conquer human frailty through progress and higher education, so that a happy ending was at least conceivable. Only Beethoven, *achieved* a happy ending in entering paradise, but that is a solution apprehensible only by one capable of Beethovenian transcendence. Most of us have to be content with evasion, whether by way of dream, like Tchaikovsky, or, like Offenbach, by way of cynicism. Stravinsky, however – this is his discomforting modernity – rejects dream *and* cynicism, even though he is incapable of transcendence. He shifts brusquely from Orpheus's failure to his destruction. Summoning the avenging Maenads whom Monteverdi and Gluck had shudderingly sidestepped, he has them tear Orpheus to pieces to a music venomously Dionysiac, stuttering, splintering, spitting. However frenzied, it has none of the animal vigour of *The Rite of*

Spring – though it is relevant to note that the ambiguity of that great work lies in the fact that its energy is also disruptive, asymmetrical.

After the final grunts of the dismemberment – which sounds like an ultimate admission of the dry savagery occasionally discernible beneath the elegant surfaces of *Apollon Musagètes* – Apollo appears from the sky as *deus ex machina*. He *wrests* the harp-lyre (the stage direction is Stravinsky's) from broken Orpheus. The god claims back his own from presumptuous man, and in the coda plays an ostinato similar to that of the aeolian Prelude. Then, Orpheus had been the lyre player, aspiring to godhead. Now Stravinsky himself, the Artist, emulates the Apollonian god in the *otherness* of this Apollonian apotheosis, in which trumpets and horns, the sacral brass of the dead, weave nobly ritualistic polyphony. In this funeral lament Art may live on, in the skies, for the stage direction tells us that Apollo, playing the lyre, 'élève son chant vers les cieux'. But it is only man's art – indeed a heroic achievement – that is thus elevated, as the crotchet ostinato rises scalewise from D instead of falling from A, as in the Prelude. Man's broken body, as distinct from his art, is left on earth, to rot. The final triad, which adds a blue flat seventh as did the final chord of the Prelude, hints that this is not a consummated end. The Orphic experience is 'open'; it will happen again.

The 'terrifying honesty' of Stravinsky's version of the Orpheus story was, however, the end of the equilibrium between Dionysos and Apollo, out of which he had created music so immediately and profoundly relevant to the twentieth century. *Orpheus* was the first major work he composed in his third home, the New World; soon after he produced his first serial work. While it is not impossible that a consciously intellectual approach like serialism might be used to Dionysiac effect, it is improbable, and in Stravinsky's case did not happen. An interesting transitional work is the *Cantata 1952* for soprano, tenor, women's chorus and small instrumental ensemble. The English texts are medieval; poems and music deal with love sacred and profane. The soprano represents a woman whose marriage is a fleshly sacrament; the tenor represents a man (Christ) who is God become human lover for our redemption. The girl's love song is warmly lyrical, yet gradually embraces 'doctrinal' counterpoint as her human passion aspires to divine unity; the man's love song is strictly canonic (*rectus, inversus, cancrizans* and *cancrizans inversues*, always so specified by the composer), since his truth is 'mathematically' eternal, without beginning or end, though from his contrapuntally serial law 'humane' harmonies are intermittently precipitated. Moreover the stanzas of his ricercar – Stravinsky pointedly uses the archaic term – all canonically treat the same circular (tail-eating) theme, but are interspersed with a lyrical Refrain similar in character to the girl's music, since as man needs God, so God needs man. There could not be a neater instance of our two-way Mercurian theme.

God and Man (only it is significantly an 'intuitive' woman) end up singing a duet, 'O Western Wind', which is in origin a secular love-song, in an idiom less divinely contrapuntal, more humanely baroque. The agitation of the faintly Dionysiac music suggests that, buffeted by the wind and the rain, we cannot be self-subsistent but desperately need God's succour. This is touchingly reinforced by the fact that the two ricercars and the duet are separated rondo-wise by a setting for *women's* chorus of the stanzas of the Lyke-Wake Dirge. This music is so simple, folk-like, non-developing, that it sounds almost pre-conscious – a keening for the dead, intuitively aware of elemental mystery as lover approaches beloved. The conception is beautiful, and the scoring for flutes, oboes and cello so cunning that the piece sounds deeply medieval, yet inimitably Stravinskyan, and therefore twentieth century. The rigidity of Christ's cantus firmus is forbidding, but is meant to be; the semitonic modulation, or change of gear, when Christ ascends to heaven, momentarily breaking the key-cycles which are as hieratic as those of *Symphony of Psalms,* is at once pagan magic and Christian grace. It could hardly make such an effect if the ricercar were less long and less remorselessly predetermined.

Stravinsky and Schoenberg have always been regarded as polar opposites of modern music, and they have little in common apart from the fact that both improbably ended up in Holywood. Hostile critics were quick to dismiss Stravinsky's espousal of chromatic serialism (which followed in the wake of the *Cantata*) as the latest turn of the weathervane, though at this date it seems that no composer has been more consistent than Stravinsky in the human and religious themes he has explored, and in the complexly evolving techniques he has used to that end. If Schoenberg's search for a new linear order proved, in *Moses and Aaron,* inseparable from the religious nature of his quest, Stravinsky's serialism also grew along with the exploration of a faith. His serial processes have little similarity to Schoenberg's, for the obvious reason that he was never a chromatic-harmonic expressionist; they do resemble Webern's, which were in turn related to medieval theory and practice. The ballet *Agon* suggests how authentically 'theological' Stravinsky's serialism is; the rhythms remain those of body and blood, while the textures are bonily skeletonic. Corporeal energy seems to have evaporated from the very last serial pieces, the *Canticum Sacrum*, the *Requiem Canticles* and *Threni*; yet if these are an old man's music, there is evidence enough that their Apollonian precision is a purgation of what had once been Dionysiac. They are an astonishing testament to the survival of the human spirit, life-enhancing in their tingling linearity. This serial unity sounds no less a historical necessity than were the fragmentation of line and disintegration of metre at the expiring twilight of the Middle Ages.

Stravinsky's moderninity is inherent in his uncompromising acceptance of the severance of Orpheus's head from his body. Only one composer is 'more' modern and that is Beethoven: who, having wrestled with the furies and learned that without his demons paradise would have been unattainable, discovered that heads and bodies are not really separable entities since man's elevation to divinity and the descent of the dayspring from on high are identical processes. It is interesting that Stravinsky, in many ways an un- or even anti-Beethovenian artist, came at the end of his life to recognise Beethoven's singular pre-eminence, remarking of the *Grosse Fugue* that this extraordinary music can never become 'dated' since it embraces 'consciousness' and 'unconsciousness' in a realm outside time. But although we must never forget Beethoven when we reflect on the crisis of modern man, we must also admit that Stravinsky, of all twentieth-century composers, most courageously confronts our predicament 'head on'. For although only rarely – notably in *Oedipus Rex* and the *Symphony of Psalms* – does he succeed in reintegrating Orpheus's head and torso, he recurrently reminds us that the need for such reintegration is a, perhaps the, basic impulse behind all the arts, at many levels, in our bruised and battered century. The heritage of Christian Europe must, if civilisation is to survive, come to terms with the eternal goddesses of earth and moon. Only thus may we attain a re-cognition that 'atonement' is also 'at-one-ment'.

Epilogue

We have traced the story of Orpheus through many musical vicissitudes and, since *rénouvellement* is the heart of his myth, through many rebirths. We have noted his origins in classical antiquity, as a poet-composer-shaman-priest who, through art and reason, attempted to play God and even to challenge death itself. Many other stories, such as Persephone's descent to nether-earth at the winter solstice, accrued barnacle-like around the original tale, which was reinterpreted in the context of changing needs.

For Christian Alonzo X, in thirteenth-century Léon, Orpheus was harping King David, seeking return to the One as he conversed with the birds and beasts. For High Renaissance Monteverdi Orpheus sang of a hero's courage and glory which, since man was not in fact God but fallibly mortal, turned out to be vain-glory. Monteverdi thus revealed the tragedy inherent in man's Orphic enterprise, though he cheated with his transubstantiating epilogue. Two hundred and fifty years later Gluck could believe enough in man's self-sufficiency to envisage a happy ending: paradise on earth might be feasible, given Enlightened benevolence and the benefits of higher education. Mozart, in *Die Zauberflöte*, reintroduced the mystic strands of Orphism latent in however Enlightened Freemasonry, while Beethoven identified it with his search for the undivided self – using the term more or less in the sense in which it has been employed by R. D. Laing in our own day. Later in the nineteenth century Liszt turned God-presuming Orpheus into a romantic play-actor like himself; inversely, Offenbach debunked him, leaving him happy in hell, though teetering on the edge of the Second Empire abyss. Stravinsky, in the Waste Land of the twentieth century and in the wake of two world wars to destroy, not save, Civilisation, restated the pristine savagery of the original myth, allowing the Terrible Mothers to rend Orpheus to pieces in revenge on his patriarchal pride.

With Stravinsky the wheel has come full circle: a fact that may lend credence to the view that the Western world is entering on its last lap. But of course Orpheus did not finally die with Stravinsky. Many other composers have toyed with him during the twentieth century: from Milhaud who in his short opera democratically yanks Orpheus into the context of post-Puccinian *verismo*; to Henze, who in a ballet and a large-scale choral work relates the story's mythical aspects to the heroism of social reconstruction, and even to the revolt of the downtrodden proletariat. Nor have his inward, psychological springs been forgotten: as we may hear in the slow movement of Elliott Carter's First String Quartet of 1951 – a piece that has been construed as a dialogue between Orpheus and the Furies and is certainly comparable with Beethoven's music of inner confrontation, such as the slow movement of the Fourth Piano Concerto.

But these works of Milhaud, Henze and Carter do not add new, post-Stravinskian dimensions to the Orpheus story. Such do not occur until, with the century's declension in the seventies and eighties, Messiaen and Birtwistle produce two works, each a cross between opera, masque and rite. Messiaen's monumental *St Francis* is not directly Orphic, though the saint, in his parleyings with the creatures, may be seen as an Orpheus in a medieval context recreated in the light and dark of contemporary experience. Since Messiaen has been throughout a long life a dedicated Roman Catholic this is hardly surprising. His St Francis is an operatic ritual about what a Christian Orpheus means today, subsumed into a 'global' world embracing within Christianity many other cultures and creeds. This is what Messiaen has done throughout his work, of which *St Francis* is an ultimate consummation. It is not extravagent to regard Messiaen as one of the handful of *great* living composers; since, however, *St Francis* depends on its Christian context we can hardly consider it a 'representative' statement of the Orphic theme today. That might be claimed for the other major work referred to, Harrison Birtwistle's *The Masks of Orpheus*, first presented in 1986. Now is probably too early to assess it; and it is certainly too late to attempt to do so in a book conceived and substantially completed before the opera was born. Something must none the less be said of it, since what it tells us about Orpheus's present destiny is relevant to the future of 'civilisation', if it has one.

That so Protean a myth is pertinent to our pluralistic world is demonstrated by Peter Zinoviev's psychologically and philosophically sophisticated libretto. Read as a dramatic poem it lacks verbal trenchancy, and may seem pretentious as well as confused. In the theatre, however, it proves to be what the composer needed, for its Jungian-Freudian-Levi-Straussian anthropology and mythology are exactly in tune with the music Birtwistle had to create. That music – although the composer worked at it on and off for fifteen years – is immediate enough totally to absorb us over a period of three and a half hours. Birtwistle has made what Harry Partch called corporeal music: sounds, such as we had long forgotten, to our bitter cost, that involve bodily action along with words so that, as with real primitive musics, we live, move and have our being in them while they last. It is worth noting that Partch, though he did not compose an explicitly Orphic theatre piece, may be said to be himself an Orpheus to disfunctioning industrial technocracy since, reared in the parched and parching wastes of the Californian deserts, he disavowed the trappings of Western harmony and tonality and assayed a new start, renewing Just Intonation and building his own sound-producing instruments from the materials in the world around him. Birtwistle's opera does not thus radically dispose of his European heritage, yet his score parallels the work of Partch in that it functions, in alliance with visual images and mimetic movement, as a rite pertinent to our global village. Certainly it operates – more than any previous music of the Western world with the possible exception of Janáček and Varèse, if we may count him as Western – in the shamanistic terms of the authentic Orpheus, not so much *acting*, as does Stravinsky, but comprehensively *enacting*, the Eternal Return. Following up his 'Greek' experiments at the National Theatre, Birtwistle evokes worlds alien to yet deeply within us. Music, decor, costumes and mime call on diverse cultures from Old English fertility plays and Aboriginal and Polynesian rites of passage to the sophistications of Japanese *Noh* and *Kabuki* theatre. What comes out is neither Greek or Japanese nor Old English for, as Birtwistle puts it, this is a world not imitated but made. The slow birth of the first act, the terrifying hurlyburly of the second act in hell, the retrospective resolution of the third act, are sublimely simple in their very complexity. Although Orpheus is once more annihilated, he is also reborn. Perhaps no modern theatre piece so overwhelmingly achieves, at its mysteriously serene end, the catharsis that was the goal of and justification for the 'pity and terror' of

Aeschylean and Shakesperean tragedy.

Like the primitive and oriental artifactors whom he has drawn on but not emulated, Birtwistle thinks not linearly but circularly, refashioning the myths outside Time, in ever fluctuating permutations. This multiple vision – seeing things simultaneously from several angles – accords both with Blake's cosmography and with the findings of our psychology, while allowing for musical recapitulations helpful to those too entrenched in linearity to shake out of it. In the theatre doubts do not occur, so gripped and on occasion griped are we by the vitality of the sounds and the startlements of the spectacle. Birtwistle deploys his bands of woodwind, brass and percussion – one does not miss the strings, even over so long a stretch – in manners closer to Australian Aboriginal and Japanese or Javanese theatre musics than to Western symphony; yet he creates sonorities that belong irresistibly to us, and convince us that the protagonists' three identities – as man or woman, as hero or heroine, and as myth – coexist, here in the late twentieth century. The stage-craft, with the heroic dimension mimed by awesomely gargantuan puppets, is as stunningly immediate as the music, and is likewise multi-ethnic. The many-layered approach works because we now accept such concepts viscerally as well as intellectually, though it could hardly succeed without inspired dedication comparable with that of the initial production.

Practical realisation of the imaginative enterprise proves, indeed, to be part of the philosophical and psychological theme. Opera singers, portraying the two Orpheuses and Eurydices, Aristeus the honey-gathering alternative lover, black Hecate and the horrendous Oracle of the Dead, can hardly be restricted to conventional *bel canto*; their multifarious vocal techniques, from Western to Eastern and from civilised to savage, are themselves rebirths; as is the fact that the singers, as well as professional dancers, are called on to move, mime and *run* as to the manner born. Animated by the blazing grandeur of Birtwistle's score, they sing the taxing vocal lines with a paradoxically disciplined exuberance, while their corporeal energy is in no wise inhibited. And the 'new' dimension of electrophonics at once endorses and qualifies the live music: for representing Apollo, the sun-god and ultimate source of life who has his own (to us inarticulate) language, it powerfully relates natural to (strictly speaking) supernatural sound-sources. This too is what one might expect: mechanistic techniques must themselves renew our fallen world. *The Masks of*

Orpheus, in 1986, genuinely remakes a story of vast breadth and immense antiquity.

It is true that 'opera', after *The Masks of Orpheus,* will never be the same, nor will we who have experienced it. The world has come a long way, for better and worse, since post-Renaissance Francis Bacon wrote in his *Advancement of Learning:*

Which merit was lively set forth by the Ancients in that feigned relation or Orpheus theatre; where all birds and beasts assembled, and forgetting their several appetites, some of prey, some of game, some of quarrel, stood all sociably together listening unto the airs and accords of the harp; the sound whereof no sooner ceased, or was drowned by some louder noise, but every beast returned to his own nature: wherein is aptly described the nature and condition of men; who are full of savage and unreclaimed desires, of profit, of lust, of revenge, which as long as they give ear to precepts, to laws, to religion, sweetly touched with the eloquence and persuastion of books, of sermons, of harangues, so long is society and peace maintained.

The religion Birtwistle celebrates is not Bacon's, nor does the advancement of Learning ('books, sermons, harangues') have relevance to his masque and masks. He begins his opera with the metaphor of an egg, and prophesies new births, *ab ovo*. He does not tell us, since no-one can know, what 'new beast' may 'shamble towards Bethlehem to be born'.

Index